BREATHING

AND

RISING

The Journey of a Mixed-Race Peacemaker

A memoir by: Curtis Monroe Griffin

Dedication

This work is for all those who have suffered due to one of the most prolific lies in human history. Those who know there's just one human race. And those who wish to celebrate human diversity.

Breathing and Rising

Acknowledgements

As in all my accomplishments, I owe many thanks to those who helped me complete this book.

First, those who contribute most—my family: Christiane, Ilse, Paul, Nicole, and Allie. Your love and support brings me immeasurable happiness.

Also, the many whose friendship and wisdom greatly impacted me, especially: Todd Rowley, Ed Gille, Anne Wilson, Wallace Martin, Todd Robertson, Megan Mickle, Dane Hanson, Adam Rothberg, Jim Downton, Jen Moore, Melanie & Christopher Howard.

Special thanks to Tim Hillmer and Randy Rothberg, whose expertise and feedback gave me the tools I used most in crafting this book.

Contents

Opening

I'm a half white, half black (identified black), 50-year old American male raised in a white community, by a white mother and grandmother from Germany.

In the 1999 – 2000 school year, I taught literacy at two elementary schools in the Boulder Valley School District. That year played as much havoc with my sense of identity as my previous 30. So, being fortunate enough to have the resources, I quit and went to attend the Creating Peaceable Schools conference at Lesley College in Cambridge, MA that summer. Opening speaker, Dr. Ulric Johnson, introduced the lead article to the core readings, The Ten C's: A Model of Diversity Awareness and Social Change. First five C's are what to be aware of:

Color – refers to "race," or skin color. But also all aspects of one's core identity, such as, gender, sexual orientation, and physical appearance and abilities.

Culture – values, beliefs, symbols, behaviors and ways of living, and the shared history of a group of people. All have positive and negative sides such as great music and food, but can promote racism or sexism.

Class – individual and group identity relative to power, authority, hierarchy, and status. It effects access to, control over, or ownership of resources like wealth, education, employment, housing etc. Denying *class* is a key obstacle to productive and authentic dialogue about diversity and oppression.

Context – the reality in which individuals and groups exist based on time, location, environment, and the socio-political, economic and historical conditions. Context helps people get over the tendency to compare and build oppressions into a hierarchy, or prioritize particular oppressions without minimizing or devaluing the pain caused by another.

Character – refers to the unique aspect of each individual person, including personal preferences, idiosyncrasies, and personality traits. We are all individuals, and must always recognize that *Character* is shaped by *Color, Culture, Class,* and *Context.*

For the first time, I had a tool to understand myself and millions more born into centuries of hatred and violence based on race, nationality, class, religion, culture, gender. Then I began to think about cultivating change with the next five C's: *Conflict, Courage, Confidence, Commitment,* and *Community.* And I soon realized that Truth is both personal and universal.

~

Many stories have given me the courage and stamina to write mine. One of an acclaimed writer being approached by a fan at a dinner party helped push me over the finish line.

"You're such an amazing writer," the fan exclaims, "I feel like I know you so well."

"Oh darling," the writer responds, "it's just a book."

Some will want to discredit me and this book. And given my afflictions with fear, anger, jealousy, and lust, they could write their own stories about me and claim my memory is selective. They'll try to make me out as another wacky lefty liberal who may have had a point in the 1960's, but has turned into a tyrant in the wake of one black president.

Still, stories of liberal bullies are overplayed. So are stories that liken Southern pride with racism, Muslims with terrorists, Mexicans with rapists, the poor with criminals, the rich with criminals—the list goes on and on. And while I have little desire to drag any of us through the mud we've all been sloshing around in, I have to tell my truth.

~

From individual words to entire stories, life is woven with paradox: good and bad, right and wrong, fear and love. My hope is that this memoir inspires people to hold two opposing ideas in mind at the same time, and still be courageous enough to love. So that we may speak, listen, read, write, apologize, forgive, and be happy.

Like striking the floor with a stick—BAM! Now!

Introduction: One

Courage is the thing.
All goes if courage goes.

J. M. Barrie

Conviction

In December 2010, I was 41 years old and got a job driving buses for the Boulder Valley School District. Aside from "pre-tripping" (checking the engine, fluids, lights, brakes, tires, etc.) on frigid winter mornings before the sun is up, it's been a good job. There's significant responsibility because the cargo is priceless. But the training and my excellent driving and student management skills lower the risks. And keeping everyone's safety in mind makes it easy to be present and enjoy the work.

Another reason I chose to drive was the hours: Monday thru Friday, roughly 7 am to 9 am, and 3 pm to 5 pm, which meant I could spend "mid-day" taking care of our daughter and writing this book. Three days a week were Daddy-Daughter days, and I'm among the richest in the world for having spent that time with her. Twice a week our daughter was in my mom's care, which if we could bottle it, would soon have everyone believing in love.

Though I wrote when our daughter was with my mom, most of this memoir was written during breaks: Summer, Thanksgiving, Winter, Spring, and weekends. 90% of those days I woke up at 5 am and wrote for six to eight hours. And my kind beautiful wife kept me nourished with breakfast and lunch in front of the computer (along with a long list of other support) as I spouted regularly, "I'm really close now!" It's hard to believe it's been more than eight years.

~

In 1989, sophomore year in College, I began thinking I was destined to be an elementary school teacher. For the next 17 years I was a pro athlete, coach, teacher, and grad student. I started a dream job teaching fifth grade in Boulder, Colorado in fall 2006. By late April 2009, principals, teachers, staff, parents, and students said my strengths were superb, weaknesses were minimal, and that I'd improved every year. I thought I was on the brink of an illustrious 20-year career. A week later I was fired.

To salvage my career I contacted principals and teachers I'd worked with at a dozen schools and applied for dozens of jobs in BVSD. I got a couple of interviews but no offers. I also sent out hundreds of applications to a dozen other districts. My first call-back came a year later. I was offered and accepted a long term substitute position at a private school that provided other teaching and coaching opportunities. The principal and teachers were nice, but the aggression and ignorance with which some parents challenged me was alarming. And after BVSD, I wasn't sticking around to see what kind of witch hunt they might conjure up. Also, the school's high tuition, minimal resources, and exclusive policies, hardened my support for Public Education—our best chance of overcoming the conflict rooted in centuries of violence and selective poverty.

~

BVSD provides first-year teachers with a mentor. My students and I loved when mine came to read or give a lesson. He also gave productive feedback about my teaching and by everyone's account, we had a successful year. We didn't speak for two years, but have met every six to twelve months since I was fired. He, like most teachers, staff, and administrators, was confused and angry that I was let go. He helped me prepare for interviews. We met not long after I started driving buses.

"40 years is enough," I said referring to my time in education with BVSD (Kindergarten through 12th grade and two decades as coach and teacher). I am a male elementary teacher, bi-racial (looks black), calls Boulder home, an experienced expert in diversity, improved in academics every year of his life (especially Language Arts), and a first-rate product of BVSD's own goals—a life-long learner of "Excellence and Equity". Still, a few BVSD administrators thought my 40 years of experience and committed work ethic didn't amount to enough. "So, I'm driving buses," I concluded, "and am going to teach excellence and equity on my own."

My mentor smiled and vowed to help. A 25-year BVSD employee and award winning author, he's given priceless feedback and editing for this book. He's one of many friends—the irony of my life in Boulder— headlined by smart, open minded, generous people helping me overcome a powerful few who came up with ignorant reasons to exclude me.

Introduction: Two

All [great writers] have learned
the one lesson that must be learned:
How to control their material.
You can too.

William Zinsser

Language

I would rarely read or write on my own until I was 24. I'd just finished the fall semester as a coach and teacher's assistant and began to train full time for the Association of Volleyball Professionals beach tour. My mom gave me Bill Bryson's book, <u>the mother tongue: english and how it got that way</u>. I broke from my cocoon in January, 1994.

~

"English grammar is so complex and confusing," Bryson explains in chapter 9, Good English and Bad, "for the one very simple reason that its rules and terminology are based on Latin—a language with which it has precariously little in common ... It is a patent absurdity ... Once this insane notion became established grammarians found themselves having to draw up ever more complicated and circular arguments to accommodate the inconsistencies ... As Burchfield notes in *The English Language*, F. Th. Visser, found it necessary to devote 200 pages to discussing just one aspect of the present participle. That is as crazy as it is amazing."

"Academic bull shit," I angrily barked, stood, threw the book onto the couch and kicked the air like I could leg sweep social hierarchies.

I first felt the power of scholarly excellence in Kindergarten. Classmates and I launched our reading and writing skills off pads right next to each other, they in their rockets, me on my pogo stick. Over the years they got better grades, read better books, wrote and told better stories, went to better universities, and got higher-paying jobs. Many are in our government, justice system, health care, education and powerful businesses. And many buzz around continuing America's long tradition of ignoring millions of under-educated, impoverished citizens. And had one of those worker-bees with their condescending smiles been transported in front of me, I would've beaten them senseless. Instead, I went for a run in the foothills.

Given that reaction, and after reading a dozen other chapters which prove the rules of English are asinine while condemning grammar grouches, one might picture me running through the streets beating strangers about the head. But it was sobering to lift weights, run trails, and hit volleyballs. And <u>the mother tongue</u> showed me the light.

~

The idea that I'd always fail Language Arts grew throughout elementary school. Roots inched deeper each week as the teacher announced it was time for a spelling test. My heart raced and I grew flush over how I was about to, once again, prove my intelligence was years behind my grade. Nonsensical rules and self-hate drove me to justify guessing, a strategy which, in English, guarantees failure. One week I'd miss: supersede; concede; proceed, by spelling them: superseed; conseed; proseed. The next week I'd miss them: supercede, conceed, procede.

"Just as a quick test," Bryson details in the chapter Spelling, "see if you can tell which of the following words are mispelled:

- idiosyncracy
- accomodate
- irresistable
- rhythym
- diptheria
- anamoly

"In fact, they all are," Bryson continues, "So was *misspelled* at the end of the preceeding paragraph. So was *preceding* just there. I'm sorry, I'll stop. But I trust you get the point that English can be a maddeningly difficult language to spell correctly."

I knew it was hard to spell in English, but it started to sink in.

Good spelling, like good grammar helps to improve comprehension, my thoughts rolled. *But I'd met intelligent people who struggled with spelling. I'd also read and understood a paragraph that had every word misspelled. So I'm going to spend less time judging people's words, and more time honoring the thoughts and ideas behind them. Especially my own.*

~

By fourth grade I despised the chuckles of classmates and condemning looks of teachers when I mispronounced words. Like when I said *ped* instead of *paid*, because *paid* reminded me of *said*. Or, *breek* instead of *break*, because *break* reminded me of *speak*.

"If there is one thing certain about English pronunciation," Bryson begins the chapter, Pronunciation, "is that there is almost nothing certain about it. No other language in the world has more words spelled the same way and yet pronounced differently. Consider just a few."

- heard – beard
- road – broad
- five – give
- fillet – skillet
- beau – beauty
- low – how

"English pronunciation is so various—one might almost say random—that not one of our twenty-six letters can be relied on for constancy. Either they clasp themselves to a variety of pronunciations, as with the *c* in *race, rack,* and *rich*, or they sulk in silence, like the *b* in *debt,* the *a* in *bread*, the second *t* in *thistle*. In combinations they become even more unruly and unpredictable, most famously in the letter cluster *ough,* which can be pronounced in any of eight ways … *through, though, thought, tough, plough, thorough, hiccough and lough* …"

Yes! I thought feeling warm, vindicated.

~

Throughout school I lamented the constant push to expand my vocabulary. Like spelling, vocabulary was usually built on prior knowledge and once I was behind, gave me regular feedback about how stupid I was. But my sense of exoneration continued when Bryson highlighted the absurdity of having an immense vocabulary in the chapter, Where Words Come From.

"If you have a morbid fear of peanut butter sticking to the roof of your mouth," Bryson continues, "There is a word for it: *arachibutyrophobia*. There is a word to describe the state of being a woman: *muliebrity*. And there is a word to describe the sudden breaking off of thought: *aposiopesis*. If you harbor an urge to look through the windows of the homes you pass, there is a word for the condition: *crytiscopophilia*."

"English retains probably the richest vocabulary and most diverse shadings of meanings of any language," Bryson continued, "We can distinguish between house and home (as for instance the French cannot), between continual and continuous, sensual and sensuous, forceful and forcible, childish and childlike ... For almost every word we have a multiplicity of synonyms. Something is not just big, it is large, immense, vast, capacious, bulky, massive, whopping, humongous. No other language has so many words all saying the same thing."

"This abundance of terms is often cited as a virtue. And yet a critic," Bryson clarified, "could equally argue that English is an untidy and acquisitive language, cluttered with a plethora of needless words."

Yes! I thought again, delighted by the idea that English snobs toil in the absurd.

"We have a strange—and to foreigners it must seem maddening— tendency to load a single word with a whole galaxy of meanings," Bryson pours it on, "*Fine*, for instance, has fourteen definitions as an adjective, six as a noun and two as an adverb. In the *Oxford English Dictionary* it fills two full pages and takes 5,000 words of description ... But the polysemic champion must be *set*. Superficially it looks a wholly un- seeming monosyllable, the verbal equivalent of the single-celled organism. Yet it has 58 uses as a noun, 126 as a verb, and 10 as a participial adjective. Its meanings are so various and scattered that it takes the *OED* 60,000 words—the length of a short novel—to discuss them all."

Wow! I laughed at the mind-boggling amount of wasted time.

~

While grammarians can get caught up in the absurd, there are advantages to knowing the rules. In the chapter, Word Play, Bryson describes Roy Dean's ability to do crossword puzzles, which to me was like reading a play-by-play of Michael Jordan splitting a double team, jumping through the lane and dunking on a seven foot tall center. Extraordinary.

"Six days a week an Englishman named Roy Dean," Bryson explains, "sits down and does in a matter of minutes something that many of us cannot do at all. He completes the crossword puzzle in the London Times. Dean is the, well, the dean of the British crossword. In 1970, under test conditions, he solved a London Times crossword in just 3 minutes and 45 seconds, a feat so phenomenal that it has stood unchallenged for twenty years."

"[American cross words puzzles are] generally a straightforward affair," Bryson further details Dean's skills, "requiring you merely fit a word to a definition. The British variety are infinitely more fiendish, demanding mastery of the whole armory of verbal possibilities—puns, anagrams, palindromes, lipograms, and whatever else springs to the devisor's devious mind. British crosswords require you to realize that *carthorse* is an anagram of *orchestra,* that *contaminated* can be made into *no admittance,* that *emigrates* can be made into *streaming, Cinerama* into *American, Old Testament* into *most talented*, and *World Cup team* into (a stroke of genius, this one) *talcum powder*."

It's hard not to stare and want to emulate the masters.

~

My resentment towards English's vast vocabulary was eased further when Bryson described the effects of immigration. Different races, cultures, religions, and nationalities coming together from all over the world. And English, for better and worse, has adopted/coopted more words than any other language and is the most commonly spoken.

"The first American pilgrims," Bryson explains in the chapter, Old World, New World, "happened to live in the midst of perhaps the most exciting period in the history of the English language—a time when 12,000 words were being added to the language and revolutionary activities were taking place in almost every realm of human endeavor. It was also a time of considerable change in the structure of the language."

"Total immigration between 1607 and 1840 was no more than one million," Bryson continues, "In the second half of the nineteenth century, thirty million people poured into the country ... in just four years at its peak 1901 – 1905 ... America absorbed a million Italians, a million Austro-Hungarians, and half a million Russians, plus tens of thousands of other people from scores of other places. At the turn of the century New York had more speakers of German than anywhere in the world except Vienna and Berlin, more Irish than anywhere but Dublin, more Russians than in Kiev, and more Italians than in Milan or Naples."

"This [the tendency to adopt words] is of course one of the glories of English—its willingness to take in words from abroad, rather as if they were refugees. We take words from almost anywhere – *shampoo* from India, *ketchup* from China, *potato* from Haiti, *sofa* from Arabia, *boondocks* from the Tagalog language of the Philippines, *slogan* from Gaelic. You can't get much more eclectic than that. And we have been doing it for centuries."

America is a stew that's been simmering for 400 years, our many flavors starting to come together.

~

While it's easy to romanticize America as a melting pot, Bryson also illustrates that living with diversity is hard. He describes the tip of the iceberg in the Chapter, *Varieties of English.*

"In Britain *homely* is a flattering expression (equivalent to *homey*); in America it means '*ugly.*' In Britain upstairs is the first floor; in America it is the second. In Britain *to table a motion* means to put it forward for discussion, in America it means to put it aside. *Presently*, means 'now' in America; in Britain it means 'in a little while' ... *To keep your pecker up* is an innocuous expression in Britain (even though, curiously, *pecker* has the same slang meaning there), but *to be stuffed* is distinctly rude, so that if you say at a dinner party, 'I couldn't eat another thing; I'm stuffed,' an embarrassing silence will fall over the table."

"Whether you call a long cylindrical sandwich a hero, a submarine, a hoagy, a torpedo, a garibaldi, a poor boy, or any of at least half a dozen other names tells us something about where you come from. Whether you call it cottage cheese, Dutch cheese, pot cheese, smearcase, clabber cheese, or curd cheese tells us something more ... If you have a catch rather than play catch or stand on line rather than in line clearly you are a New Yorker. Whether you call it pop or soda, bucket or pail, baby carriage or baby buggy, scat or gesundheit, the beach or the shore—all these and countless others tell us a little something about where you come from."

People make language their own, I realized. *Words are born, grow cute tenors or harsh tones and then fade. It's the circle of life. It also produces pride and confusion.*

~

Misunderstandings can be benign and funny. But in the Chapter, Swearing, Bryson demonstrates the destructive potential of words. Conflict is a breath away, especially between people who come from different cultures and backgrounds, and use different languages.

"Among the Chinese," Bryson details, "to be called a turtle is the worst possible insult. In Norwegian, *devil* is highly taboo—roughly equivalent to our *fuck*. Among the Xoxa tribe of South Africa the most provocative possible remark is *hlebeshako* – 'your mother's ears.' Incest is so serious in many cultures that often it need be implied in only the vaguest terms, as with *tu madre* in Spanish and *your mama* among blacks in America. Often national terms of abuse are nonsensical, as in the German *schweinehund,* which means "pig-dog.""

"Swearing seems to have some near-universal qualities," Bryson concludes about words that get children punished and spur adults into verbal and physical fights, "In almost all cultures, swearing involves one or more of the following: filth, the forbidden (particularly incest), and the sacred, and usually all three. Most cultures have two levels of swearing—relatively mild and highly profane."

Some words should have more power and at times be off limits. Still, while all words need to be respected, I vow not to take words too seriously. Because if you're willing to get into a fight over something someone says, you're an easy target for those who hunt in packs or pack heat.

~

The mother tongue awakened me to two things. One, I'll be learning rules and definitions in English and other languages until I die. Two, those who excel at reading and writing have power. Then, like former boxing promoter Don King, I had a moment of religious "epiphanosity," and vowed not to let grammar grouches and language snobs embarrass me into silence.

I wrote about being biracial, dealing with a girlfriend's death, and playing beach volleyball. I thought about submitting my work to publishers, but imagined rejection letters reading: "Mr. Griffin, The good news is we liked the idea of a biracial kid overcoming racism, death of a friend and becoming a champion. The bad news is your grammar and structure are so flawed we shredded your manuscript after reading the first couple chapters. Spend a year or two with an editor or back in school. Until then, future submissions will meet the same fate. Good luck."

So I kept writing, because after my teammate and I dominated the professional beach volleyball qualifying tour, I understood the power of language. And I wanted more.

*   *   *

Seven years after reading the mother tongue I began graduate school in the Jack Kerouac School of Disembodied Poetics at Naropa University.

One of my favorite classes was Tai Chi, which I took as my contemplative requirement each semester. For those two years I started every morning inhaling and exhaling long perfect breaths, rooting my feet to the earth, and doing what my teacher—and his teacher—and his teacher—and his teacher—and so on for the last two thousand years, had said was Tai Chi's most important mantra: Relax. Relax. Relax. Relax.

~

Documentary in Poetry was my most spiritual class. I took the advice of a Native American spirit I'd met on Independence Pass, and researched Chief Joseph and the Nez Perce. I illustrated the cover and self-published several dozen copies. After graduation (first fall I hadn't coached volleyball at Fairview High School in a decade), I took a ten-day road trip through the north-west, including three nights in the birthplace of the Nez Perce, the Wallowa Valley.

First afternoon of the road trip I camped near Steamboat Springs, fished the Yampa River from late afternoon until dark and didn't see a single fish. The next night I camped near a hot springs outside Boise Idaho, hit the road in the morning and checked into my cabin in Wallowa Valley that evening.

I was wading the Lostine River at first light. The fishing was slow—a few strikes and one bull netted. That evening I went to an art show featuring Native American artists to benefit the Nez Perce. The art was excellent: sculptures, paintings, rugs, pottery. I talked with locals, a few from out of state, and a member of the Nez Perce who agreed to speak with me about my documentary. We talked about my life-long interests in the northwest, Native Americans, and our shared humanity.

First thing the next morning I was back in the Lostine River and the fishing picked up—a couple bulls and brooks netted. The following night I went to a community dinner and one-man-show on a slave's struggle for freedom in the 1850's, which was written and performed by an African American from Seattle. More nice people; good conversations.

To get back to Colorado I drove east to spend a night camped near Lolo Pass.

Chief Joseph and the Nez Perce escaped over Lolo Pass when the US Army attacked them in 1877. The heavily armored US Army struggled pursuing the Nez Perce across the Salmon River, so the Nez Perce doubled back and then crossed LoLo Pass, leaving the trail littered with fallen trees and rocks. With a three-day lead and having left their home, the Nez Perce didn't think the US Army would continue their pursuit, so they brought their rear guard back to camp. Before sunrise the US Army attacked and killed 95 of 600 Nez Perce. The assault on sleeping men, women, children, and elderly was called the Battle of Big Hole.

I set up my tent and meditated late into the night, then woke early to the call of eagles before driving to the Grand Tetons.

That evening I waded through the Yellowstone River and a robust hatch. I judged the currents, rocks, and slight breeze. Felt the crisp rhythm in my cast. Gently landed a #20 Blue Wing-Olive. Stripped my line. Watched a Brown rise and gulp my fly. Set the hook, turned her and reeled—turned her and reeled—turned her and reeled. Turned her again, raised my pole, then scooped with my net, removed the hook and marveled. 15 inches of perfect design, stunning colors.

"Thank you," I said like always, before watching her disappear into the current like a wisp of smoke into air.

I netted a dozen Browns and Cutthroats. Halfway between sunset and dark I sat on the bank. The Yellowstone rippled a tune the big browns like. I thought about people I met at the art show and dinner and looked forward to hearing from those who agreed to read my documentary. I hoped they'd be impressed with my thorough research. And how my prose made it clear that the age-old tactic of 'divide and conquer' is working as well as ever. I went so far as to imagine being invited to do a workshop as an honorary member of the Nez Perce, but didn't get my hopes too high. A semester of research didn't make me an expert. And although many expressed gratitude, many also suggested I do a book on the struggles of African Americans.

Some might say I'm an outgoing, quick witted, exuberant person (perhaps including a few I met in Wallowa Valley that weekend). But everyone else would tell you I'm practically a recluse, and must get a nasty rash every time I touch a phone. Which is why I only made a few follow-up calls to those in Wallowa Valley. Instead I focused on connecting with teachers I'd worked with in the Boulder Valley School District, and writing grants to do my poetry workshops.

~

Another inspiring class came in the fall of my first year. We studied Karl Marx, philosopher, economist, journalist, and socialist born in Prussia in 1818. And Frederick Engels, German philosopher, social scientist, journalist, and business man.

There are reasons to disagree with Marx and Engels, I know. But I agree with my mom, who said the problems with many communist and socialist governments aren't the systems. It's that the people in charge can easily abuse them to feather their own nest. A problem, by the way, no system, including capitalism, is immune to. Besides, Marx and Engels have some important ideas about how to minimize greed.

Marx thought the essence of humanity is relationship. So he praised capitalism for creating a world market, world literature, and cosmopolitanism. But he also criticized capitalism for turning money into the primary connection between people.

Exactly! Money determines neighborhoods, friends, and schools. And prioritizes things like profits over people and lobbyists over democracy.

Marx also predicted capitalism won't rule for long because it prioritizes greed, which will cause too many to become oppressed and turn violent.

Right.

"Ruling ideas of an age," Marx observed, keeping the thought-provoking ideas coming, "are the ideas of the ruling class naturalized."

Like the illogical rules of English, and white babies who listen to successful white English speakers from womb to adulthood.

These are advantages white Americans often ignore when boasting about how far equality has come. Which means when they look at poverty, school drop-out, incarceration, drug addiction, and violent crime statistics, it seems reasonable to conclude that dark-skinned people are not that smart.

For 5000 years, people of all colors have been enslaved or oppressed by a "ruling class" which made it illegal for them to learn how to read and write. In America, dark-skinned people (with the help of many whites) fought and died to be educated. And they've been successful enough that unless all Americans learn to speak and act differently in the next two or three generations, minorities are going to be the majority, and whites will be the ones labeled poor and stupid.

"Age" and "class" could refer to labels used in grades K-12: boys vs. girls, jocks vs. nerds, preppies vs. smokers. And how the education of what Marx called the Bourgeoisie—the mass of working class people who are the unwitting carriers of "false consciousness"—begins in elementary school.

Two months into two years of full-time school and, as I had throughout my life, I was thinking about teaching those with whom I have the best rapport, elementary-age kids. Mostly I dreamt about teaching language arts; reading and writing books, reports, stories, and personal goals. Then share and rewrite, share and rewrite, share and rewrite. And watch our dreams come true.

~

"Speak, write, and let no one stop you!" Professor Taylor wrote on the board to begin one of the most transformative lessons in my life.

"Words tell us very little about what something *is*," Taylor said, "mostly words tell us what something *is not*. For example, someone tells you to look at that 'tree.' You could name millions of things you're *not* looking for, anything with fur, skin, scales, feathers, etc. You can name some things you *are* looking for, roots, trunk, bark, branches, leaves or needles. But you know nothing about the *actual* tree. Is it the evergreen standing tall in the middle of the cliff? The aspen, largest living organism on earth? The ironwood, living up to its name as it decays? The rosewood, made of porcelain and crafted 1500 years ago?"

Trees are simple compared to people: the twelfth generation Irish American or twelfth generation African American. The communist who works like a capitalist or a capitalist who labors like a socialist. The scholarly athlete or artistic mathematician. The socially liberal conservative or fiscally conservative liberal. The soft-spoken extremist or hard-line moderate. Or those with a religious experience similar to mine, when I became more Lutheran after reading a Buddhist's thoughts on Jesus.

Then I thought about growing up in Boulder, going to college in Kansas, living four years in LA and traveling coast to coast 25 weekends a year. I also considered my enthusiasm for liberals and distaste for conservatives. Suddenly I recognized that my passion for one position made it easy to dismiss another. Then it hit me—a diamond bullet through my forehead.

We're born prejudiced! From our first moments in the womb, we feel rhythms of our mother's heart, lungs, and blood streams. We feel when she lies down, runs, and accelerates in a car. We feel with a mass that grows 600% in 24 weeks, then the vibrations hit our ear drums: loud and quiet sounds and voices and their effect on our mother. Scientists say people do better when parents talk and sing to babies in the womb. Few successful societies in history would tell you otherwise. It's Language 101. It means everyone is born prejudiced!

So I vowed to study those who loved their enemies. Peace-makers like Jesus, Gandhi, Martin Luther King Jr., Thich Nhat Hahn, Chief Joseph, Chief Niwot, The Dalai Lama, and many more. I used their work as a foundation for my poetry workshops. I was dreaming about teaching kids the power in language. And the joy we can create when we celebrate everyone.

PART I

Pain makes man think.
Thought makes man wise.
Wisdom makes life endurable.

John Patrick

Breathing and Rising

Roots

My mom is a blond, blue-eyed Caucasian born into the middle-class in Hamburg, Germany. My father was a tall, athletic, dark African American born in the ghettos of Trenton, New Jersey. In 1963, they each turned 13 and moved to Boulder, Colorado.

It's hard to know who went through the bigger culture shock, but they each used their intelligence, good looks and talent to fit in. As well as to rebel.

~

I was born with dark skin, tightly curled black hair and in 1969—making me part of the first generation of black Americans to be born free. It feels strange to write that the first generation of black Americans born free came in the 1960's, 1970's and 1980's. I too get lost in the semantics of Reconstruction: Blacks were freed in 1864; 100 years of Jim Crow, KKK and Segregation were about "rights," not "freedom." Still, while a second-class citizen is more free than a slave, blacks were actually freed on July 2, 1964. My dad was 14.

After moving from the black ghettos in New Jersey, my dad's family celebrated the Civil Rights Act among the 90% white, largely rural and conservative population in Colorado. Some whites didn't like the changes. And even though most celebrated our Constitution being amended, many assumed police, lawyers and judges would uphold the new law. This made it all too easy to dismiss the hatred many had already learned to ignore.

It must have been harder for blacks to forget which water fountains, restrooms, restaurants, and hotels were "white only." Or which bars men stumbled out of, itching to maintain social order. Where school-aged boys roamed, looking to make their dads and heritage proud. Where girls and women gathered and squawked about the unnatural, unkempt look of dark skin and afros.

It must have been harder for blacks to forget what it took for white America to wake up: Step one, let your enemy beat you with a club. Step two, get wealthy and powerful whites to film it. Step three, get whites who are more wealthy and powerful to ok it for broadcasting. Finally, have the US military escort some blacks into schools. And still, some wealthy and powerful whites vowed never to cave to our government, which they branded unlawful and immoral.

My dad focused his fear and anger into athletics. He spent most of his time in weight rooms, on football fields and basketball courts nurturing a discipline that made him a star at Fairview High School. When he wasn't playing sports, he hung out with and fell for a beautiful blond who hadn't been taught the American social norms most girls had.

~

Even though it took most of Germany's cities being reduced to rubble (and Germans emotionally so), many were thankful to be rid of Hitler and a chance to start anew. Given no choice, the Germans invested in their people, in infrastructure, manufacturing, education. And they were intolerant of hateful, divisive rhetoric, even if only a small minority claimed offense.

My mom was born five years into the rebuilding, and often spoke of the lessons her mother and father taught: watch for the pitfalls in patriotism! Debate all the good and horror before going to war, and remember that if we try to understand another's point of view, we just might learn to get along.

My mom quickly lost her German accent and learned the idiosyncrasies of American teen life. While she played along with fancy hair, make-up, hip clothes, and finding a boyfriend (in sharp contrast to her tomboy elementary years in Germany), she never understood, nor cared to maintain America's dark secret. Consequently, despite vast disapproval (and in some ways because of it), my mom fell for the darkest of the tall and handsome athletes at Fairview High School.

In the fall of her Senior year, mom learned she was pregnant. Abortion was never an option. Friends, teachers, pastors, and school counselors talked about the difficulties, and praised the benefits of giving me up to a black family. Still, my mom vowed to prove love overcomes.

Nurses took me shortly after my birth and gave me to a foster family (standard practice for young, unwed mothers at that time). First thing after the 30-day waiting period, my mom went to court, addressed the judge, signed the paper work, and brought me home.

The women in my mom's church choir confessed many years later, they'd have visited us in the hospital but, "Just didn't know what to say." And she began to ignore the questioning glances of strangers who wouldn't have noticed her if she wasn't so young and carrying a black baby.

Not everyone would be so hard to convince. My mom's high school French teacher visited us in the hospital. She brought a small gift with a handwritten note saying, "Every child comes with the message that God is not yet disappointed in humanity." Also, my mom's parents vowed to help.

~

My parents agreed to marry and raise me. They regretted their lack of maturity. A mere high school education and few resources would compound the difficulty of my having to grow up biracial in America. But they never regretted their decision. They often told me I was the best thing they would ever do. And while some may have thought I was a mistake, I never thought that about myself.

While I've never thought of myself as a mistake, I have often wished people spent more time talking about "race"—calling it the myth it is. A lie. A 5000 year-old illusion that enabled millions of people to call themselves "civil" while doing unspeakable things. And like in most societies that enslaved others, many Americans didn't witness the horror that provided them economic power. So sixteen generations of whites obeyed the law that equated black people with cattle. While sixteen generations of blacks lived being treated like cattle.

America lost powerful voices for equality and love with the assassinations of John F. Kennedy, the first President to speak of blacks as equals; Malcom X, best known for "bullet or the ballot box," but preaching love and unity after traveling the world; and Martin Luther King Jr., who survived a decade fighting the KKK, but was murdered only a few years after confronting those who get rich off poverty and war. Love can overcome. But when bodies crumple under bullets, they provide fertile ground for myths, lies, and illusions.

Being so young, my parents probably would've divorced anyway. But being an interracial couple significantly increased the odds (it would've been *illegal* for them to marry just two years earlier!). Race riots erupted across the nation. The University of Colorado's campus burned the year I was born. And while my parents never blamed race for their relationship deteriorating into frustration, faithlessness, and violence, raising a biracial child in a nation and town that were literally on fire created enormous pressure. They divorced before my second birthday.

~

The most common childhood memory I have of my dad is a Saturday or Sunday spent looking out my living room window, waiting for him to pick me up. He rarely came on time and often didn't show at all.

When he did pick me up, we usually went to watch and play basketball at the University of Colorado. Two dozen wide sandstone steps lead to the tall heavy wooden doors. Once inside, you're met by the smells of a gym built in 1924 and used ever since. Then came the sounds of squeaking sneakers and bouncing balls echoing off the stone walls. My heart still jumps with excitement.

My dad was 6'2", 220 pounds of chiseled muscle. He usually played in sweatpants, to hide his "chicken legs" (enormous thighs and bone-thin calves) as he called them. Watching my dad pile more weights on the calf machine after some huge white guy finished lifting was the first of many lessons in how the biggest aren't always the strongest.

On a basketball court, as in all aspects of his life, my dad was aggressive. His jump shot was flat, as if it had to get to the rim in a hurry. Time and again my dad would shoot so low the ball seemed certain to clang off the front of the rim but … swish. And he drove hard to the basket, through defenders.

"Football is *not* a contact sport," my dad often said, "Football is a collision sport. Basketball," he'd emphasize, "is a contact sport."

I'd hear my dad bark over all the other noise in the gym, "Move!" "Set a pick!" "D-up!" and inevitably, "Foul!"

"Come on Chico," my dad's defenders sometimes pleaded using his nickname which means, 'Little Man,' "If you're going to come at me like that … I gotta play too."

"BALL," my dad would command and walk to the top of the key.

"Come on," they'd insist.

"The ball stays here!" he'd whip the ball to the defender and bark, "Check it up!" then step forward like he was going to start throwing punches if the ball didn't come back in play.

I had a hard time understanding my dad's anger over a game. Maybe because I didn't grow up when hanging "White Only" signs was legal. Maybe because the thought of hurting anything larger than an ant made me sick. Maybe because my mother and her parents denounced violence and demanded I be thoughtful and kind. Whatever the reason, this distance between my dad and me was not lost on him. "Sometimes," he said when I was twelve and we were talking about people we didn't like, "I think you're the adult."

~

While nothing could replace my dad's broken promises and absence, my mom did her best, by sharing the kind of unrelenting support she learned from her mother and grandmother.

My great-great-grandmother stayed with her husband even though he regularly spent his small paychecks on beer instead of food for his hungry family of fifteen. Still, my great-grandmother taught my grandmother and her sister how to make-do while respecting the needs of others.

My grandmother would jump to my beck-and-call nearly as often as my mom. Though even she wished my mom were more strict with my dad who never paid child support. And with me, who weaseled chocolate, video games, less homework, and days off from school when I didn't feel that sick.

The first time my mom told me my dad hit her I was 42 (writing this memoir). My mom's silence may have helped save what little relationship I've had with my dad and kept my thoughts of black people more positive. On the other hand, maybe I would've better understood their divorce and gotten over my dad's broken promises more quickly. Maybe things would've ended up virtually the same.

"This world is a tough enough place to live," the women in my mom's family have said for generations, just before committing yet another act of forgiveness and kindness.

~

I was 23 when my dad first told me that he hit my mom. He came to the school where I worked as a teacher's assistant. I hadn't seen or spoken to him in months and was surprised he knew where to find me.

I was about to move to Southern California to pursue a career in pro beach volleyball. We went outside. He talked about regrets, shame for hitting my mom and not being there for me. "I saw how the anger was poison," he explained, "the hatred in me and our family was toxic, and I knew you didn't need to be around it."

He cried, asked for forgiveness and we hugged. I told him it was ok. I could understand his anger at the injustice we face as black men, and his not wanting to expose me to the unproductive aspects of it.

"You and your great-grandmother are so alike," he said.

From what I heard, my paternal great grand-mother was every bit of what you'd expect from a black woman who earned a college degree and raised a family in the early 1900's. "It's too bad you didn't get the chance to know her better," my dad often lamented.

My memories are from early elementary school. I'd step into my grandma's dark house (shades on every window always drawn shut). First thing my dad and grandma would say is to give great-grandma a kiss and hug. She was usually resting in her bedroom at the end of the dark hallway. Small, dark, wrinkled and nice, she raved about how good I was at coloring. She pulled a new coloring book from her nightstand almost every time I came.

Years after she passed, my dad told me he'd been like the walking dead for most his life. That his Grandma implored him to do the right thing, but he couldn't hear her until he was forty and she was gone. Still, he was happy to hear her now, providing insight that helped him in all aspects of life, including his job as a bouncer in a club that saw its share of conflict.

"People just want respect," he emphasized, "so I watch—walk around and talk—let people know I'm on their side. I want them to have a good time. All the fighting and other nonsense can be avoided. People just want respect."

~

My mom's ability to put a positive spin on things is a big part of my becoming a pro athlete, coach, teacher, graduate student, and writer. Still, my mom had her practical side, too. Like when our church's charity towards our family included sending her to Seminary. And after graduating, she nevertheless told them she couldn't serve a congregation because church politics made it too difficult for her to be a pastor and remain faithful.

While my mom couldn't make it her profession, church was a staple. I have fond memories. Good friends in Sunday school, confirmation and other classes. The quick recognition and inflection of pride my dark skin afforded me around the older white congregation. And the music— watching my mom stand tall in the choir, her strong, low soprano voice crisply singing her favorite Christmas Hymn, *Lo, How a Rose e'er Blooming*.

The shades in our house were always pulled open at first light. Our cats and dogs would bask in a spot of sun. I would squint and recoil under my blankets, then slowly warm and wake. And though I don't like being seen through an open window, opening my shades is a habit, spurred by memories of my mom pushing back the curtains and humming:

How Can I Keep from Singing

Though winds will rage on the storm-tossed sea
While to the rock I'm clinging
Since love is lord o'er heaven and earth
How can I keep from singing?

~

Every year my journey has grown more complex—new rights, wrongs—and most especially my experiences with the countless shades of gray. Still, aside from a few, I've enjoyed life more each year. Mostly because I learned early on that within all the madness, there's grace.

Culture

My Opa (German for grandfather) was born into a life of privilege in Hamburg, Germany in 1921. He had two siblings and all three had their own floor in their home: bedroom, music room, and library. The most poetic illustration of his mother's fearful expectations and demands was that it'd be easier for her to let food rot than to give it away.

My Oma (German for Grandmother), was also born in Hamburg, Germany in 1923. Her family was poor but not without. Her father worked for the railroad and owned a plot of land in the woods outside Hamburg. Oma spoke fondly of frequent weekend getaways from their home in the city's poor neighborhoods, even though they took a train and then still had to carry food, water and other essentials a few miles down a dirt road to their "cabin" (a well-built shed with a stove).

Oma's mother was short, stout, walked the walk, talked the talk, and most respected her authority. While shopping during the Nazi era, she'd firmly take my Oma's hand and lead her into the butcher shop. Since this was the same kind and skilled butcher they'd gone to for years, she continued to patronize him into the late 1930's, despite the Jewish star in the window and the posted order not to shop there amid the Nazis staging their menacing presence.

~

My Oma and Opa were skilled classical musicians who met studying at the Music School in Lübeck. Not long after they married the United States carpet-bombed Hamburg. My Oma was fortunate to be with Opa at the time, because seventeen in Oma's family burned in their basements the night her neighborhood turned into an inferno. As is often the case in war, the poor are the first to go.

For those who lose wars, the rich take a beating too. My Opa's family lost their house, possessions, and savings to bombing fires.

Time does heal. But in some ways, Oma and Opa never overcame being citizens of the country that gave rise to Hitler, and surviving the carnage as the world's armies put a stop to what they couldn't. Sometimes their guilt and pain would show, like when talking about flags. They'd sit up like King Cobras—hoods spread—hissing, "We hate *all* flags for the unthinking, blind allegiances, and frightening loyalties they evoke in people."

~

Opa was a linguist and received his PhD at the University of Hamburg where he also became a professor. He told me he liked how different languages and perspectives can reveal similarities in people. He was also the kind of person who knew things would get better as soon as everyone understood he was always right. When university politics turned sour in Hamburg, he was offered a fresh start at the University of Colorado in Boulder, and moved his wife and two children to the United States.

Oma hated leaving family, friends, Hamburg's forests and harbors, and vacations in the Swiss Alps. Nevertheless, Oma did what she did best; she created a home overflowing with comfort, support, and love.

Six years after leaving Germany, Oma's and Opa's teenage daughter got pregnant and they turned their basement into a nursery. While my mom went to school and work, I thrived under Oma's doting care. And the male role model position left vacant by my dad was filled by Opa.

Opa left when I was 10. He'd fallen in love with his research assistant who accepted a position in Germany. He took me for a drive before leaving, apologized and assured me his leaving had nothing to do with me. He also said he could best continue his work of understanding different languages and cultures in Germany. Then he promised to fly me over to visit.

I never went and only received rare random post cards and letters over the years. He retired, then moved around the US with his wife who had teaching positions in Washington State, Wisconsin, Alabama and finally, Pennsylvania.

My mom and I went to see him in Pennsylvania in my early twenties. His wife was nice and I felt welcomed in their home surrounded by a few acres with a garden, goats and chickens. At dinner he talked about his time in America's South, and how he saw racism still existing in its educational and judicial systems. Though I liked catching up and hearing his perspective, I was ready to get home by the end of the long weekend. We never spoke again.

~

After 40 years of love and friendship, Oma landed in hospital with a nervous breakdown when Opa moved back to Germany with a woman their daughter's age.

Though never quite the same, Oma's gentle, contagious laugh returned. She worked in the kitchen at Boulder High School for a decade, with a boss who was "mean and nasty" for no reason (though after Oma retired her boss regularly invited her to lunch and, naturally, Oma went). Oma's soups were loved and requested by staff and students. She regularly gave to charity, church, and families (especially children).

Oma almost always condemned violence, and looked for the best ways to straddle the line between doing what's right and what's best. Like when she and Opa decided to speak only English to me. They loved German, from the staccato sounds matching the stern culture, to use of the masculine, feminine and other grammatical structure they felt better expressed what they were thinking. Still, they thought my being black and raised by whites in a white community would make it hard enough for me to fit in, so they exposed me to as much English as possible.

Oma met Thekla not long after Opa left. Thekla was from Hamburg, but Oma didn't know exactly where until she visited Thekla at her assisted living facility. Oma arrived early (as always) and while waiting in Thekla's room, saw a painting of my Opa's house before it was bombed and burned down. Thekla had painted the house she saw across the street from her bedroom window! She and Oma became dear friends. They criticized America sharply and loved America for being able to do so. Like Oma always said, "Most Americans are so very kind."

~

I flew to Germany and stayed with a friend for a couple weeks after graduate school in 2003. I visited the Alte Pinakothe where a highlight was a wall sized Monet Water Lily. I gazed for 20 minutes. The science and technology at The Deutsches Museum had me believing in miracles. I also walked and sketched in and around Munich: Neuschwanstein, Peterskirche Cathedral, Marienplatz, and English Gardens. I met family for the first time and we went to their favorite beer garden for a large pretzel and larger beer. Then to their living room for coffee, photo albums, and more stories. They dropped me off and as I walked the busy streets, thought of my mom, Oma and Opa talking in the kitchen, and took a liking to the German being spoken around me.

I also visited the Dachau Concentration camp—a museum to remind people how dangerous we can be. I sketched and took deep breaths. I thought about my great grandmother taking my Oma's hand while walking past the Nazis and into the Jewish-owned butcher shop. I remembered American bombs killing seventeen in our family. And heard my Oma, from 1982 to 1999, objecting to US bombing campaigns: Lebanon, Panama, Gulf War, Bosnia, Haiti, and Kosovo.

"Stop the bombing," she'd say, "too many innocent people die." We never talked about her family, but I saw her freeze up from time to time. It must be hard to forget the smell of burnt steel, glass, and flesh.

~

For a long time I tried to laugh and join the banter in satire and caricatures (like Hogan's Heroes). But it's like my mom always said, "Language is not just reflective, language creates!" And I developed a strong distaste for negative stereotypes of all kinds.

Potential

In first grade, I remember brightly colored numbers and letters on a thick rug; perfectly sized chairs and tables; carousels of glue, scissors, and markers; a castle with a small metal crank to lower and raise the drawbridge; two exit doors, one was the fastest way out to recess. I also remember a day when the teacher didn't understand me.

It was a warm spring Saint Patrick's Day. The game of tag was loud and fast. And it had a new rule: if the person you tag isn't wearing green, you get to pinch them.

I wasn't wearing green. I also got distracted and was tagged. The pinch hurt and pissed me off. A burst of adrenalin and I chased someone down. I wanted to pinch hard but didn't (one of many examples of when I decided to hurt something, but my muscles fell limp as I went to strike). Then I ran to a safe distance.

Heart pounding I vowed not to get caught again. I darted and prowled behind the fort, swings, and monkey bars. Most who were "it" barely looked at me. A few of the faster boys stalked, but no one sprinted.

One boy was targeted a lot. I thought his shirt was green enough. A couple of kids said his shirt was blue and pinched hard. Recess dragged to an end.

~

That afternoon, our class did a worksheet on colors. There was a row of circles down the left and the names of colors down the right. Our assignment was to color in a circle and to draw a line to the corresponding name. If needed, there was a large color wheel posted on the wall: detailed, neatly labeled, beautiful. My mind wandered.

Some greens look bluish, yellows greenish, reds purplish, I thought then I realized, *there are millions of blues, yellows, and reds.*

Breathing and Rising

Thrilled about my revelation I raised my hand. The teacher came over.

"When someone says something is blue, we still don't know what color it is," I explained.

She stared for a moment.

Such "looks" are common. Variations include lowered or raised eyebrows and slightly open or pursed lips. Over the years I've learned they can mean anything. Someone may dislike my clothes, or want to flirt with me. Maybe they didn't get enough sleep, or are trying to decide if they're going to tell me about the food on my face. Once, while in a bar in Kansas, a stranger gave me the "look" and after I wiped my mouth, called me a nigger.

"People don't see blue and call it pink," she politely stated.

"At recess, my classmates and I called the same color something different," I said.

"It doesn't work like that," she replied.

"It wouldn't happen a lot," I clarified knowing the kids at recess were just being mean, "Still, it could happen, right?"

"No. Finish your worksheet," she said then walked away.

Wait! Get back here! I thought, heart beating as it had after being caught and pinched at morning recess. I wanted to scream, *don't you get it? I'm right!*

Wisdom

I remember going to the library in fourth grade. The lesson began with students taking turns reading aloud. Classmates were mostly patient, but my stammering was excruciating to me. Fortunately, the text ended before my turn. Then we were allowed to explore the library. I loved going at my own pace among the seemingly endless possibilities.

A <u>John Henry</u> picture book was displayed. My dad's name is John and the man on the cover had the same hair, skin and physique. I picked it up.

John Henry was gifted with size and strength. After working the railroads for years, he could swing a hammer better than anyone. Then, someone built a machine to replace the railroad worker. To prove a person's worth, John challenged the machine to see who could dig a tunnel faster. My heart and mind raced. John had to win!

The illustrations were finely drawn: huge iron wheels and blades pulverized rock; the curves of John's thick thighs, shoulders, and forearms blasted with the hammer. Exhaust spewed. John sweat. The lead traded back and forth.

Moments after winning John collapsed and died. He also won the admiration of those who favored the machine. It was shocking, sad and beautiful. I checked it out.

Each time I read it, I grew more sick over the illustration of John's dark powerful body on the ground, with the pale man sitting in the machine behind him.

Overdue notices piled up in my desk. The librarian paid me a visit. Embarrassed for being spellbound by a picture book, I gave it back.

~

In my twenties, I saw a <u>John Henry</u> picture book read on television. Illustrations were brilliantly detailed and colored. The narrator sounded like James Earl Jones. During the race, choir voices rose and soared, percussions thumped, clanged, and rolled. John broke through the wall first and fell in silence.

I was training for a career in pro beach volleyball and as I lifted weights and ran the foothills, pictured myself in a race against the machine like John Henry.

~

In my late thirties I fulfilled a dream of learning to play the guitar and some Blues. To improve finger picking, I researched and found Mississippi John Hurt. His songs sounded simple but cool, so I got a book and learned Hurt played complex arrangements with ease. I also learned Hurt was an extraordinary man.

John Hurt was born in Mississippi in 1893. Discrimination was law. African Americans were beaten, raped and murdered without consequence, but the legend of John Henry inspired hard work to overcome impossible odds. From 1908 to 1963 Hurt provided for his family by jacking up and leveling railroad ties; cutting oak, pine and cypress trees into cross ties; building dams and levees; cutting trees and gravel roads; tending cows, filing hoes and farming other people's land.

Hurt also loved music. At 12 years old he taught himself to play guitar and performed for house parties. At 23 he worked the Illinois Central line and a rail-hand named Walter Jackson taught him "Spike Driver's Blues" (a version on John Henry). He had his first recording session in Memphis at 35, and played saloons and roadhouses for the next 35 years.

In 1964, the same year the Civil Rights Act set black Americans free, Hurt turned 70 and was "discovered." He moved to Washington D.C. to pursue music full time. He was invited to play folk clubs, The Newport Folk Festival, college campuses and Johnny Carson's Tonight Show. The New York Times praised his "compelling artistry" adding, "His performances have the quiet introspective quality of chamber music." Fellow musicians said Hurt was patient, wise, and gentle. Stefan Grossman studied guitar with Hurt and admired how he lived by the saying, "When in Rome, do Rome," which made him, "very Christ-like and perfect."

Hurt could afford a small house and a bit of land in the summer of 1965, so he moved to Mississippi with his wife and grandchildren. The next summer, Hurt visited New York City to record for Vanguard. "He got uncomfortable with people fighting to control his recordings," Grossman wrote, "so he went back home and died in his sleep [November 2, 1966]. He came in gently, left gently."

~

The first song I learned, because it was the easiest to play, was "Spike Driver's Blues."

Spike Driver's Blues
John Henry was a steel-drivin man,
Oh, he went down, yes, he went down.
John Henry he had a little wife,
Name was Poly Anne, name was Poly Anne.
John Henry took sick in the bed,
She drove steel like a man, drove steel like a man.
John Henry he left his hammer
Layin' 'side the road, layin' 'side the road.
John Henry, he left his hammer
Painted in red, all painted in red.
You just take this hammer and carry it to my captain
Tell him I'm gone, tell him I'm gone, tell him I'm gone.

I savored playing and singing it every day for months. The rolling base line, smooth melody and insightful lyrics steam-rolled the melancholy I'd felt since reading John Henry in fourth grade.

Hell yah, tell him I'm gone! Or better yet, I'll tell him "Take this job and shove it!" Or "Go fuck yourself!"

~

For 55 years, Hurt had no choice but to work railroads and farms. Still, he never lost his passion to play guitar and sing. Hurt had been a star throughout the south for half a century before being "discovered." And when Hurt could finally earn a good living as a musician, he bought a small house, a little land, and spent as much time as he could with his family.

Nigger

The first time someone called me a nigger was the summer after fifth grade.

I was on the large gravel field by my elementary school. On the southwest border of the field were two baseball diamonds with ten-foot tall chain link fences for backstops, the bases were old tires buried in the dirt. Some were soft, slick, and crumpled under my weight. Others were hard and deeply grooved. They could be treacherous. A misstep could mean a broken ankle.

I practiced running them—full speed. One stutter step too many and I'd repeat the loop. I was learning precision, focus, and courage. It wasn't long before other kids had a hard time throwing me out.

~

Summer after 5th grade I was returning home through the diamonds. Though late, I decided to sprint the bases. I saw three kids on the southern edge of the field walking my way. After a poor performance around the first diamond and improvement around the second, I jogged through the infield, hustling home. I glanced at the kids—boys, two my size, the other smaller.

I preferred a short cut home, a trail where I could dart between tunnels of bushes and trees and leap on boulders for dry passage over Bear Creek. Just before reaching the trail I heard yelling and glanced back. The boys again. One was shouting. I couldn't hear him.

"What?" I inquired.

"Fucking nigger," he yelled.

"What?" I said again.

"Fucking N-I-G-G-E-R!" he repeated.

"What?!" I was confused.

They laughed.

I needed to get home. I started walking.

A rock tumbled by my feet. I turned to see all three pick up more rocks. They wound up. I planned my exit strategy—side step and run. One rock stopped ten feet in front of me. The others rolled harmlessly by.

They can't hit me. Fuck them!

Now it was my turn. I picked up a rock, threw it and watched it sail over their heads. We continued our exchange—my rocks flying left, right and long—theirs tumbling weakly by. I found bigger and heavier rocks, then chuckled over how certain I was they were going to lose.

As soon as the rock left my hand I knew it had a chance. The rock hit the boy who shouted on top of the head, bounced remarkably high, and sounded a hollow knock I'd never heard before. The kid grabbed his head, bent over and screamed. The others rushed to his side.

Now I was scared. Really scared. I ran.

~

Once home, I debated whether or not to tell my mom and Oma. Since it took half the world's armies to end Hitler and his regime, my mom and Oma understood the need for self-defense. On occasion my Oma told me to "box" a bully on the nose. Then she'd strike the air, demonstrating she had no idea how to throw a damaging punch.

I was in my thirties the last time my Oma advised me to hit someone. I visited her at an assisted living facility. Alzheimer's had taken her ability to recognize most, but she always knew me. Walking arm in arm from the lounge to her room a man called me a nigger. We looked at each other and kept walking. Then she boxed the air and we laughed at the poor fundamentals in her jab and our desire to flatten a frail old man who thought it was 1950.

Still, my mom and Oma drew a hard line when it comes to violence. They cited the cycles: the horror of WWI's aftermath giving rise to Hitler and his followers; gang members exacting revenge for murdered friends; abused children who should know best that it's wrong, but are more likely to abuse their own. Plus, when I replayed the rock throwing incident in my mind I felt bad, like watching my friend shoot at birds with his bb gun. I decided not to tell my mom and Oma.

~

A few weeks later I saw my dad and confessed. His head and shoulders slumped. He spoke with that intense but resigned tone that often came when he talked about race, "Curtis," he said, "someday you may have to pick up a rock, stick, brick—anything."

My dad seemed to be missing the point. I didn't really want to hurt that kid.

"Listen," my dad continued, "'nigger' is not only an insult but a warning—there's no telling how far that person is willing to go." My dad straightened his back, arms hanging comfortably, veins bulging across his thick hands and running up his dark, muscular forearms and biceps. He leaned forward, elbows resting on his gigantic thighs. "Promise me Curtis, you'll do what you have to in order to protect yourself."

My dad could be more aggressive than he had to be, like when he'd bark at the T.V. during football games, or plowed through defenders on a basketball court. But I remembered the pictures of America's "Strange Fruit" in our history books.

"Southern trees bear strange fruit
Blood on the leaves and blood at the root
Black bodies swinging in the southern breeze
Strange fruit hanging from the poplar trees

Here is fruit for the crows to pluck
For the rain to gather, for the wind to suck
For the sun to rot, for the trees to drop
Here is a strange and bitter crop."

I felt justified hitting that kid. I even wished I'd thrown a few more. They were easy targets huddled around their injured friend. Plus, my arm was just getting warm, and like I'd done in many games of dodge ball, I could've brought more heat, closed in, and taken out all three.

"You understand, right?" my dad's black eyes searched mine.

"Yes," I stated.

"Whatever it takes," his tone penetrated.

"I understand," I said with conviction.

~

The rest of that summer I worried the boys would seek revenge, so I picked up rocks before entering the seclusion of the short cut.

My vigilance dissolved in the fall of 6th grade. No one in school called me a nigger. I didn't know anyone who disliked me. Many told me being black was cool. Besides, I was strong and fast, so most wouldn't consider messing with me.

In the spring I was crossing the field and thought about the incident.

Those boys might have hurt me if they got close and surrounded me. It's good to know what it means to be called a nigger. Next time, I decided as I dashed down the path and over a creek that roared on that hot spring day, *I'll bolt for the bushes and disappear.*

~

I love to disappear. Going to the mountains is my favorite way. But I like to vanish in all environments. Which isn't easy when you're black in a sea of whites. And a big part of why I'm good at smiling and finding common ground.

Dreams

I remember about half a dozen dreams a year. In elementary school, a few were about a flood. But most had to do with either medieval warfare, running from a monster, or flying.

~

The first medieval war dream I had was in first grade. I was the best knight in our kingdom. All the people in our land were happy. The neighboring kingdom was ruled by a mean king. All his people were unhappy.

Our king ordered me to lead our army to vanquish the mean king.

> *I led the charge. When I swung my sword it glowed and ten enemy soldiers flew through the air and landed unconscious.*
>
> *My soldiers didn't have to fight as I swept the enemy like dust off a porch. Then I point my sword at the chest of the mean king and he surrenders.*
>
> *Suddenly the enemy soldiers regain consciousness and everyone celebrates.*
>
> *Soon, we were off to vanquish the next mean king.*
>
> *Kingdom after kingdom, we marched around the world.*

~

In 5th and 6th grade I had a friend who loved medieval war. He owned a number of dice playing games. Each game presented many different strategies, and we used different kinds of dice, with anywhere from four sides—25%, 50% or 75% chances—to twenty sides, 5%, 10%, or 15% chances.

One game was like a chess board on a map with rivers, plains, forests, lakes and mountains. Playing-pieces represented infantries with leather or plate armor, cavalries, archers, catapults, battering rams and ladders. Advance your army, engage the enemy and capture his castle. Plate armored infantry had great odds against leather armor, except in the forest. Armored cavalry had great odds against plate armored infantry, and guaranteed odds against leather, except in the forest. It took extra turns to get the armored troops across the river. It helped to have archers, catapults, battering rams, and ladders.

Some games focused on individual skill, strength, and endurance. Duels were long: high and low strikes and blocks: duck, thrust. Side-step ... Roll the dice again ... and again ... and again ... and again ...

I quickly learned the value of getting the odds in your favor.

~

When I dreamed of war in sixth grade I didn't have superhero strength or weapons. No one fell unconscious and popped back up.

We charge. Scream. I run with my friends until the last twenty yards, then accelerate into the lead, raise my sword and strike at the head of the first enemy in my path. He deflects. I explode deeper into their line, wheel my sword and strike the head of another enemy. He stands dazed as I spin and strike low across his shin. Compound fracture.

Advance, high guard, strike, spin. Advance, high guard, strike ... always looking past who I'm striking, to where I can advance and strike someone who doesn't see me coming. I keep dancing through the forest of bodies—cracking arms, legs and necks like branches that leave behind pools of blood and bone marrow. The enemy retreats. Screams give way to night and a chorus of moans with the occasional wail. The sun rises in unspeakable silence.

The war lasts years and I become a legend. But friends die and small wounds add up. I'm slow in my last battle. Never see it coming: an arrow through my chest; a mace pulverizes my knee; a broadsword knocks off my forearm at the elbow. Friends help me to safety.

Whether internal bleeding causes blood to bubble like a softball under my skin, which feels better to drain but does nothing to slow the advancing chill. Or my blood flows while the gangrene thrives. I spend two long days and nights with the sobs and silence of a field hospital.

On the third morning, I see half the sun over the horizon and begin my last breath.

Then I wake cold, sweating, exhausted.

~

In fifth grade art class we were given paper that was three times as wide as it was tall. Then we painted colored squares down the middle of the paper. To the left, we mixed the color with some black and painted another square. Then we mixed in more black and painted another square. We continued until the last square, which was black. On the right, we mixed the color with white and made each square lighter.

Another assignment was to paint and label a large color wheel—mixing a range of hues to fill a dozen circles between primary colors. We debated when red becomes orange, or yellow becomes green, or blue becomes purple. And when any color becomes black or white.

I thought about first grade, and my teacher who said no one would call the same color by a different name and walked away.

Fifth grade is also when I started having dreams about being chased by a monster.

I'm standing in acres of thigh-deep mud and a monster closes in. I try to run, but am barely able to pull my feet from the mud. My heart pounds louder and louder. The monster closes in. After five exhausting steps I collapse. When my body relaxes I start to float up through the mud like a buoy through water. When my feet hit the top, I take off running.

Before long I'm bounding over dirt, darting between trees, fallen logs, boulders, and distancing myself from the monster. I go faster and faster and realize I can't slow down. "Slow down," I tell myself as I pick up speed and—BAM! I run into the trunk of a large blue spruce. I drop to my knees, touch my numb cheek and it feels like bloody hamburger. The monster closes in. I stand. "Slow down," I tell myself, "Jog and you'll get away."

Again I pick up speed, "Slower," I say picking up speed, "Slower." WHAM! Trunk of a large evergreen. I drop. My shoulder took the brunt. The monster closes in.

I rise, focusing on going slow but pick up speed faster than before. SMACK! Aspen and large head contusion. I hear the monster's steps.

When I stumble to my feet I have rockets strapped to my back and my next step triggers the ignition—SSHHHHH—CRUNCH. Sequoia.

I clinch my thigh muscles to hold my broken femur together, wobble to my feet, feel the monster's breath on my neck and know my next step will fire the rockets.

I bolt upright in bed, drenched in sweat.

~

My flying dreams start on one of the trails that sprawl through Boulder's foothills behind the National Center for Atmospheric Research (NCAR).

NCAR was built in 1970, atop a mesa on a large, steep hill just below the Flatirons. The building looks like a castle with a modern flair: 40-foot high red sand-stone walls, long narrow windows, and blocks of stone overlap top corners like guard towers.

Bright day. Perfect temperature. I hike past NCAR, higher into the steep hills. On my way down I start stepping from rock to rock with such ease that I begin to jump, further and further down the hill. With each jump I feel more relaxed; land more lightly. Like a feather.

"It's all about relaxing," I tell myself. Soon, I jump off a cliff, sail, and swoop onto a tree branch like a hawk.

I breathe, my muscles relax further, and then I begin to levitate. As my confidence grows I drift up. When I'm hundreds of feet off the ground I start thinking about what would happen if I fell. My heart beats faster. My muscles grow tense and I begin to fall. The more I fall, the more tense I get. The more tense I get, the faster I fall. When it feels inevitable that I'll crash into the ground I relax, which slows my descent, which relaxes and slows me more. Just above the ground I stop, completely relaxed.

Soon I start floating straight up again. My confidence grows with every foot until I suddenly transform—and, light as air—am able to instantly and effortlessly accelerate to high speeds in any direction.

I soar over Devils Thumb, Skunk Canyon, and Bear Creek Park. Speed over the St. Vrain and Big Thompson rivers (covering a forty-five minute drive in ten). Then I enjoy the beauty over Lake Estes before shooting to the top of Longs Peak. Where I hover, watch the sky turn crimson and violet over the city lights. Then I fly home.

~

I always woke up energized after a flying dream. A seed that spawned decades of study and practice with breathing and relaxation. And while it's true that for 33 years my morning grumpiness rivaled the Scrooge (and there are still days when it's best just to give me some space). It's also true that 95% of the time, all I remembered was a dark quiet that, once I actually woke up, rejuvenated me and my quest to fulfill the dreams I had while awake.

Fight

At a birthday party in Jr. High we watched Saturday Night Live. Eddie Murphy thinks whites have it easy. To prove his theory, professional make-up artists color his skin and fix a wig creating a stunning transformation. Then Eddy goes around town: buses, stores, and a bank.

Each scene begins with a few black people around. Then the blacks leave and a party breaks out. The bus driver starts the music and a disco ball falls from the roof. Everyone dances. Champagne and hors d'oeuvres are served. The banker asks Eddy, "How much do you need?" Then hands Eddy fists full of money, "Take it! Take it all!"

We all laughed, but I stopped sooner than my friends. I remembered walking around Boulder, and the looks my mom received, as opposed to those my dad received. She did get the "you repulse me" looks too. But she didn't get them as often, and they weren't as severe.

Some men looked at my dad like he was an ogre, and they were thinking about getting their pitch forks. They were often big, strong, and/or wearing suits. My dad would lift his chest and strut. I could feel the tension. Like when my dad pulled out of a parking lot and merged into traffic. A man believed my dad cut him off. At the light the large man got out of his car, started yelling and walked towards us. My dad told me to stay put and stood just outside the door.

The man approached and shoved my dad, who responded with a three punch combination that left the man on his back, unconscious, and bleeding. 15 minutes later the paramedics put him in a neck brace, on a stretcher, and into an ambulance.

My dad explained to the policeman that he feared for his and his son's safety. The officer had spoken with witnesses, nodded, and said he probably would've done the same thing. Many black men in similar situations have gone to jail. My dad drove me home.

Later, the man filed a lawsuit including court costs and lawyer fees. Everyone lost time and resources.

That man may have had the right to be mad, I thought, *but he damn sure should've thought twice about what he asked for.*

~

In the first week of Jr. High two of my friends decided to fight (they didn't know each other, I knew one from school and the other from church). I tried to talk them out of it.

"Look at him," one said, "I just hate him."

"I'm not backing down," said the other.

They exchanged a few flurries. Then one put the other in a head lock and they tumbled to the ground. The one in a head lock slipped out and got on top. They grabbed, rolled and threw weak punches. They broke apart, stood, and gasped for air. Then threw more weak punches, grabbed and gasped some more. Soon, it looked more like they'd fall down if they weren't holding on to each other. Mercifully, they separated for good with only a few cuts and bruises each.

First, I figured, *I could beat the hell out of either.* But then I considered the last look they gave each other—as much hatred as before the fight. *What a waste of time.*

~

I saw the movie "Gandhi" in eighth grade. Mohandas Gandhi, 1869–1948, was a political and spiritual leader in India who used nonviolence to lead a revolution against the oppressive British rule and eventually win India's independence. I was spell-bound by a man who freed the people of his nation by leading them to be beaten.

Though India freed itself from British rule, many in India didn't learn the lesson and fell victim to the cycles of violence. Hindus and Muslims started killing each other. Gandhi went on a hunger strike and nearly died before extremists on both sides promised to keep the peace. The movie concludes with Gandhi, old and frail, shuffling through a large crowd shouting his praise. Then a man steps forward, pulls a gun and shoots Gandhi in the chest.

"When I despair, I remember that all through history the way of truth and love has always won. There have been tyrants, and murderers, and for a time they can seem invincible, but in the end they always fall. Think of it. Always." – Gandhi

I loved Gandhi's pragmatism, the small number of oppressors simply couldn't control India's population (like the North winning the Civil War). I admired Gandhi's courage to say and do things that might get him or loved ones killed. Then I learned that Martin Luther King Jr. modeled the Civil Rights Movement after Gandhi's strategies, and realized nonviolence as the most powerful tool for positive change. If I wanted to be a peacemaker, I'd have to work harder.

Because these are my heroes! Like Jesus, they prove peace is made when we learn to love our enemies. I doubt I'll ever be as good as Jesus, MLK Jr., or Gandhi, but I'll do my best.

~

In 8th grade some boys played a game called "Dead Leg." The object was to sneak up on someone and knee them in the thigh. One boy kneed me hard. I wanted revenge. I watched him for days: in and out of classrooms, talking in the hall. Finally, I stood behind a door outside one of his classrooms. He didn't see me coming. I kneed as hard as I could. He let out a high pitched whimper that turned into a wheeze and tears fell from his unblinking eyes.

I often thought of his look of pain and disbelief, and of Gandhi saying, "An eye for an eye only makes the whole world blind." And of half a dozen stories where a man spends his life seeking revenge, only to discover exacting it doesn't ease the pain. And my mom quoting Oscar Wilde, "The best revenge," she said again and again, "is a life well lived."

~

The best part about Jr. High was Art class, which I took all three years.

Each day we got our drawing/painting and pencils/paints, then sat at our desk. The bell rang, the teacher turned on the radio, and we'd start working. Soft music. Calm. Sometimes we worked all period and the teacher just walked around and checked in with students.

Sometimes, 10 minutes after the bell, the teacher gave a lesson. She taught how colors and tints would complement and contrast, could make the audience feel elated, aggravated, or serene. How lines and dots create perspective, focusing eyes in and out, this way and that. She helped me see the brilliance of Picasso, Rembrandt and my favorite, Monet.

In ninth grade I painted an under-water ocean scene: fish, coral, seaweed, streams of light and bubbles. My teacher often liked my work, but raved about this painting, "The colors, complements and contrasts, my eyes move throughout the painting. Gorgeous!" she said. "I can't wait to enter it into a contest."

"Hi, I'm Curtis Griffin," I told the greeter when my mom, Oma and I arrived at the award ceremony at a beautiful auditorium in Denver, "I won the Gold Key award."

"Sorry, I can't find your name," she said after checking the list, "Let me see your invitation. Oh, you're a Gold Key Finalist," she corrected then said, "Your painting is going to be shown in New York, maybe Paris, France [it wasn't]. Your seat is in the front row."

~

When I was bored in an 8th grade Language Arts class I drew a cartoon picture of some black men from Africa: black afros, large lips, pierced noses, head dresses, no shirts or shoes, muscular, holding spears. Classmates were impressed.

They told the girl who sat in front of me to check it out. She was a quiet blond from Australia or New Zealand.

"That's cool," she said before asking in her charming accent, "You drew those niggers?"

My classmates' eyes went wide. They looked at me.

I slid forward in my chair and kicked her in the leg.

"Ow," she said, "What was that for?"

"Nigger is not a nice word," one of my classmates said.

"Well, that's what we call them," she sounded confused and turned back around.

I didn't kick her hard, but regretted it because she seemed genuinely surprised. Maybe she thought nigger was just a physical description, no bearing on character and intelligence. I wished we had talked. But my ability to deal with girls in Jr. High was a lot like 2nd grade, and since she was kind of cute, a gentle kick was the best thing she was going to get from me.

~

I played football in 9th grade. I was small and not very fast, but had a quick first step and nose for the ball. I played defensive safety. Safeties are like the clean-up guy, they start behind all other defenders and whether the other team runs or passes, they run to the ball at full speed and deliver a punishing hit.

Once we played a team that had five huge linemen, three big tight ends, two large fullbacks, and a massive running-back who was fast. On almost every play they snapped the ball to the running-back—sweep left or sweep right.

Early in the game our linemen and linebackers aggressively met their linemen and fullbacks, which gave their running back a small gap. I met him head on and tackled him on the spot. My head rang. Everyone cheered. As the game went on I met the running back and got knocked backwards, dragging him down by his legs and feet—head ringing— everyone yelling. In the fourth quarter our front line was consumed by blockers, the running-back had a huge hole, made a cut, I grabbed air, and lost ground on the way to our end zone. Head still ringing.

A few weeks later we played a smaller team. Our linemen and line backers engulfed their blockers, forcing the small running-back to stop and change directions. I flew toward the line of scrimmage—the predictable gap—where the running-back crumpled under my weight.

This team, I marveled, *must have gotten killed by the team we played a few weeks ago.*

At the end of the season, I was relieved to turn in my pads and helmet. I knew I'd never play tackle football again. I wasn't going to risk severe injury (one player broke his femur). I also would no longer endure hits that made my head ring. Nor would I have to watch or be a part of my least favorite play, when a defender runs full speed and gets blindsided by a blocker. The defender writhes on the ground as oohs and laughter erupt from practically everywhere while a few announce, "Got to keep your head on a swivel out there."

My distaste for hitting (especially those who don't see it coming), extended beyond the football field.

I don't want anyone, anywhere, anytime, I knew, *to feel like they have to keep their head on a swivel around me.*

~

I'd heard of a fight club in a classmate's garage. The toughest from other schools were invited to face our toughest. I never saw one, but imagined their speed, strength and stamina made it more exciting than the fight between my friends from church and school.

I ran into our School's toughest in a bar twenty years later. He had a wife and kids. I had a Master's degree in writing and was teaching the poetry workshop curriculum I developed to foster peace and respect.

"I don't know why I fought those guys," he said, "my mom was one of the Ladies in Black (a group that held weekly peace vigils in downtown Boulder)," and closed, "I guess I did it because my friends encouraged me."

~

I'll never forget how I felt leaving school on the last day of Jr. High. I would miss art: the teacher, drawing, painting, and other rewards. But just a few steps out the door it sank in. I'd never enter that school—where loving your enemy was out of the question—again. Then I looked up at the warm sun and sapphire sky and every part of my face smiled.

Kindness

"You're so nice," people often said to me. Melted by my thoughtful words and gentle tones, their faces and bodies went from sharp and hunched to soft and relaxed.

I heard praise throughout elementary school. I heard less in my late teens though, when being taller with broader shoulders and thighs meant some girls looked more adoringly, but some older women stepped aside or crossed the street. Such avoidances happened enough so that if an older white woman didn't see me coming, I might feign a cough to announce my approach or cross the street myself. The wide eyes and startled twitches weren't so bad. I just thought it smarter not to chance her misreading me or the situation.

Some, perhaps many, will think that's crazy. No one should see (or even care) whether prejudice is behind what could also be the result of a poor night's sleep, a random thought, sudden itch, or a million other things. They might call me paranoid; accuse me of "playing the race card." Ideally they're right. But in reality, the color of their skin hasn't made them a threat nearly as often as others have seen my skin as a threat.

~

While on vacation in the small mountain town of Estes Park, I went swimming and met a boy who was a few years younger than me. We played a modified version of Marco Polo—touch the dark blue tiles on the pool wall and get a point. That way, as he insisted, we could determine a winner. Being bigger and faster I got bored. I wanted to go hard and to feel the thrill of the chase; I began to swim under water. Still, I could dive and touch the tiles three of four times before oxygen debt slowed me enough for him to catch me.

After a while I tagged the tile, sprang out of the water and shouted, "Point."

"Cheater," he yelled back.

"No," I said, "I touched it."

"No way, you're a cheater," he said, "I quit."

"Ok, since I'm bigger," I suggested, "How about if I get one point for touching the tile and you get five?"

"I guess," he said.

"Marco," I began.

"Polo," he replied.

I reached and missed.

"Five points," he shouted.

After tagging him I dove in, "One point," I said, "Two … Three …" oxygen debt and I slowed.

"Got you," he exclaimed, "I'm still winning!"

"Marco," I called.

"Polo," he replied and dove for the wall.

Awesome, I thought before diving after him, *all he needed was to win.*

~

Throughout high school I worked in a church daycare, looking after three, four, and five- year olds during Sunday services. I loved to play and make up games with kids. And to show them the importance of respect and kind words.

The kids mirrored Boulder's population, one minority for every ten whites. Which meant for many, my easy going manner and smile were an invitation to ask about my dark skin and curly black hair. I loved how easily they embraced differences, seeing how diversity makes the world interesting and beautiful.

It'd be nice if no one knew the meaning of words like nigger, honky, spic, gook, Injun … all those ugly words.

~

I don't remember much of what I read in high school. I was a painfully slow reader and reading the first and last pages of every chapter isn't the comprehension strategy I made it out to be. Still, I remember reading about the Civil War.

The Civil War began because the south wanted rights like the right to own slaves. The war's outcome was in doubt until Lincoln promised to abolish slavery and four million blacks joined the fight. That's why I can't fathom why some Southerners claim the Civil War was not about slavery. It's also the reason the "ignorant redneck southerner" is one of the harder stereotypes for me to overcome.

One of the most memorable chapters I read was on Sherman's "March to the Sea." Sherman used an ancient military tactic called, "Scorched Earth."

First thing that stood out was that Sherman's escort was the 1st Alabama Cavalry.

Perhaps not all Southerners were heartless idiots. It's going to be great reading how these Southerners and Northerners shoved cannon balls and bayonets up the stupid Southerners' asses.

The march lasted from November 15th until December 21st. Sherman wrecked 300 miles of railroad, numerous bridges and miles of telegraph lines. He seized 5,000 horses, 4,000 mules, and 13,000 head of cattle; confiscated 9.5 million pounds of corn and 10.5 million pounds of fodder; and destroyed uncounted cotton gins, mills and homes. "Sherman," David J. Eicher wrote in his account, "destroyed much of the South's potential and psychology to wage war."

Reading the devastation didn't make me feel as good as I thought it would. It's hard to read how your side's peacemaking destroyed so much. I felt worse after reading many of the 10,000 slaves Sherman liberated suffered right along with their owners. And hundreds more died of hunger, disease or exposure as they fled with Sherman's army which had confiscated vast amounts of resources.

Then I thought about WWII, when the Allies bombed Germany. And my Oma survived American bombers because she was with my Opa, but

17 in her family burned to death. Then I thought of Hiroshima. And Nagasaki.

I also had the first of a few dreams in which I was Sherman. The dream repeated the same scene over and over all night. The only difference was that I was a little older each time.

> *I awake from a nightmare drenched in sweat. I get up, go to the kitchen, wash my face, pour a tall glass of whiskey, sit, and mumble with each tiny sip, "If only I couldn't still hear the screams and smell the smoke."*

Throughout high school I had about four war-dreams a year (including a few when I was Sherman), which means I started a dozen mornings feeling like I hadn't slept for days. Still, I was thankful because I also had about four flying dreams a year, and woke energized. But more to my being grateful, over 350 nights a year, all I remembered was dark rejuvenating silence.

~

I ran Cross Country in high school. Our head coach was the quintessential Boulder athlete, a world class climber who pioneered some of Colorado's most treacherous rock walls. Muscular, lean, streaked with veins, he ran so balanced and relaxed it looked effortless. An assistant told us coach fell into a trance running up and down two peaks in the foothills. After using a common calculation that translates elevation into distance, they figured coach ran a marathon in a time that would've shattered the world record.

My first practice was the summer before high school. We met at Fairview and drove an hour into the foothills. As we stretched, seniors from the girls and boys teams talked about how they were going to win State (they did). Shortly into the run my muscles were screaming, I was nearly out of breath, and we were still on the part of the trail where coach said, "Really shake it out. Make sure you're warm because the next half mile is steep."

I stopped soon after the steep part began. We'd talked about how I wouldn't be able to keep up and that I should continue at my own pace. The others' breathing and footsteps quickly disappeared up the trail. I caught my breath. It was silent and beautiful. I ran in spits and spurts for 30 minutes before they came bounding back down and I jumped in the back of the line.

Though never very good, by senior year I could keep up with the top runners on easy days and made friends.

The team went on a retreat senior year and we explored the power of our minds. We had fingers hooked up to equipment that measured heart rate and temperature, and were told to try to raise and lower both. Deep breaths, relaxation, and mantras like: my heart beat is slow/fast; my body is cold/hot. Most could raise and lower their heart beat and temperature.

Like when I felt the "runners high" and my flying dreams. The more relaxed, the more power and control.

Some teammates complained about coach, "He knows what he's talking about, but is too quiet." They wanted more fire to motivate and excite them. I welcomed coach's approach. I had plenty of fire: Dad and Opa not being there; people expecting me to answer for all blacks; my knowing little about blacks; watching out for strangers who'd call me nigger; violence and dealing with the extraordinary wealth around me while knowing children are hungry ...

Running the foothills recharged me: quiet, smell of pines, wild flowers, grasses, streams and groves of fern. Skunk Canyon. Bear Peak. I had a number of favorite perches to sit on, look over the valley, breathe, and listen. The hills always told me everything would be ok; that I should charge back down like a warrior—balanced, fast, unstoppable.

~

Summer before my junior year I bought Confederate flag running shorts. My Oma and Opa would *not* have approved. They didn't like any flags (let alone one that stood for a nation that tried to enslave four million people). Like Oma and Opa, I was afraid of the way flags evoke unthinking and frightening loyalties in people. But this was America, "land of the free." Perhaps Confederate flags flew on State capital buildings to represent those in the South who never agreed with slavery (the way my family disagreed with Hitler). So I ran the foothills in confederate shorts as a reminder, and charged for millions of victims of Scorched Earth: Southerners, Germans, Mexicans, Japanese, Christians, Muslims, Jews and many, many more.

I wore the confederate shorts to a team practice once and received looks of bewilderment. I thought about explaining, but buried the shorts in the bottom of a drawer instead.

~

Junior year, our church group was given a presentation on poverty and ghettos throughout America.

"They should just move," one girl scowled, "get a job as a dish washer."

"They're in the only place they can afford," I countered, "and can't buy a job."

"Whatever," she closed after we had gone back and forth a few times.

Afterwards, the pastor took me aside, praised my awareness and compassion, and asked if I would like to attend a leadership and cultural awareness conference.

So my senior year I flew to Miami and stayed in a beautiful hotel for a week with a few dozen high school students from across America. We visited Haitian, Latino and other poor communities to learn about their hardships and triumphs. We listened to teachers, parents, kids and other community leaders talk about neighborhoods overrun with drugs and violence. Homes where family members and friends are in jail or dead, where folks go to bed and school hungry. And we learned how friends, families and mentors provided them with opportunities and hope.

The most memorable experience was a couple of hours in fields with migrant farmers—hot, muggy, working low bushes to fill a huge basket for a few dimes. My shirt was soaked in sweat, even though we sat in the truck because we weren't allowed to pick fruit as was originally planned.

Back in Boulder, there weren't many opportunities to talk about the privileges our parents and town provided. Prom was the preferred topic. How we'd earned the right to spend hundreds or thousands of dollars on suits, dresses, shoes, limousines, and a few plates of food.

I don't want to bum people out. But we can't come up with ways to help fellow Americans if we can't talk about how and why so many are struggling.

~

A dozen or so friends (one black the rest white), were in my social circle for lunch, parties, and ski trips.

"Scholarships for African Americans? Ridiculous!" A white friend quipped after an assembly where students who earned scholarships were honored, "Seriously, a scholarship for being black?" He droned on for a while before ending with, "What a joke!"

I thought about telling him that I didn't get the scholarship *just* for being black. I had to compete: GPA, community service, letters of recommendation, a mission statement and an essay all counted toward my achievement. I beat out students from single-parent families like mine, but who went to school hungry and lived in drug-infested, violent neighborhoods. I thought about reminding him I had nothing to do with my parent's divorce or living in Boulder, like he had nothing to do with his parents staying married. Or living in a home and property worth millions, perched on a ridge of the valley, surrounded by "open space" (a belt of land voted on and paid for by citizen's tax dollars, where residential and commercial building is banned, effectively turning Boulder into one of the more envied and exclusive communities in America). But he and I had been down that road before. So I didn't say anything—but was never closer to telling him to go to hell.

~

I fell in love with George Carlin's comedy in high school.

"America's leading industry is still the manufacture, distribution, packaging and marketing of bullshit. High quality bullshit. World class designer bullshit to be sure. Hospital tested, clinically approved bullshit. But bullshit none the less.

It always amuses me that people seem to think that bullshit only comes from certain sources: advertising salesmen, politicians. *Not true. Bullshit is everywhere.*

Bullshit is rampant. Parents are full of shit. Teachers are full of shit. Clergymen are full of shit. Law enforcement people are full of shit. The entire country is completely full of shit.

In fact, this country was founded by a group of slave owners that told us all men are created equal. That's what's known as being stunningly full of shit."

~

Carlin inspired me to think of my own skit.

I walk on stage and sit next to an old, rich, white lady.

"Taxes steal from those who earn money," she complains, "and gives it to the welfare queens!"

"Why can't she see," my thoughts play over the speakers, "that her argument is just another version of the arguments white people made during Segregation and Slavery?"

"We have to show tough love to blacks making bad decisions," she continues.

I nod because tough love can prove helpful, "Still," I say, "many were dealt a terrible hand. When living in dire conditions our harsh judgment isn't the answer."

"Maybe," she replies, "but many blacks are lazy."

"Like many of all colors," I confirm and take a deep breath.

Feeling like I might boil over I change the subject. I talk instead about my pre-school teaching days and how honest, non-judgmental, and kind children can be.

"You're so nice," she says.

Then I stand, hover over her frail little body and start screaming: "Anton, Ashley, Steve, Mary, Henry, Sara ..." I continue to scream names until the audience starts to fidget.

"All those names," I continue to yell, "Are a fraction of those who are smart, work their ass off and still can't feed, educate or keep their children safe!"

Then I start screaming names again. After about a minute I end with, "All of whom are still only a fraction of those, including myself, who would like to say, FUCK OFF!"

Then I walk off stage.

My humor would come out from time to time. Many times people responded that I was "Not that funny" or "A little harsh." Though I spent decades trying to lighten up, my humor hasn't changed much—I still want to jump on the hypocritical words and actions some are unwilling to recognize. Yet another reason why I'm a quiet person.

~

In order to be truly kind, you have to take the time to go beyond stereotypes and understand others. You have to know where they're coming from. Some blacks like to call each other nigger, some don't. Some parents use corporal punishment, some don't. Some volleyball players I coached fell apart when I yelled, some asked for a profanity-laced tirade if I saw them do any, as one put it, "Weak ass shit."

Silence

I went to college at Bethany in Lindsborg Kansas. I was no stranger to being stereotyped, but felt ambushed in Kansas, where political correctness is dead on arrival. And like getting flicked between the eyes, the relentless judgement drove me crazy.

"You look just like _____." *Insert famous black man.*

"You look exotic." *Though meant as a compliment, it's actually just a meaningless generalization, a lot like saying you look white.*

"You're so well spoken." *Any scholar would say I spent decades butchering English.*

"Black people just look scary." *What kind of person says that*?!

While my distaste for such dialogue grew, I was still sympathetic to how easily it occurs. I don't always look closely at everyone, and have confused people who were the same color but looked different. Perfect grammar isn't always a sign of speaking well, especially if you want to sound cool. And when walking past big, strong men, I, too, was often more afraid of black ones.

Nevertheless, the constant lazy associations made it difficult to be myself; and that's one of many reasons I don't live in Kansas.

~

A few weeks into my freshman year I sat outside my dorm and marveled at the muggy air and massive swarms of bugs around the street lights (more reasons why I don't live in Kansas). Then I had a conversation with a group of white guys.

"I hope you don't take this the wrong way," one said after a while, "but you're the whitest black guy I've ever met."

I thought about Bethany's cafeteria. For the first time I had to choose between tables filled with all blacks or all whites. I chose whites.

"I guess it's because I grew up around whites," I said.

"To me," one guy clarified as the conversation evolved, "calling someone a nigger is like calling someone an asshole, they just happen to be black."

Given the sincerity in his voice and that some blacks actually call each other nigger affectionately, I believed him. Still, I had to protest.

"Calling someone a nigger means more than calling them an asshole," I emphasized, "the word comes from centuries of slavery, theft, murder, and rape," I continued, "Every black person my dad's age and older was born and raised a second class citizen."

"Between those who vow never to say nigger and those who aren't in a joking mood," I continued, "don't be surprised if some blacks make a bigger deal out of being called a nigger. If someone's an asshole, it's best to call them an asshole."

"I understand," he said and vowed to be more cautious. Others nodded.

~

Junior year I was an assistant coach for the women's volleyball team and a white player came to me for advice. She was in love, but her parents were pressuring her to end the relationship because he was black. Her parents liked him as a person, they explained, but feared what "others" might say and do. Also, they'd heard that bi-racial children struggle in our society.

"It's not that bad, is it?" she inquired, "I mean, you're happy and doing well, right?"

"Yes," I confirmed "I'm thankful to be here and am doing well."

"What really matters," she continued, "is the love you have between you, right?"

"Definitely," I assured her, "My mom and Oma are proof that love provides. Plus, violence towards blacks continues to decline."

"Right," she said and her shoulders relaxed.

"Still, it's not always easy," I had to be honest, "Your parents are a good example. They say your boyfriend is good-looking and smart, and that they want what's best for your children, that the problem is this crazy mixed up world we live in. Still, it's your parents' words and actions that are racist, because they're also saying they'd support your relationship if he was white."

"My parents are good people," she said like she had a few times already, eyes welling with tears, begging for the magic bullet.

We smiled meekly at each other, thin layers of hope trying desperately not to pop.

"I'm sure your parents are fine people," I concluded, "Tell them as long as your children are supported by a loving family, they can overcome any crazy fools. Show them the love you have for each other and you'll be happy."

"Thank you," she said, eyes drying.

~

I had the same three white roommates for three years. Two from the towns of Byers and Strasburg in eastern Colorado, where vast plains and conservative mindsets are so prevalent it feels more like Western Kansas. The other was from Topeka.

One was 6'4", skinny, pale, red hair, and loved the band, The Cure. Like its members, he kept the sides and back of his head shaved and let his bangs grow long into a large curly bushel that would hang above his forehead when dry, and touch his chin when wet. He was bullied for his looks and taste in music while growing up. And was quick to dismiss those who attacked others for being different. "The Cure sells out stadiums around the world," he'd rant, "crowds that dwarf the populations of most towns in this state. The haters are the minority!"

Another had passion for business. Donald Trump was his hero. He lent me money, kept close tabs on my debt and was flexible if I needed a new deadline. He offered to pay for a program to help one roommate quit smoking. He also regularly lent me his car, so I could get to volleyball practices and tournaments. 70 miles to Wichita, where teammates taught me winning takes confidence, serious and lighthearted accountability, and hard work.

My third roommate gave 110% in the classroom and on the basketball court. A few times a year he talked us into watching the movie "Hoosiers" (it wasn't hard). 1950's, in small town Indiana. Basketball is practically religion. The high school team gets a new head coach. Coaches, players, teachers, parents and most in the town overcome prejudice and adversity, and the team wins a State Championship. That roommate wanted to get married, raise kids, teach, and coach. When I couldn't use our other roommate's car to get to volleyball, I drove his truck.

Over the years, we discussed the death penalty, war, and Affirmative Action.

They were quick to point out the failed logic of discriminating to eliminate discrimination.

"Affirmative Action is good," I argued, "blacks don't get into college for being black. There's a competitive process and still, deserving kids are left behind. If whites or people of other races deserve to go to college," I continued, "We should create new laws that, combined with present Affirmative Action laws, would send more kids to college. I'd gladly pay higher taxes to educate more people."

In the end, they seemed to warm to the actions they had shown me all along, and we agreed that those who need and deserve help should receive help.

~

Senior year, a group of students were concerned about racial divides around campus (like blacks and whites sitting at separate tables in the cafeteria), so they held a symposium. The cafeteria was packed. Panelists introduced themselves and talked about how they hoped to bring Bethany's community together. They stressed that to be successful we had to have open minds. We need to respect that we come from different backgrounds and have different values, beliefs and experiences. Then some panelists shared.

My favorite story was about a white student who lent his fishing pole to a black student.

"My fishing pole is a prized possession," he explained, "I wouldn't lend it to anyone."

"Early in the year," he continued, "a white guy asked to borrow my pole and I said no. A few weeks later a black guy asked. But I was afraid that if I said 'no' he'd think I was prejudiced," the speaker confessed, "So I said yes."

The black guy who borrowed his pole came to the podium and said he'd always been interested in fishing, but never had the opportunity.

The black guy and white guy put their arms around each other's shoulders, smiled, and spoke of how thankful they were for their friendship.

The white guy who first asked to borrow the pole was smiling too. He got to borrow the pole after the owner saw how happy the black guy was and wanted to spread the joy.

Laughter and smiles rippled through the audience.

~

"You should say something." one roommate urged and the others nodded.

The fishing pole story said it all, I thought and frantically tried to think of something constructive to add. I certainly had stories: *strangers calling me a nigger and my looking for escape routes; my rich high school friend making fun of my measly scholarship for blacks; blacks who alienate me for how I act; whites who alienate me for how I look; the volleyball player's parents telling her to break up with her black boyfriend; my white girlfriend cursing and crying over her parent's wanting us to break up because I'm identified as black.*

"I really think you should say something," my roommate prodded with his elbow.

My heart pounded, temperature skyrocketed.

Race is a bullshit idea, I wanted to say, *made up by people too lazy to do their own damn work and too greedy to pay someone to do it. And stupid mother fuckers have been playing along for centuries.*

Again, my roommates motioned for me to go speak … last chance.

You're a stupid mother fucker, my heart fired like pistons and thoughts ran like a train, *if you think calling a black person a "nigger" is the same as calling them an "asshole"; a racist if you want a bi-racial relationship to end for the good of the children; a moron if you think 25 years of the Civil Rights Act has reversed centuries of Slavery, Jim Crow and Segregation; an asshole if you think impoverished children deserve what they inherit; an idiot if you don't like Affirmative Action, but like the story of a white guy who found friendship when he lent his fishing pole to a guy because he was black.*

I didn't think the words coming to my mind would be productive. So I just shrugged.

Breathing and Rising

PART II

Every great person
Has first learned
How to obey
Whom to obey
And when to obey.

William Ward

Breathing and Rising

Lessons

Spring, 1989, sophomore year at Bethany. I entered Presser Hall, a rectangular three-story red brick building constructed as the heart of campus in 1929. Inside, there's an auditorium that seats 1,700, and offices for admissions, financial aid, and registration. I declared my major, sailed down the front steps, stopped, and took a deep breath. Small bright green buds on the branches of the large maples. I'd always loved working with kids and knew I was born to teach.

~

I spent most of my time in college with roommates, girlfriends, and volleyball players I either played with or coached.

Around campus, my white mannerisms were noticed. Black extremists saw me as a traitor. White extremists saw me as a "wannabe." A few saw me as a hero. Even fewer took the time to see *me*.

The twelve women in the elementary program mostly talked about boyfriends, marriage and having children. The other guy was quiet and read and wrote a lot (activities I did only when I had to). My advisor said little, except for how I needed to improve lesson and unit planning, especially in Language Arts.

I was friends with a white guy who grew up in a black community in Wichita. We joked and bonded over how God must have switched our colors at birth. He transferred to a place with a little more color.

One girlfriend went to Emporia College. I liked the drive to visit her in Emporia. I rarely regretted leaving Lindsborg. But the cowboy boots, big belt buckle, and southern drawl of the guy who called me a nigger assured me I was still in Kansas.

~

Senior year, I student taught a 5th grade class in the town of McPherson, 20 miles south of Lindsborg. For over half a century the town's population has stayed between 13,000 and 14,000. McPherson's Industrial

Development Company is the key to its success, pulling in a workforce of over half a million people from near-by counties. Located at the intersection of I-135 and US-56, the commute is fast and easy.

McPherson has an early education program, four elementary schools, a middle school, high school, and an alternative high school. K-12 enrollment is 2,400. McPherson school district was the first in the nation to opt out of President George W. Bush's flagship bill for education, No Child Left Behind. As part of the agreement, students are required to earn a Silver Level Work Ready certificate in order to graduate. Though schools in the district have plummeted in state rankings ever since, many still regard McPherson as one of the best in Kansas.

I taught at Eisenhower Elementary, where the racial diversity reflected the overall population: 95% White; 4% Hispanic or Latino; 1% Black.

My cooperating teacher was excellent. John was small, fit, and had the energy of a large generator. His students plugged in the moment he stepped in the room. He'd taught his students' older brothers, sisters, cousins, even a few parents.

Between lessons, students talked and joked to themselves, but the second the lesson was scheduled to begin, they sat quietly, right books opened to the right pages, all eyes on him. He taught social studies during language arts, math during science, and music during math.

When I taught literacy I basically read from the teacher's guide. Before long, when I'd announce to the students it was time for Language Arts their eyes rolled, yawns sprung up, and bodies went limp. A few told me to work on my language arts lessons, but they liked my social studies lessons.

~

One day, a student came to me in tears because some girls were picking on her, "I just want to be friends," she said.

We talked for ten minutes. "You should try to be friends with whoever you like," I advised, "But, if you're nice to them and they put you down, they aren't being friends. At some point you may need to find new friends."

John overheard and marveled, "Where did you learn to be so sensitive?"

"I don't know," I wondered, "guess I was just raised that way."

"Well," he concluded, "you handled that great."

~

For my student teaching to have been successful, I would've had to put more time into preparation. But while I may have dreaded my Language Arts lessons as much as if not more than my students did, I wasn't giving up lifting weights, basketball or indoor volleyball. Because after living in Kansas and realizing how much bias and prejudice would impact my life, I wouldn't have had the composure to teach at all if I hadn't been able to sweat, grunt, and scream while doing squats. Or boxing people out and snatching rebounds. Or hitting volleyballs.

I failed the student teaching assignment. My advisor cited poor literacy lessons. Still, John thought my overall performance was pretty good, believing I just needed more practice.

I had the credits to graduate in spring 1991, but failing student teaching meant I wasn't eligible for a teacher's license. Thanks to the generosity of another advisor and his wife letting me live in their home, I could afford to return to Lindsborg for a second student teaching assignment fall 1992. This time in a school in Salina, 20 miles north of Lindsborg.

Salina is the seventh-largest city in Kansas and sits at the intersection of I-70 and I-135, in the center of one of the largest wheat producing areas in the world. With Kansas City 180 miles east, Wichita 95 miles south, Denver 425 miles west, and Lincoln 200 miles north, Salina primarily serves as a trade center. The population grew 65% after the 1951 opening of Schilling (Smokey Hill) Air Force Base. In 1965, the base closed and the "Golden Era" ended. The population increased only from 44,000 to 48,000 between 1992 and 2012. Salina has eight elementary schools and in half of them 80% of the students or more qualify for "Free and reduced lunch." That's a nice way of saying their parents can't afford to feed them.

When I taught at Oakdale, the population of Salina was 86% White and 14% minority. Oakdale served students from "the wrong side of the tracks." Many came from poor single-parent homes and/or with a family member in jail. The principal and my cooperating teacher were black women. The class was 60% white, 40% minority. And everyone was excited about my being a positive black male role model for these 5th graders.

~

I was also excited because Salina was my ex-girlfriend's home town. After we lived together in Boulder that summer, she told me I was the most beautiful and thoughtful person she'd met. But her parent's racist fear grew and they threatened to cut her off, so she moved back. Now I'd have a chance to earn a teacher's license and prove myself in their community.

~

My cooperating teacher in my second student teaching experience was also excellent. Millie was short, round, dark skinned, bright as the sun, and from the south. She had marched with Martin Luther King Jr., became a teacher right out of college and taught for 30 years.

On my first day, one outspoken black boy refused to take a "Stupid test." Millie said that he'd take it after school. Under her supervision.

When the dismissal bell rang, Millie was bombarded by students to clarify homework, review lessons, and just talk. The boy who was supposed to take the test slipped out. When she looked for him the other students told her he left.

"Oh no," she replied and ran out the door.

"Ooooooo," the students exclaimed, then went to the second-story window. I followed. We watched the round, grey-haired lady run over the blacktop, across the street and disappear into the neighborhood. She went to the student's house and with his sister's help, found him hiding in the basement.

A group of students and I hung out by the windows. As they walked back over the blacktop Millie's pace was crisp and the student struggled to keep up, as if Millie was tugging him by his ear though she wasn't touching him. Everyone at the window laughed.

The student's performance on the test was average. Millie told him that considering his lack of effort, his score was evidence of his brilliance. "You'll be good at whatever you choose to do," she said adding something she announced to the class regularly, "An education gives you the best chance of doing what you want."

"You have to be part of the community," she explained to me after everyone left, "I've known a lot of these students since they were born. I know their families."

~

Sometimes, Millie turned the air dark, quiet, and still—like right before a tornado hits. Her hook was especially potent because of a story she read at the beginning of the year. There's a character that coldly stares to let people know he's not taking any more crap. They called him, "Dead Eye Dan."

After every lesson she made sure everyone knew what was expected and sometimes she'd announce "Watch out for Dead Eye Dan!" Which meant if they saw her staring—furrowed brow, wide eyes, pursed lips— they had two seconds to be doing what they should be doing.

When I began teaching and Millie left the room, two black boys raised their hands to say they hated me because I talked and acted too white.

Salina is not only a hub for trading wheat, but for stolen goods and illegal drugs. The same two boys often expressed pride in their gang affiliations: family, friends, and other powerful connections from Denver to Kansas City, Omaha to Oklahoma City.

During a social studies lesson, the boys argued that history books glorify whites and perpetuate oppression. I responded with how far we've come, which was bait for their anger over how far we still have to go. That led to cussing, a flying pencil, and one using the chaos to smack another student with a book (retaliation for an unrelated incident). I used my long frame to separate the boys, then Millie stepped in the doorway. DEAD EYE DAN!

"Disrespecting Mr. Griffin," Millie reiterated, "is like disrespecting me." She also reminded them that they were there to get an education, "because an education gives you the best chance of doing what you want."

A week later I gave a black girl the "Dead Eye Dan." She rolled her eyes and muttered, "*You* can't make *me* do anything." I was relieved she didn't cuss me out again. "I don't hate you now," she said on my last day, "I even like you a little."

There were a few good moments. But I don't think either of the boys ever trusted or liked me.

My teaching improved in every subject, including, most importantly, Language Arts. I passed the assignment.

I was thankful to have worked with two master teachers. They knew their students, their student's families, and their communities. They had the resources and ability to teach a variety of subjects in a variety of ways. They planned meticulously, improvised brilliantly, and gave their time and energy to everyone.

Why in God's name do even mediocre professional athletes, I kept asking myself in awe of these teachers' dedication and skill, *earn so much more money and status than the best teachers?*

~

I met with my ex-girlfriend a couple of times. Moments were awkward, but we also talked and laughed like old times. I called her a week before student teaching ended, "She doesn't want to speak to you," her mother explained, "Don't call again," then hung up.

Great teachers are invested in their communities, I thought.

I moved back to Boulder and learned that requirements for a teacher's license vary from state to state, and that I had to take classes to be eligible for a license in Colorado. So I enrolled at the University of Colorado. Then I fell in love with volleyball.

Volleyball

For many, volleyball conjures up images of picnic blankets, saggy nets, and a rock-hard ball. They know each team has three hits to get the ball over the net. So they try to hit the ball over in one shot. If that attempt falls short, their teammate tries. If that attempt fails, one more chance.

Though small, there is another network that spans coast to coast. We know the proper inflation of the ball, along with the height and tension of the net. We also know that to win, you have to pass to a teammate, get set, approach fast, jump high, and smash the ball off your opponent's court.

~

The first time I saw men play competitive volleyball was in high school. Boulder Parks and Recreation hosted an Association of Volleyball Professionals (AVP) beach volleyball tournament a few blocks from my house.

Initially, I was struck by the women in bikinis. Then I noticed there were just two guys covering the entire court. They were big, strong, fast, and moved with precision and skill. They wore only shorts and sunglasses, and competed like their lives were on the line.

I'd watched great athletes my whole life. My dad was a high school basketball and football star. He played football at the University of Colorado until his shoulders gave out. Still, he was a regular in weight rooms and gyms, worked out six or seven days a week, and was friends with professional athletes. He took me to watch and play basketball at the University of Colorado. The pick-up games resembled a fight: yelling, bodies colliding, passes rocketing like missiles, men sprinting like lions, and bombs going off when a big man dunked.

Beach volleyball was similar.

~

One star was Randy Stoklos, 6'4" tall and built like a linebacker. When Randy hit, the ball seemed to turn to smoke and detonate when it hit the sand. When blocking, he jumped with his head above the eight-foot net and pressed his broad shoulders, arms, and hands over like a wall, rejecting hitters and forcing errors.

The thin 6'5" frame, long arms, and lighting quick jump of Tim Hovland reminded me of basketball players who swat lay-ups off backboards. Tim, affectionately known as "The Hov," was passionate and controversial. He screamed at referees, opponents and fans. I envied how he told people they were acting a fool.

The players I most wanted to be like were Randy's and The Hov's partners, Sinjin Smith and Mike Dodd. They showed that a hitter didn't have to crush the ball. Take something off and hit accurately—it's impossible for your opponents to defend every corner of their court. Plus, a great off-speed shot makes a fast ball more effective.

Sinjin and Mike specialized in playing defense behind the block. When a back row defender pops the ball up to a teammate, it's called a "Dig." Great defenders watch the direction of the hitter's approach, the position of their shoulders, and know how a hitter prefers to swing at a ball (across or away from the body). The defender shuffles into position: knees bent, back straight, arms extended low, palms up.

Sometimes the ball is hit so hard and flat that defenders can't get their hands up, so they tilt their chest, using it to paddle the ball straight up like off a table (bragging rights for the seams and logo imprinted in their skin). If the ball hits the defender in the face it's called a "six pack." Shattered sunglasses, a cut on the nose, plus the defender owes the hitter a six-pack of beer.

Sinjin and Mike were in the right position time and again. Sometimes they'd take one in the chest. But usually, they'd extend their forearms and absorb the force of the ball so it would rebound softly, arch neatly through the air to where their partner could easily step under it and set.

When the ball was hit away from Sinjin and Mike they'd sprint and dive. Sometimes they weren't close. Sometimes they slid a fist under the ball just before it'd hit the ground, making the ball arch up high and smooth, to where their teammate can easily step under it and set.

The most accurate way to set is overhand. Randy was one of the best (which is unusual because like outside shooting in basketball, big men rarely have the finesse to master the skill). Elbows bent. Hands above the forehead, palms up. Supple wrists. Receive the ball with fingers and thumbs simultaneously. Fling it like it bounced off the middle of a trampoline. When The Hov set overhand however, it looked more like his fingers were prongs of a fork and he was trying to pop the ball; a motion that usually results in an illegal contact. The Hov was an excellent bump setter though: elbows straight, arms perpendicular to the ground, shoulders shrugged, and the ball came off his forearms like off a table.

The moments I savored most came after digging the ball, "Set it! Set it!" I'd command my partner. For the first time in my life I had a taste for hitting something.

~

Timing is the key to hitting. Track the set. Start slowly and reach full speed in a few steps. Plant both feet, jump up and forward for maximum height and power, and at the peak of your jump and full extent of your reach, hit the ball with the palm of your hand and snap your wrist for topspin. Hit the ball with a fist when you can pound it straight down.

My hitting improved thanks to a training device—a long pole attached to an upside down U with two foam blocks at the bottom. I'd wedge the ball between the foam blocks and set the frame on a basketball hoop with the ball sitting just in front of the rim. Then I'd approach, jump and hit the ball from between the foam blocks. Retrieve and repeat.

Freshman year I could barely touch the rim, which meant I regularly missed the ball with the palm of my hand and jammed my fingers. For the next three years I played six-man indoors and lifted weights. I watched AVP stars compete a few blocks from my home. And all summer on "Hot Tuesday Nights," a weekly televised broadcast from across the country featuring world class athletes, sky rocketing prize money, and gorgeous women. The scene in Colorado was exploding too. I played five or six days a week. Tournaments almost every weekend.

I liked winning prizes and the attention of women. But really savored releasing a lifetime of anger generated by the laughter and ridicule over my poor academics, blacks who saw me as a traitor, whites who saw me as a wannabe, my ex-girlfriend's racist parents … *The best revenge*, my mom's voice often rang in my head, *is a life well lived!*

The last time I trained in Kansas was shortly after my ex-girlfriend refused to speak with me. I wedged the ball, hung it on the rim and used my fist to pound it straight down. Again and again and again—for an hour—with only one thought, *Pop the fucking thing!*

Warriors

I was a junior at Bethany when I saw "Apocalypse Now" for the first time. It was the most horrifying and beautiful thing I'd seen. It also reminded me of my war dreams. Short bursts of extreme violence followed by long periods of boredom and misery.

Between the white half of my family needing the world to take out Hitler, and the black half needing the threat of the National Guard in order to attend public school, I believe in having and using military force when necessary. Still, after watching "Apocalypse Now," I knew I'd made the right choice in becoming a Conscientious Objector. Sure, there are selfish reasons not to go to war. But the point is that the cycles of violence are powerful, and I don't want *anyone* to have to try and make it out. As comedian George Carlin observed, too many are trying to minimize the devastating outcomes of war.

"During WWI," Carlin explains, "they said a traumatized soldier has, 'Shell Shock.' In WWII it was 'Battle Fatigue.' During Korea, 'Operational Exhaustion.' And now 'Post-traumatic Stress Disorder.' The humanity has been squeezed completely out of the phrase. And the pain is completely buried under jargon ... I'll bet you if we'd still been calling it, 'Shell Shock,' some of those Vietnam veterans might have gotten the attention they needed at the time."

Maybe they should use the term for soldiers traumatized during the Civil War "Soldier's Heart."

~

Another terrifying aspect of war is the double agent. Most militaries have them. They add new dimensions of fear and betrayal that make dangerous people that much more paranoid and determined to respond in kind.

In "Apocalypse Now," US Colonel Walter Kurtz executes four allied South Vietnamese officers for spying. Despite Kurtz' evidence and a drop in enemy North Vietnamese activity, the US military charged Kurtz with murder. So he went AWOL and enlisted an army of natives to fight the North Vietnamese. The US Army called up special-forces assassin Captain Benjamin Willard.

"Well, you see Willard," the commander explains, "In this war things get confused out there. Power, ideals, the old morality and practical military necessity ... Because there is a conflict in every human heart, between the rational and irrational, between good and evil. And good does not always triumph. Sometimes the dark side overcomes what Lincoln called 'the better angels of our nature.' Every man has a breaking point. You and I have it. Kurtz has reached his and very obviously," the commander concludes, "has gone insane."

"Obviously," Willard assured his commanders, "Completely insane."

Willard accepts the mission to find Kurtz and 'exterminate with extreme prejudice'. "Of course," the commander clarifies, "as far as the US Army is concerned, this mission does not exist."

While being ferried up-river, Willard reads Kurtz's dossier: Top of his class third-generation West Point graduate who served in Korea, Vietnam, and received dozens of decorations. "I couldn't believe they wanted this guy dead," Willard marveled, "He was being groomed for the highest commands in the corporation, General, Chief of Staff, etc."

At 38, Kurtz relinquished his command and joined an elite training program that 95% of the military's youngest and toughest fail. "I did it when I was 19 and it nearly wasted me," Willard thought, "[the young cadets] must have thought [Kurtz] was one far out old man humping it around that course."

Willard also read a letter Kurtz sent to his son, "I have been officially accused of murder by the Army," Kurtz wrote, "The alleged victims were four Vietnamese double agents. We spent months uncovering them, accumulated evidence and when absolute proof was created we acted like soldiers. The charges are unjustified and in the circumstances of this conflict, quite completely insane."

"In a war there are many moments for compassion and tender action," Kurtz continued the letter to his son, "There are many moments for ruthless action that may, in many circumstances, be only clarity—seeing clearly what there is to be done and doing it—directly, quickly, awake. As for the charges against me I am unconcerned. I am beyond their timid, lying morality," Kurtz concluded, "and so I am beyond caring."

~

Part of my vow to work hard at volleyball was recognizing that whether I agreed with our military or not, American soldiers were putting everything on the line while I was playing a game. So when I stepped onto the court, like many athletes, I imagined I was charging into battle. My imagination was aided because when a volleyball player hits the ball onto their opponent's court or off their opponent's body and out of bounds, it's called a "kill."

At 6'2", 170 pounds I was small for getting "kills" in the indoor game—six defenders on the 30 by 30 ft. court. 6'8", 240 pounds brings the preferred kind of heat. Still, most indoor setters I played with raved of times when they kept setting me because I killed every good and bad set they threw my way. In the two-man beach game, I was a stone cold killer all the time.

"Nobody! NOBODY!" partners yell during those glorious moments in doubles, when the hitter gets set close to the net and no one is blocking. To further announce the other team's grave mistake, hitters start yelling as they approach and then scream as they blast the ball off the vast amount of court their opponents left unguarded. If the hitter is a "Real Man" they'll pound the ball straight down and bounce it 30 feet in the air. If the hitter is "The Man" they'll pound the ball 30 feet out of bounds, off their opponent's chest. Ba-boom!

I was a calculated attacker. I had a quick arm-swing and there's nothing like bringing too much heat. I'd blast the ball every now and again. But mostly I hit for accuracy, 60% to 80% power. Strong approach, jump, good timing, and full reach meant I'd contact the ball well above the net. Take a peek at the defense and I'd have one or two shots my opponents simply could not defend. Many thought my softer swings looked easier to defend. I savored watching their frustration grow. And saving the energy to do it all day long.

~

Captain Kilgore commands the attack helicopters assigned to escort Willard, the boat and its crew to the mouth of a river. Captain Kilgore is an avid surfer, and when he learns one of the crew on the boat is a world class surfer, he attacks a village controlled by the Viet Cong, so they might hold the beach long enough for them to surf the best breaks in Vietnam.

Helicopters descend blasting 'Ride of the Valkyries' over speakers. Women and children run for cover. Enemy soldiers run for weapons. Gunfire, explosions and death rock the village.

Taking fire, Willard and the crew land on the beach, sprint, dive, and dig in the sand. Walking slowly and upright, Kilgore surveys the waves.

"Kilgore is one of those soldiers with a strange light around him," Willard thought looking up from his shallow fox hole, "You just knew nothing was going to happen to him."

"What do you think?" Kilgore motions for the surfing star to stand and check the waves.

"I don't know Sir," the surfing star stands, twitching and ducking at the sounds of bullets whizzing by, "I think we ought to wait six hours for the tide to come in," he exclaims before diving back into his fox hole.

"You want to wait around here another six hours?" Kilgore asks standing tall, looking around.

~

In Jr. and Sr. high school, I rarely played sports as aggressively or skillfully as I could. I was paralyzed by fear over how either I or my opponents might be labeled losers. But by 18 I didn't care. Winners in pick-up games got to play again. I wanted to play all day. It was either my dreams or theirs. So I studied, saw clearly what needed to be done and did it—directly, quickly, awake. The more I won, the stronger I got. The only times I was lazy I was like my cat, basking belly up in the sun before again pouncing on the mouse flopping towards its hole with three legs, one ear and a broken hip.

~

Unlike war movies from John Wayne's era, I liked "Apocalypse Now" because it more closely resembled my dreams, and portrayed what I felt was a more full account of war—even those who win lose too much. Like how half a dozen unarmed, innocent Vietnamese are gunned down during a misunderstanding over a puppy. And the boat Captain is killed, struck in the back. "A fucking spear," he marveled looking at the large iron arrow protruding from his chest, dripping with his blood.

The pragmatism in Kurtz' madness struck me too. How he captured and tortured Willard for days, then left him unguarded and nursed him back to health. The same thing Kurtz did to the first assassin the US Army sent to kill Kurtz, and who ended up joining his army.

"I've seen horrors," Kurtz explains to Willard as he recovered, "horrors that you've seen. But you have no right to call me a murderer. You have a right to kill me. You have a right to do that," Kurtz clarifies, "But you have no right to judge me."

"We went into a camp to inoculate some children [for polio]," Kurtz further detailed, "We'd left the camp and this old man came running after us and he was crying. We went back there ... and they had hacked off every inoculated arm. There they were, a pile of little arms. And I remember I cried. I wept ... Then, I realized like I was shot with a diamond. A diamond bullet right through my forehead ... The genius of the will to do that: perfect, genuine, complete, crystalline, pure ... These men fought with their hearts, who have families, who have children, who are filled with love, but they had the strength, the *strength* to do that. If I had 10 divisions of these men then our troubles here would be over very quickly."

"I worry that my family, that my son will not understand what I have tried to do here," Kurtz concluded, "If I were to die—and I hope you understand my meaning here Willard—if I were to die, I hope someone would go and tell him everything, everything they saw here. Because there is nothing that disgusts me more than the stench of lies."

"[Kurtz] just wanted to go out like a soldier," Willard thought, "Standing up."

That night, Kurtz stood just before Willard closed in and split him open with a machete.

~

The weapons and strategy in "Apocalypse Now" brought new horrors to my war dreams. Two scenes impacted the dreams I had during the day.

The first is the opening scene in the movie. Willard in a hotel room in Saigon, waiting for a mission. The Door's song "Riders on the Storm" plays over a montage of Willard getting drunk, sleeping on the floor, smashing mirrors with his fists, bleeding all over, and weeping like a baby.

"Every time I think I'm going to wake up back in the jungle," Willard thinks, "When I was home after my first tour it was worse. I'd wake up and there'd be nothing. I hardly said a word to my wife 'til I said 'yes' to a divorce. When I was here I wanted to be there. When I was there all I could think of was getting back into the jungle. I'm here a week now, waiting for a mission, getting softer. Every minute I stay in this room I get weaker. And, every minute Charlie squats in the bush he gets stronger."

The second scene is when Willard and the crew stop for supplies. They noticed a glow in the night sky and hear construction a few bends down-river from the outpost. Coming around the final bend they see a stadium being built on the bank of the river. USO is putting on a show. Willard and the crew get complimentary tickets.

A helicopter lands on stage. Three Playboy Bunnies step out and dance. The soldiers go wild. The Bunnies strip a layer, dance, flirt, and soon soldiers rush the stage. The Bunnies and their agent run for the helicopter. The MP's hold the soldiers back long enough for the Bunnies to get away (though one soldier got close enough to grab a landing skid as the helicopter took off and hung on for a short ride before dropping into the river).

"Charlie didn't get much USO," Willard thought smirking at the sight, "He was dug in too deep or moving too fast. His idea of R & R was cold rice and a little rat meat. He had only two ways home, death or victory. No wonder Kurtz put a weed up command's ass. The war was being run by a bunch of four-star clowns who'd end up giving the whole circus away."

Winning takes 100% effort, I thought before turning it into my mantra, *100% focus*.

~

At tournaments I sat in the shade with a good view of the courts. I didn't pay much attention to women in bikinis, instead staying focused on the best teams. I imagined being a sniper, learning how to pick off opponents one point at a time.

The summers of 1988, '89, and '90 I played a few dozen tournaments. I won all the lower divisions: BB, A, and AA with different partners. In my first six Open tournaments (top division), I placed between 13th and 4th with a few different partners, and always stayed to watch the finals. At night I'd get into bed, picture myself in the bush eating cold rice, rat meat, and thinking of ways to improve my game and exploit my opponent's weaknesses.

~

There's a good chance I would've picked up a gun and fought against the American South in the 1860's, or Hitler in the 1940's, or maybe even been drawn in by a young and charismatic Malcolm X in the 1950's. But it's never been legal to hang "white only" signs while I've been alive. And I think most people, including many I'd often disagree with, would like to see an end to violence. So following MLK Jr. and the pacifists made the most sense.

Still, I was outraged by white supremacists in our government and bars in Kansas and Boulder. Frustrated with those who ignore the lessons of 1930's Germany by tolerating hateful rhetoric and disheartened by Desert Storm because our soldiers and their families were the only Americans taking risks to stop a dictator. And they risked everything. I was exasperated by the fact that America's economics and demographics still looked a lot like they did in the 1960's, and infuriated with the war on drugs, three strikes you're out, and racial profiling. I was also incensed by those trying to cut programs that educate the under-educated and feed the hungry.

While playing volleyball I pictured my opponents with the face of someone I wanted to beat the crap out of.

One favorite image was of an older man with cowboy boots, big belt buckle, and plaid shirt. I took a few pennies from the 'take a penny cup' at a Kwik Mart in Lindsborg. He followed me outside and called me a cheap nigger. I laughed it off in the moment but spent the next few years getting more and more angry about it.

Another was a small, poorly-shaven middle aged man. I passed him five minutes into a run on Bear Mountain Drive in Boulder. He called me a nigger and though I knew better than to respond (perfect record since the rock throwing incident in elementary school), I stopped, turned, pointed, and yelled, "Fuck you!"

"Ok, man," he said putting both hands up like I'd drawn a gun.

My heartbeat was steady and rapid. Muscles felt loose and explosive. I was a step away—could've knocked out a tooth or two so he'd remember not to use that word. But a judge and jury would probably find my reaction excessive, perhaps even think such violence typical of my race. Or the guy might get angry, find some friends and lash out with more than hateful words next time.

Not a teachable moment, crossed my mind so I turned and ran, adding a hundred push-ups and squats to my routine up Bear Mountain. And still thinking about the man on the way back down, added another mile by circling around the mesa the NCAR building sits on.

~

I won my first Open tournament in 1991. By 1993 I'd won a dozen with half a dozen different partners. I also started to overhear people talk.

Like the father of a former partner saying, "Looks like Curtis is trying to prove he can win with anyone."

Which wasn't entirely true. I chose partners who could play. But I was committed to the process of no excuses and accepting full responsibility. I wanted to learn how to play with, and against, many different strengths and weaknesses. And I began to step onto the court with that glow of invincibility that accompanies some warriors.

Champions

I met Nick Petterssen and Dave Mardoz at the South Boulder Rec Center's sand courts on a sunny 50° day in December. They played on the six-man indoor club team at the University of Colorado and encouraged me to try out when I told them I was enrolled. "What our team really needs," they emphasized, "is an outside hitter that can pass."

There are two kinds of serves. Top Spin, when the server snaps his wrist when he hits, generating top spin so the ball dives into the court. And Float, when the server hits with a stiff wrist, so the ball comes off with no spin and knuckles through the air. If you can't pass someone's serve, you belong in a different league.

"I'm a great passer," I lied.

While I was effective in doubles, the outdoor ball and game are more forgiving. But the precision required for sixes indoors meant that my teammates in Kansas told me to stand in the corner during serve-receive and, "Don't touch the serve. Ever." Mike Steele was our specialist. Like a spider, he scurried short, deep, left, and right, covering two thirds of our court. Mike beat the ball to where the serve was going to land. Knees bent, back straight, shoulders shrugged, arms extended, elbows locked. Time and again the ball rebounded off his forearms, cut a neat arc through the air, and fell softly into our setter's hands.

I lived my lie, shrugging off months of poor passing like it was just a bad night. Every time I stepped on the court I tried to be like Mike, and made a habit out of using the kind of confidence that goes on recon missions with arrogance. I would go on to be a strong passer at the professional level. And given my speed and hand-eye coordination, I could've become one the greatest ever at passing a volleyball.

~

In spring of 1992, the only way we could afford to go to nationals in Buffalo, New York was to rent a van. 60 hours on the road; we played because we loved it.

We went undefeated in the early rounds, but our inexperience showed when we faced perennial power UC-Davis in the first round of the elimination bracket. We finished 9th.

We watched UC-Berkley play Graceland College in the finals. I'd won a couple of Open doubles tournaments in Colorado with Graceland's starting setter, so I knew his weaknesses. It wasn't just the Utica Club beer talking when I vowed CU would be in the finals next year.

~

"This isn't picnic volleyball," Coach Dave Blessing announced to 80 young men at the 1992 fall tryouts. "If you're not here to play volleyball at the highest level, you should leave." Then returning players demonstrated offensive and defensive drills and Blessing concluded, "Come spring, we're going to be National Champions."

Everyone knew that for us to win, six would play the majority of points: Ryan Post, and five returning starters, Jesse Mahoney, Nick Petterssen, Guy Swope, Mark Lindstrom, and me. Still, 24 players made the program. And for eight months we competed like Silverback Gorillas—every point was a female in heat.

Though a non-starter, Steve Mckowski was a defensive genius. At Nationals, we played Sacramento State in the quarter finals. Players on both teams ranged from 5'8" to 6'8", jumped 32-42 inches and hit the ball 70-80 mph. Many thought the winner of that match would go on to win the tournament. We won the first game by a few points. Lost the second by a few. Won the third by two in overtime. Steve made a number of diving one-arm digs we converted into points.

John Umaki was a non-starter from a renowned high school program in Hawaii. He was only 5'10" but could pass, jump high, and hit hard. I loved watching his powerful approach and swing in warm-ups, when the ball is set on top of the net, and the hitter pounds it straight down trying to bounce it into the ceiling. It's not a practical play. Sets on top of the net in a game are easily grabbed by a blocker and shoved down the hitter's throat. Still, in warm-ups, the best teams fill gyms with thunderous echoes of balls rocketing off the floor and crashing into the lights.

In the national finals we played Rhode Island, and John subbed in for a cramping Ryan Post. That season all of us had come off the bench and played poorly, resulting in painful losses (the worst were to our rival Colorado State University). So our motto was, "Ready to play at game pace" and in the national finals, John did just that. He hit the first set he saw high and hard, off the blocker's hands and out of bounds.

Hitting high and hard is like football's three-and-a-half yard run between the tackles. It doesn't look fancy. Most find it boring. But it's how the war is won.

In football, the best knock their opponents off the line of scrimmage. If the offense pushes the defense three and a half yards on every play, the drive is a foregone conclusion ... play after play ... a slow march ... touchdown. On the next drive, demoralized and tired, the defense loses another half step ... play after play ... a slow march ...

In volleyball the best jump high and hit hard. If blockers have to turn their palms up to avoid having their fingers broken, their block will likely deflect the ball out of bounds. Big hitters often try to hit small blocker's hands, a target that is only a few feet away, usually scores points, and sometimes inflicts a great deal of pain.

John got set and hit high and hard a couple more times. Then he hit his silky off-speed shot—same aggressive approach, jump, and swing—only he used a supple wrist to roll the ball inches over the block and land it in the middle of Rhode Island's court, their six defenders standing around a campfire. Smiles and high fives all around for us.

We extended our lead while John was in. When a cramp-free Post got up off the bench to check back into the game, I thought about his hitting against Sacramento State.

Sac State fans led by a dozen nearly deafening cow bells. John on the bench, jumping like a wild man, waving a towel, directing our fans,

"The Post man delivers! The Post man delivers! The Post man delivers!"

I gave Post a high-five. We settled into serve receive. I knew we were going to win.

~

The first time I played against Post was in a doubles tournament in Vail, Colorado. 6'3", thin and fast, he jumped high, had great ball control and rarely made mistakes. I was grateful his partner wasn't that good. And thrilled when he became CU's starting outside hitter opposite me.

"Be greedy," coach Blessing demanded of us, "any time the ball comes over the net and one of you can touch it, call it and go get it!" In serve receive, whether opponents served Post, me, or up the middle, we usually started our offense off with an excellent first pass.

We didn't blow doors off defenders when hitting, but we each jumped 38 inches, had deceptive arm swings, and were able to put the ball in any corner.

On defense we would step in front of our opponent's hardest hits and pop it softly into the air. Or sprint and dive to keep balls in play that few could touch. The kinds of plays that turn tides and open flood gates. Roll to victory.

~

Jesse Mahoney was our setter, the position with the greatest responsibility. Setters receive the ball with both hands above their forehead, palms up. Then, use fingers and thumbs to fling the ball along the net and into positions that give hitters the best chance of pounding it onto their opponent's court. Good setters play the second of your team's three touches on every play. Great setters deliver the ball to the right hitter at the right time.

Aside from being 6'3" with large strong hands, Jesse was pragmatic. His astute observations took him to law school. He also excelled at calling plays and talking smack. Once, our opponent's setter gave his left side hitter a good set, but Nick Petterssen stuff-blocked the hitter, making it clear Nick out-classed the hitter.

"Don't set that guy again," Jesse announced.

On the next play, their setter set the middle. Guy Swope stuffed him. "Better choice, but I wouldn't set him either," Jesse cackled.

Then their setter set his right side hitter. A good set and best choice given I was the weakest blocker and on that side. Still, I stuffed that hitter.

"Maybe you should set that guy on the bench," Jesse brayed and pointed.

Their setter set the first hitter again. Stuffed again.

"I told you not to set that guy," Jesse glowed.

The other team's setter glared and yelled at his teammates, "Come on! Put the ball away!" They went on to commit a whole series of "un-forced" errors.

~

Nick Petterssen played opposite Jesse. Every good team has a terminator and Nick was ours. 6'4", long arms, huge hands and feet. Powerful. Never one to shy away from the obvious, Jesse worked hard at being able to make a deceptive back-set to Nick. I watched in awe.

Blockers were late. Back row defenders waited—knees bent, back straight, arms extended low, palms up. Nick soared, swung, and the ball turned into a missile rebounding off the defender's forehead and sailing 30 feet out of bounds. Or rocketing straight down and bouncing directly into the defender's crotch. Da-dump. A wheeze. Our point.

Nick was unique. In 1992 we teamed up and began to dominate Colorado's doubles tournaments. At the beginning of the summer he shaved his head except for one square inch on the side. He braided that patch of hair and put a couple of beads on the end. Except for that braid, he kept his head shaved all summer and by the end, it looked like, as many described, someone had glued a six inch worm to the side of his head.

Nick was extreme in everything he did. Especially skiing.

A frigid morning. The first run. A group of us skate from the lift to the top of a black diamond bowl. We ski around the cornice, slide into the bowl to take a few turns to feel the snow, loosen-up. Half a dozen turns or so and we stop to stretch and take in the view. Suddenly Nick comes flying over the cornice, 20 ft. through the air in a tuck, lands (skis pointing straight down-hill) blasts by us carving three long turns then skids into a cloud of snow at the bottom. The snow settles to reveal Nick standing— looking tall as bug—waiting.

Like Jesse, I'm partial to the obvious, so I teamed with Nick to qualify for events on the AVP Professional Beach tour the summer after Nationals.

~

Guy Swope and Mark Lindstrom were two of the most well-liked on our team. Quiet, nice, and hard-working, they fulfilled the crucial role of middle hitter/blocker. Like football teams with great offensive and defensive linemen, great middles make bad teams average, average teams great, and great teams unstoppable.

Guy was 6'6", quick, and silky smooth. Sometimes he and I played pick-up basketball. In our first game Guy sprinted down the sideline, across the baseline, and in one motion, caught a pass, squared his feet to the basket, jumped straight up and shot a 20 foot jumper ... swish (the home-crowds would have been chanting: *Lay-up! Lay-up! Lay-up!*). Next time down, Guy sprinted the sideline and baseline, caught the pass, faked a jump shot and with the defender in the air, took one dribble, three steps and rose for a two-handed dunk (*Lay-up! Lay-up! Lay-up!*).

In volleyball, middle blockers defend the middle of their court, which funnels attacks towards backrow defenders. On offense, they create high percentage hitting opportunities for everyone. It all revolves around the quick set. Timing is the key.

The moment the server makes contact with the ball, the receiving team's setter races to stand next to the net in the center of the court. As the ball is passed to the setter, the middle times his approach so he's at the peak of his jump, a few feet from the setter, ready to hit the moment the ball enters his setter's hands.

The setter looks at the defense. If the opposing middle hasn't jumped to block, he's left the center of his court undefended. So the setter flicks the ball a few feet to where his soaring middle can smack it past the flat-footed blocker and into open court. An unblocked quick set scores as easily as an ally-hoop dunk. Middles must jump to hit and block the quick set.

If the middle is blocking the quick set, the setter sets the ball forward or backward to his outside hitters. This means the middle blocker must land, take two steps left or right, then jump and block with his outside hitter. If the middle blocker doesn't get outside, he's left a hole in the defense and the other team's hitter can rip the ball into open court.

I loved to watch Guy jump, land, sprint, jump, and press his arms over the net to stuff outside hitters. He left them with that quizzical expression, "Where did he come from?" I knew they'd be less surprised if they saw Guy sail down the baseline and dunk. I wanted to counsel the hitters, "Yah, he does that," or "Watch out he'll do it again," but never said anything.

When middles block in the middle and outside, attackers must hit the ball at a back row defender. When the ball is dug into the air, the middle blocker becomes an attacker. He steps off the net, squares his feet and times his approach so that he's at the peak of his jump, ready to hit, the moment the ball enters his setter's hands. The setter looks and if the opposing middle isn't blocking—smack—into open court.

Mark was a 6'5" all-conference tennis player at his high school. His feet were as fast as Guy's and he had a lightning quick arm swing. Mark was so humble there were times when it was annoying. But humility kept him working hard. And it paved the way for my favorite moments, in private, when he would boast with a chuckle, "I knew I'd stuff that guy," or "That was great when I blasted the ball off that guy's head."

We played Kansas City in semi-finals at Nationals. Guy and Mark were instrumental in our overcoming the big win let-down after Sacramento State. They made stuff-blocks, funneled hitters into easy digs and errors, and after making difficult transitions, bombed the ball past their defense. We won the best of a three game match in two games.

~

We beat Rhode Island in two games for the title. Afterwards, some of their players said they knew they were in trouble during warm-ups, when the crowd roared for hits that bounced 40 and 50 feet high. Then erupted for Nick, who bounced one into the four-foot wide air duct that hung just below the 80 foot high ceiling.

~

I often struggled to fall asleep after tournaments, tossing and turning as the good and bad replayed in my mind. I bought a journal in 1990, and though my entries were just a few sentences and/or an illustration, it was easier to get to sleep. A week after nationals I commented on the end of the Sacramento State match.

We won the first game, but in the second, Sacramento's outside hitters found a rhythm and repeatedly sizzled the ball past our middle blockers' arms and off both Post and me in the back row. Before the third game, I thought about a drill we did at every practice.

To start, one player stands in the middle of the net. Another stands on the left sideline with a few in line behind him. The player in the middle takes two steps and jump-stops shoulder to shoulder with the player on the left sideline. They jump and block together. Upon landing, both take two steps to the middle, jump-stop shoulder to shoulder and block again.

After landing, the blocker on the right goes right and jump-stops on the right sideline, while the blocker on the left goes left and jump-stops shoulder to shoulder with the next player in line. All three (one on the right side and two on the left) jump and block at the same time. Upon landing, all three step to the middle, jump-stop shoulder to shoulder, and put up a triple block.

Then two go right and one goes left to join the next player in line. With two on each sideline, all four block.

On the right, the blocker on the outside is the one who started in the middle. He's completed his first set, so he steps off the court and gets back in line. Meanwhile, the inside blocker on the right and two from the left step to the middle. Triple block.

Two step right, one steps left. Four block.

Of the two on the right, the outside blocker is the one who started on the left sideline. He's finished his first set so he steps off the court and gets back in line while the inside blocker and two from the left step to the middle. Triple block.

Everyone does three sets.

"Together!" coach Blessing shouted as a warning to get our shoulders, arms, and hands in sync. If poor form continued Blessing would command, "Start over [three more sets]!"

"Let's go!" we implored as oxygen debt-induced mistakes mounted (the worst were getting an elbow planted in your ear or knocking knees with someone taking off the wrong way).

Sometimes, it seemed like Blessing shouted "start over" just for the fun of it. Finally, when done, we caught our breath and got a drink.

Sacramento was ahead in the third game 15–14, match point, they dug my hit and set their outside hitter. He'd been getting kills by hitting the ball just inside our middle, so I followed Mark to block on the outside. A triple block was rare in those days (I hadn't and wouldn't again all tournament), but I had to take away that shot with which their outside hitter scored so many points.

I can still feel the ball squarely compress just above my right elbow. I can also hear the sounds that led to it rocketing straight down onto their court. Da-Da-Dum.

15-15. Jesse served and they set outside again. Jesse digs, Nick sets, and I smack the ball into open court, 16-15, our match point. Then, just like he often did, Jesse served a crisp knuckle ball that skipped off their passer's arms and out of bounds. We win.

~

"Be ready, you won't always play your toughest competition in the finals," I wrote in my journal, along with, "Pay attention, even the best have tendencies that can be exploited."

I also noted that everyone made great plays in tournaments and practices all season. Steve in the quarter finals. Jon in the finals. Kern, who could hit any corner with his float serve and often burned Post and me; Chuck who jumped 40" and brought high caliber hits and blocks; Craig, a 6'5" middle who learned from some of the best in Southern California. Coach Blessing, Post, Jesse, Nick, Guy, Mark, I and a dozen I didn't mention. The 1992–1993 University of Colorado men's club volleyball season was no picnic.

Fate

March 11, 1993, my girlfriend Gail Lessig died in a car accident.

Gail and I were going to volleyball tournaments in northern California. I left Boulder with the CU team a few hours before Gail left with her club team.

While driving down I-80 with CU, we saw a car drift into the tires of a semi, over-compensate and spin off the road at 65 mph. It flipped once and as we ran up to it, roof partially caved, feared what we might see. They had some cuts, bruises, and were dizzy but everyone was fine.

Gail's accident was on I-80 too.

Gail was beautiful. One of the most thoughtful and kind people I'd ever met (and an all-state volleyball player). She was eager to learn and quick to speak up for how others might feel. She wouldn't hesitate to speak against hate and everyone said they liked her. I tried to ease my grief by reminding myself that we'd only been dating for a few months, but adding to my loss was her family: mom, dad, step mom, and brothers who treated me like family. Most memorably so during a ski vacation in Aspen over Christmas break.

~

I'd always been sensitive to violence, but became hyper-sensitive after Gail died. At a tournament in Arizona with the CU team, we had an afternoon off, so we went to a movie about a quiet, depressed man that had a bad morning, found a bunch of guns and went on a killing spree. Walking out of the theater I became dizzy. I sat and the world stopped spinning. Still, a darkness set in that I would not come out of for a year. I drank a lot of alcohol to help me get to sleep.

Many aided my recovery. One that stands out was the U.C. Berkeley coach. I went to his office to take the call when my mom told me Gail had died. I hung up and felt hot, sick and kept thinking his desk was pretty well organized.

"I lost someone in an accident," he said, "it will get easier." Then he spoke about how his friend lives on in him and concluded, "It will never be right, but it gets easier."

~

One of the saddest moments in my life was right after the finals at nationals. It felt strange to feel so down after winning. I sat on the bench, watched teammates and competitors shake hands, talk, and laugh. Then I remembered a favorite movie.

"Chariots of Fire" Best Picture Award winner in 1981. A fact-based story about two of Great Britain's track athletes, Harold Abrahams and Eric Liddell, who each won gold at the 1924 Olympics in Paris.

Eric was a devout Scottish Christian who ran to prove God's glory. With his unique form (head and shoulders back, arms wheeling) he looked as if God's hand was pushing the small of his back and he was simply along for the joyous ride.

While on the boat to France, Eric learned his heat for the 100-yard dash was scheduled on a Sunday. Eric cherished running as much as any of God's gifts, but training had taken too much from his missionary work already. He could not now, in the eyes of the world, run on the Sabbath. "It's only a heat," his coach and trainer rationalized. Still, Eric pulled out of the Olympics. There was criticism and praise.

A few days later, a teammate asked Eric to take his place in the 400-yard dash, which didn't have scheduling conflicts with the Sabbath. "Just to see you run," Eric's teammate explained.

Eric wheeled to victory, carrying a note an American athlete gave him just before the race: "Those who honor me," the bible passage read, "I will honor."

Of all the characters I liked Eric best; but I identified most with Harold.

Harold and his family were discriminated against for being Jewish. Harold wanted to win because being the world's fastest man would prove racists wrong, and could help him bring awareness (and an end) to prejudice. In one scene, Harold talks about Great Britain's racist socio-economic corridors of power, and vows to, "Run them off their feet."

Harold elicited the help of a world renowned trainer Sam Mussabini. They trained day and night, rain and shine, "Mad men," his teammates chided.

Cambridge administration met with Harold to discuss concerns over his coach for being "Arab," and that they were training like professionals.

"I consider myself lucky to be worthy of his [Sam's] attention," Harold emphasized, and was insulted at the suggestion that he leave his dreams to "... playground whims of a child." Harold would hold his fate in his own hands.

After Harold was crowned fastest man alive, Harold's teammates tried to celebrate with him in the locker room. Harold ignored everyone, changed his clothes, packed his bag, and slipped out the door.

The next scene shows Harold and Sam in a bar after closing, drunk.

"Now you've got it out of your system," Sam slurs, "So go back home to that wife of yours and start some bloody living!"

It's long past closing and the bartender tells Harold and Sam they have to leave. Harold stumbles to his feet for a toast, "To Sam Mussabini, the greatest coach in the world."

~

After the finals at nationals I sat on the bench and watched the stage being set up, tables with dark blue skirts, rows of trophies and plaques for teams and all-tournament players in a dozen men's and women's divisions. It'd be a while before they'd announce Division I awards. Wally Martin sat down beside me, his 6'5" frame sitting tall like always.

Wally's a multiple time national champion as player and coach under Al Scates at the University of California, Los Angeles. Scates developed a system with world class athletes using pinpoint ball-control and impeccable timing—all of which helped the U.S. win gold at the 1984 and 1988 Olympics. In 1991, Wally came to Colorado to teach at a school for struggling kids and start a men's volleyball program at Colorado State University.

Wally first called me a few days after Gail's funeral. I only knew a few things about him: he coached our rival CSU; we called him "Dark

Man" because his large frame, black pony tail, and black trench coat reminded us of the character in Stephen King's The Stand. And once, while playing against Wally's team in a men's league tournament, I got a perfect set, saw him crouching in the cross court, and hit the ball—aiming directly at his forehead. He put his hands up like he was setting and flicked the ball perfectly to his setter. Then he stood, stretched one hand back, covered his mouth with the other and yawned.

"Come north young man," Wally would say, referencing the drive from Boulder to Ft. Collins. We'd work-out. Go to a dinner of burritos smothered in green chili and more margaritas than the limit. I'd crash in his guest room until I was awakened by the prodding cold nose and playful paws of Belle, an Australian Shepherd who made it clear the sun had been up way too long for sleeping. Then I'd smell breakfast.

"Bittersweet, huh?" is all I remember Wally saying on the bench after nationals. He was always quick to recognize there's more to life.

~

I was mad when I wasn't voted to the all-tournament team. Nick, who won MVP, and Jesse and Post who also won honors, played great. Still, I was voted MVP a few times that year and played similarly—consistent, with great plays at important moments throughout. Plus the scouting report said you could beat CU by serving the black guy, and every team tried.

But that was not my reputation in Colorado. I'd won top-level doubles tournaments with many partners: Omar Swani, Scott Smith, Scott Peters, Ed Gille, Guy Swope, and Nick Petterssen.

"Keep the ball away from Curtis," was a phrase I heard more and more. I loved controlling the ball. Especially when the game was on the line—a fire that began burning the summer after my senior year in high school, at the 1987 King of the Mountain tournament in Vail.

I played with Todd Rowley, a friend from church and school. We competed in the weakest of five divisions. After playing on Saturday we earned a spot in Sunday's bracket.

That night we drove two hours to Denver for KOOL radio's 'oldies' concert featuring The Four Tops, Supremes, Paul Revere and the Raiders. Afterwards back up the mountain, asleep by 3 a.m.

In the quarter-finals we lost the first game to eleven and were down 9 - 10 in the second, match point. One of our opponents hit a short shot that he'd scored many points with. I dove and popped the ball up, back to the hitter. He hit again. I lunged and batted the ball, back to the hitter. He took another rip. I swatted (mostly in self-defense), and the ball rebounded higher and deeper into their court. The player I just dug three times called "Mine" and established position under the ball, before suddenly stepping aside and shouting at his partner, "You take it!" The ball landed untouched. We went on to win the match.

In the semi-finals the eventual champions overwhelmed us with what seemed at the time, flawless serving, passing, setting and hitting. As we warmed up for the next match, I'd never wanted to win more, because the difference between 3rd and 4th was a trophy.

~

The 1987 King of the Mountain lowest division third place trophy started a collection. When I reached a dozen, dusting and appreciating each began to feel like a chore. Plus, while my trophies proved I had the will to win, my game had evolved. And more importantly, I knew I needed to continue to evolve.

I also admired Eric Liddell in "Chariots of Fire," when he hosted a track meet for a community and gave away his old trophies as prizes. "The smiles on these kids' faces," he said, "are worth a thousand of any of the tin pots I got gathering dust in the attic."

And I loved it when Nick brought the centerpiece of his MVP trophy (an actual volleyball), to a session of indoor deep court doubles a week after Nationals. First time in our gym since being crowned national champs and the beach doubles season was upon us—the Silverbacks were back. We introduced that ball to a life of spectacular hits and digs.

As a reminder to live in the moment, I've had ceremonies to get rid of all but two of my trophies, plaques and medals. One is a silver medal from the 1991 AAU Indoor National Championships. I played middle blocker/hitter, a position I was too small for and had only played messing around. But our team needed a middle. Throughout the tournament I had blocks and hits which proved I could be a physical force, most notably so in the finals, against a 6'9" high flyer touted as one of the nation's best. The other is a silver medal for coaching the 2001 University of Colorado's men's club team. Having competed in a national championship with CU as both a player and a coach, is a poignant summary of my most treasured accomplishments in volleyball.

~

September 1992, Colorado's professional volleyball tour held its first "King of the Beach" doubles tournament. Eight players are invited. Everyone plays once with each competitor. Whoever wins the most games is crowned "King."

Since players often finish with the same record, there's a point system to break ties. That year we received five points for winning, plus one point for every point in the margin of victory. For example, if a team wins 11-2, each player gets 14 points (5 plus 9). For an 11-9 win, players get 7 points (5 plus 2).

I competed with/against Nick Petterssen, Wally Martin, Dane Hanson (stand-out on Colorado State's indoor team that finished 5th at Nationals) and the next four top-ranked players. I finished with the best record 6-1. I also ran away with the points, scoring 75 while my opponents scored 61, 48, 41, 37, 28, 16 and 14.

The luck of the draw creates more favorable and less favorable matchups, I wrote in my journal: *Still, the talented field means everyone can strike a winner. Adjust to your partner's strengths and weaknesses. Stay positive—every moment, every point. One point at a time!*

~

In January 1992, I was King of Colorado, playing on a team with a good shot at winning nationals, and had just spent a very special long weekend in Aspen with Gail and her family. When I thought of the prejudice and ignorance I'd faced in Kansas, I was even more proud of having heeded my mom quoting Oscar Wilde, "The best revenge is a life well lived."

On the drive back from Aspen Gail ranted like she did from time to time. It was therapeutic for us both.

"So many idiots! Who cares if people are black or white or yellow or red? Where they were born or which God they pray to? Whether you're gay, straight or bi? Athletic, tall, short, fat or thin? Just be kind. All we need is love. So few get it!" She ended with her gorgeous smile beaming, "When I die, people better dance on my grave, because I got to move on from this world."

~

Between 1992 and 1998, I played five King of Colorado tournaments and won them all. Having moved to Los Angles and gotten stronger, faster and more skilled playing against the best in the world, I was favored in all but the first one. Still, aside from a five-month stretch in 1994 and a few tournaments here and there, I rarely played my best. My performances as a pro hit rock bottom in Miami in 1997. I had to make a choice, either become comfortable with being a pro beach volleyball player, compete like I can and communicate better with partners, sponsors, players, fans, and referees. Or leave L.A. and the pro tour.

I won my fifth King of Colorado title a year after leaving. There were new faces, athletic and talented players from Colorado, California and Florida. There was also a new point system, which lessened the value for a win and meant each point was more valuable (losing 11-3 as opposed to 11-2 could be the difference). I played in the moment as well as ever, won by two points, and danced when I got home.

~

Gail's death pushed me over an edge. Few could match my rage and will to win. And "Chariots of Fire" was my guide—Harold's work ethic and passion to run racists off their feet. And Eric's faith when he explained to his sister why training to run was interfering with his Mission work, "Because God made me fast! And when I run, I feel His glory."

I hoped to pound racists, sexists, classists all in the sand. Because when I'd dive, dig, get up, and put the ball away, I felt His glory too.

Qualifying

Nick and I were confident after Club Nationals and set our sights on the Association of Volleyball Professionals (AVP), "The world's best." Qualifying tournaments were held every few weeks from May through August. Top finishers won entry into the next few main events.

True to form, my Mom and Oma didn't flinch when I told them I wanted to pursue a career in professional beach volleyball. Then they gave me money for plane tickets.

Nick and I failed to qualify in Texas and Arizona.

The next qualifier for four tournaments on the AVP's swing through the north east, was in Atlantic City. We could afford the trip because Nick's grandmother lived in New Jersey. We flew to Newark, took a train, and she picked us up. When we entered her house my mouth began to water at the meal she'd prepared.

She piled huge servings on our plates. When Nick and I finished she served another large portion. "Oh, it's delicious," I said 'but I can't eat all that."

She took my plate, scooped a small spoonful back then handed me the plate and said, "Eat." After that she brought out desert.

I had a refreshing sleep. We got up in the dark, took Nick's grandmother's car (that would also be our bed and roof that night), and drove to Atlantic City.

~

Like most tournaments, the qualifier was "double elimination." Every team gets ranked based on past performances, called a "seed." 1st seed is the team with best record, 2nd seed, second best, etc. down to the team with the worst record at 32nd. Initially, all teams are placed in the "winners" bracket: highest against lowest, 1st vs 32nd, 2nd vs 31st, and so on. If the bracket plays out according to seed, semi-finals are 1st vs 4th and 2nd vs 3rd, the finals are 1st vs 2nd, and when 1st wins, they wait to play in the championship.

After a loss, teams play in the "contenders" bracket. If that bracket plays out according to seed, the 2nd will eventually face the 1st, meaning in order to win the championship, they must beat the 1st seed twice.

In Atlantic City, Nick and I received a terrible seed and lost to the 1st seed in the second round. We focused our anger, one point at a time. When I made a poor play, he made a great one and vice versa. Back-to-back games all day. We got better with each game.

One win before the finals and qualifying for four AVP tournaments, the sun was setting. Since it might get too dark to play before finishing, the tournament director asked both teams if we wanted to start now or wait until morning. "Now," Nick snapped. I wanted to play right then too, but meekly agreed so our opponents wouldn't think we were too excited and postpone. They agreed. We finished them off with light to spare.

~

Our first two AVP events were in Seaside Heights, New Jersey and Ocean City, Maryland. Again, we stayed at Nick's grandmothers, ate fantastic food and borrowed her car.

The first lesson in our first AVP tournament was don't try to sleep in a car. It heats up like a sauna, but cracking a window for air lets the mosquitoes in.

The top seeded team, Karch Kiraly and Kent Steffes, beat us 15-4. Karch is a three-time Olympic gold medalist: two indoor six man and one on the beach. At 144 pro tour wins, the most ever, Karch is widely regarded as the best player of all time. Kent was a gifted young player who worked hard and teamed with Karch to dominate the tour from 1993 to 1996. They were the first team to win Olympic gold in beach volleyball in Atlanta in 1996.

Nick and I were also soundly beaten by young stars from Brazil, Eduardo Bacil and Jose Loiola, and two other teams. We placed 25th in both events. No prize money. The irony of earning more at the qualifier than at both main events was lost in our thrill to compete against the best—

a pride we felt every time we put on our shorts, which now displayed the official AVP patch.

The next AVP tournament was the Grand Daddy of them all, The Manhattan Beach Open. Unfortunately we were broke so we played in a Colorado tournament to collect the thousand dollar first prize. We crushed three opponents and were winning big when Nick dug a ball, planted his foot and "pop." Torn ACL.

It was a huge loss. I don't like to spend much time on 'what ifs'. But after placing 7th in the US Championships in 1995, it was a shame Nick and I didn't get a chance to play with a little more experience and while we were hot.

With Nick out, the AVP let me choose a partner.

~

I asked Dane Hanson (standout on Colorado State University's six-man indoor team that placed 5th at Nationals). Like me, Dane was better at doubles and had quickly moved up the ranks in Colorado. He often trained with us when Wally invited me to Ft. Collins. Dane was an excellent passer and backrow defender. I hoped we'd play like the small but accomplished teams of Larry Mear and Eric Wurts, or Leif Hanson and Scott Friederichsen.

Dane and I played Sinjin Smith and Ricci Luyties on Cape Cod, MA. Sinjin is one of the winningest players ever with 124. Ricci is 1988 six-man indoor Olympic gold medalist and seven-time AVP champion. Though the game was to 15, the AVP had newly implemented a game clock, so games fit into time slots for television. We lost 9 - 8.

If we played old school rules (side out scoring, must score 15), Sinjin and Ricci might have beaten us 15-10. After all, they finished 4th while we finished 25th. Still, we were just two plays from a big win and I choked. Late in the game, Sinjin hit a ball I would have dug ninety-nine times out of a hundred. But I shanked this one out of play. Another play I timed an approach so badly I hit the ball with my forearm, sailing it 15 feet out of bounds (not the last time I'd make horrendous plays because I was thinking about winning).

Dane and I placed 25th in three AVP tournaments that summer, each riddled with rookie mistakes. The worst was Seal Beach, CA, when we missed our entire warm-up because we were watching a game on the outer courts like a couple of fans.

Dane and I finished our season at the Motherlode pro/am tournament in Aspen CO. Over 600 teams from all over North America came to Aspen on Labor Day weekend: thousands in prize money. Plus hiking, mountain biking, world class fly fishing, more. And while most players focus as much on family, friends, and what Aspen has to offer, when players from the AVP, US national team, Olympians and top ranked College programs step on the court, they compete with pride. The Motherlode is a coveted title.

~

I played my first of twelve Motherlodes sophomore year in College. I left Kansas at seven Friday morning. Twelve hours later I drove by the tiny town that sits at the east entrance of Independence Pass: a 40 mile stretch of narrow, barely two-lane road with switchbacks, 500 foot drops off the edge of the road, an 11,000 ft. summit with stunning views, and the town of Aspen sitting at the west entrance. I parked at the summit. The sun had set but it wasn't dark. I walked to the scenic overlook. The air was crisp and cool. Rocky Mountain peaks in all directions. Clouds streaked rose and lavender under the sapphire and indigo sky.

~

In 1993, my first Motherlode with Dane, I also coached the girls' sophomore team at Fairview high school.

I loved coaching, especially after learning from Wally Martin and Andy Klussman. Andy moved from Southern California to Ft. Collins the same time as Wally, and was an indoor national champion as a player and coach at UCLA as well. He also played on the four-man professional beach tour. Andy and Wally coached camps all year and asked me to guest coach from time to time. I'd regularly parrot their phrases and jokes, many of which they'd credit to legends like Al Scates, Karch Kiraly, and others.

I was also an assistant coach at Bethany and for junior club teams in Colorado. I loved it when players would make a play and light up. Or when they'd make a mistake, adjust on the next play, then light up. Or when I learned new ways to say the same thing, to help more players and teams be better. I also liked how, after being crowned "King of Colorado," becoming a national champion, and playing on the AVP, players listened more closely and worked harder for me.

Fairview had a match Friday night of Labor Day weekend in 1993, so I left for Aspen around 9 pm. An hour into the four-hour drive I exited I-70 at Copper Mountain and wouldn't pass another car on the road until Aspen—three hours of Jimi Hendrix, Run DMC, and Muddy Waters.

It was raining and Run DMC was singing "Walk this way" when I drove by the iron gates that close Independence Pass in the winter. Soon the rain stopped and a thick fog moved in. Poor visibility, the slow pace and humming engine made me drowsy.

I parked at the summit. On a clear afternoon you can see hikers, like ants, inching their way over a rolling 12,000 ft. mountain to the south-west. I stepped out to stretch. The silence, dark and cold seized me.

I heard my heart beat, *Ba-boom ... Ba-boom ... Ba-boom ...*

And my breath, *Sshhhh—hehhh ... Sshhhh—hehhhh ... Sshhhh—hehhh...*

I wanted more, so I grabbed my flashlight and started down the asphalt path to the scenic overlook. Then I veered onto the dirt trail leading to the 12,000 ft. mountain to the south-west, focusing on my breath and the next step up the rocky trail.

Ba-boom ... Sshhhh—hehhh ... ba-boom ... sshhhh—hehhh ... ba-boom ... sshhhh—hehhh.

The fog grew thicker. The incline steeper. My heartbeat and breath were strong and steady. My stride lengthened, as if I were on an escalator to the moon. I began to cry.

I cried regularly in the first six months after Gail died: shower, bed, mountain meadows. Silence can be brutal—the constant reminder of the way things are.

My pace slowed. My flashlight in the mist like a lightsaber. Rocks glistened. I thought of what so many say, "*They* would want you to go on," "*They* are in a better place," "You will see *them* again." But that answers only a few questions. Why am I still here? Why does God take those who use love to stop hate?

I stopped walking. Thought of Oma and Opa. Germans tolerating Hitler when he spent most of his time talking about national pride and jobs. But then it took the combined Allies' armies to stop him. Millions, including 17 in my own family, were killed.

I stopped crying and screamed, trying to hurt the ears of a world that doesn't miss a step. Like news broadcasters talking war, murder, and rape in the same cadence and tone they use to describe sports events and the weather. Then I thought of my Oma's favorite prayer by St. Francis of Assisi:

Prayer of Peace

Lord, make me an instrument of Thy peace:
Where there is hatred, let me sow love; where there is injury, pardon;
Where there is doubt, faith; where there is despair, hope;
Where there is darkness, light; where there is sadness, joy.
O Divine Master,
Grant that I may not so much seek to be consoled as to console;
To be understood as to understand; to be loved as to love;
For it is in the giving that we receive,
It is in the pardoning that we are pardoned,
And, it is in dying that we are born to eternal life.

I started breathing easily, stood, walked, and drove through the fog into Aspen.

~

Dane and I were seeded tenth, but had home-court advantage over the top-seeded teams. They were from sea level and consequently less comfortable with the burn that hits the lungs at 8,000 feet. They were also less familiar with the ball moving in gusty, light mountain air, as opposed to the heavy, steady ocean breeze. The crowd was in a frenzy for their local boys and we gave them reasons to cheer. We placed second.

1993 was my first of six finals appearances in a row winning four consecutive titles. As important as my excellent play, were the road trips and deep breaths atop Independence Pass.

Quest

Between 1991 and 1993, I became the best in Colorado at the fastest growing game in America and eligible for a teacher's license. I also enjoyed being back in the more liberal town of Boulder, where some are able to look more critically at things like jokes that might be racist; links between institutionalized behavior and impoverished minorities; and US military intervention overseas. Unlike in Kansas, where even my ex-girlfriend and I argued about Desert Storm and the United States' bid to throw Saddam Hussein out of Kuwait.

"Don't tell me you think it's about oil," she said.

"My mom and her family are from Germany," I said, "so I understand, some leaders need to be stopped—taken out—and I respect the hell out of those who risk everything doing so. But, too often our government has made mistakes or outright lied."

I brought up Manuel Noriega of Panama, Ferdinand Marcos of the Philippines and Mobutu Sese Seko of Zaire. I mentioned our giving weapons to Iran to sell on to the thieving, murderous Contras in Nicaragua. And the many in Congress who supported South Africa as they jailed Mandela.

I was surprised she couldn't see that our Government probably wouldn't give a rat's ass about Saddam if he didn't have oil. Or recognize the discipline it took for me to become a Conscientious Objector, following the examples of Martin Luther King Jr., Gandhi, even Jesus.

"We're not going to show up on your parent's doorstep locked and loaded," hoping a personal illustration might help, "dinner at gun point wouldn't change their hearts and minds. It's best to have faith in their intelligence and compassion. Best to channel our anger into love."

After one year of trying and two since giving up, I took solace knowing that the myths, illusions, and lies surrounding my being black weren't the only reasons we broke up. We fought the good fight, I'd moved on. And was happy to be around people who helped me understand myself in a world ripe with prejudice and violence.

~

Still, Boulder isn't the oasis many of its liberals make it out to be. I continued to run into white guys who called me nigger, fearful old white women, those dumbfounded by my white behavior, and others who assumed my skin color qualified me to talk on behalf of inner city blacks.

In 1992, the Denver Post newspaper ran an article on the annual KKK rally held on MLK Jr. Day. The KKK's "promising" young spokesman heralded Boulder as the kind of place where he'd like to live. And my wealthy high school friend who ridiculed me for receiving a scholarship for blacks, howled with laughter and boasted, "Boulderites would never tolerate racists."

~

Black football players at the University of Colorado have taken the brunt of Boulder's harsh reality.

I was a season ticket holder 4th through 8th grade. Young, hopeful, and after years of losing big—Oklahoma 82 to 10, Nebraska 63 to 3, Texas 59 to 17, I loved watching the Buffs become nationally ranked in the late 1980's and National Champions in 1990.

The Buffs were led by Coach Bill McCartney, a long-time assistant at Big Ten power Michigan, where football rules dawn to dusk, six days a week. He was also a born-again Christian.

"One of the things that happened at Michigan," Coach Mac said in "The Gospel According to Mac," a documentary in ESPN's 30 for 30 series, "is that we recruited the great black athlete. And I learned that you can't win without the great black athlete. It wasn't true in everybody's mind," he concluded, "but that's how I felt."

~

Most of Coach Mac's stars were black and came from ghettos in Southern California.

"Up through 8th grade," quarterback Charles Johnson explained, "I didn't have one white classmate, teacher, neighbor, teammate or friend. I thought white people, by and large, were television stars, you saw them on television."

"[Playing] football, I'm in my element," said tail back J.J. Flannigan, "had my helmet on, nobody could see me. But when the crowd was gone and the cheering stopped," J.J. continued, "I'm a young black kid in a big pool of white people that I don't know, that look at me strange, that I look at them strange."

"When you're from a certain neighborhood, you're not used to people calling you nigger," added running back Eric Bieniemy, "And that was just like a daily thing we went through. And it was hard to accept, you know, you got different people telling you to just turn away, don't even listen to it. But I mean, your manhood is telling you to challenge that issue."

In one incident, Eric was approached by two white guys in the bathroom. They called him racist names and punched him. He busted out of the bathroom and ran to his friend Kanavis McGee.

"Well," Kanavis explained, "my natural reaction was to hit [the white guy] back ... [the media] didn't look at the reason, they just saw a CU football player who broke someone's jaw.

On Halloween, a crowd of four or five kicked J.J. Flannigan's car and a fight ensued. "I just remember trying to explain to the police, and the girl that was with this group, she yelled why don't you just shut up you stupid 'n' word." J.J. continued, "I was young, I reacted wrong, got highly upset, and just slapped her, and I just remember the police telling me, 'Now your black ass is going to jail.'" and J.J. concluded, "I had never been in trouble a day in my life."

"[Black athletes were] recognizable," said linebacker Chad Brown, "and at times you're walking around campus and there's a cop car, just following you around campus ..."

18 arrests, 65 complaints and Sports Illustrated ran a national story, "What Price Glory?: Under Coach Bill McCartney Colorado football had

taken off, but so has ugly criminal behavior among the Buffalo players. Black and white year book photos were arranged like mug shots."

My dad played football for CU and kept tabs on the program over the years. In the same sad tone of surrender that he'd told me to defend myself after the kids on my elementary school playground threw rocks and called me a nigger, he talked about how the Sports Illustrated article was asinine. And how poorly these young men were being treated.

~

Someone called me a nigger every year or two between the ages of 10 and 33. In my mid to late thirties I only heard it once. No one's called me nigger in my forties (though someone did call my girlfriend a nigger).

Though not surprised, it was still shocking each time it happened. I was desensitized by recognizing that the right to say something hateful is more important than stopping hate ("boys will be boys"). And by excusing people for being either funny or affectionate. Assuming good intentions in others turned off my alarms, so it took a moment before I realized that the person who called me a nigger meant the worst.

Their voices often echo in my head, reminding me that racists are out there, working to convince others of "good" reasons to think badly of minorities.

When I felt overwhelmed I'd have lunch or dinner with my mom. She had a way of bringing it back to my work as a teacher, coach and role model.

"Curtis, the greatest impact you can have on social change," my mom often said, "is to be yourself."

~

When the police officers who beat Rodney King were acquitted, and then some blacks burned and looted their own neighborhoods, I dreamed of kicking the shit out of the officers *and* the looters. While CU running back Eric Bieniemy's manhood was telling him to challenge those who called him a nigger, I wanted to challenge *all* bad behavior.

If I'm going to help people see that the best way to end prejudice is for each side to focus on changing its own bigotry, I'm going to need more influence and power.

~

"I, like I think just about everyone in our freshman class," quarterback Charles Johnson explained in "The Gospel According to Mac," "went to his office at one point and said 'Mac, I want to transfer.'"

"One of the smartest things I ever did was hire Dr. Wil Miles," Coach Mac raved about the black clinical psychologist and professor in CU's Black Studies department, "you have to have advice, counsel, sensitivity … You have to tap in, you have to be led, and not just think you have all the answers because you think your heart is right."

Dr. Miles counseled the young men on how large, strong, black men from ghettos are often treated in Boulder: from police who won't give them the benefit of the doubt, to the check-out lady that puts change into the hands of white customers but sets it on the counter for them.

Coach Mac addressed Boulder's city council. "These 17 and 18-year old kids aren't the problem," he lectured, "they're here to get an education and in many cases, trying to figure out life themselves. If adults who are charged with providing them an environment to grow can't deal with them in a more constructive way," he said frankly, "then you're the problem."

"These are terrific kids," Coach Mac didn't let up, "and have come to a foreign land, and the people are treating them like foreigners. We need black educators, faculty, role models, administrators, mentors, and more black coaches … more black students that indicate, yes, ok, I belong here," Mac concluded, "There's very little."

"The thing that became apparent to me," noted receiver Lance Carl, "was a lot of the white guys on the team and a lot of the black guys on the team coming together as a team. He [Coach Mac] brought us together as a team."

"What do you do?" receiver Jeff Campbell asked, "Do you leave a teammate or family member out there to struggle? No, you say this is who we are with, we are going to help them adapt to this new environment that they're in. We're going to make this home. We're going to make a family and we're going to win."

"We had some emotional meetings," recalled receiver Mike Pritchard, "I mean, where guys were just crying about their experiences and what was going on, it was a family setting, it was as if we were around a dinner table."

Like generations of successful minority parents across America, Coach Mac also did his best to prepare his players for the prejudice they'll face by matching the severity of punishment with which whites would judge them. One arrest, one game suspension, two arrests led to a one year suspension.

Coach Mac benched his star players on a few occasions. He made one player watch every practice and game for a year. "It was hard," said defensive back Deon Figures who was arrested twice, "but I was jeopardizing everything I worked for. Still didn't go over so good with me, but looking back it was the right thing." Deon made the game clinching interception in the National Championship game, and was an All-American and first-round NFL draft pick.

"White guys don't get it. White guys are stupid," coach Mac explained in an attempt to hold everyone (not just his players) to high standards, "They don't see that they discriminate. They don't see that they have advantages."

"I think the white man needs to know that he's responsible for the repression of the black man," Coach Mac added, "He's held him down, pinned him down. He's benefited at his expense. Most white people try to excuse themselves as not having any bias. Truth of the matter is that all of us have benefited in different ways, whether we knowingly partake or not, and we need to put that right up front."

~

Winter 1993 I'd won my second King of Colorado and every big tournament in the state except the Motherlode. I'd beaten Division I national champions, professionals and top rated players from the most competitive beaches in the world. I loved the raw truth: dive, jump, scream, pound the ball off the sand, or if doubt needs to be erased, my opponent's face. The best part was I had reached full maturity, put in years of work in weight rooms, and had begun to attain, as my dad described it, "Man Strength."

This is my time. Like Harold running racists off their feet. Or Arthur Ashe. Or Jackie Robinson. Or Mack, Jackie's brother, and Ralph Metcalfe, each of whom won silver behind Jesse Owens in the 100 and 200 yard dash at the 1936 Olympics—the other black men to beat Hitler's best. Or Coach Mac, who got time with Boulder's City council because CU was in the national spotlight.

Dane was dreaming big too, so in March 1994 we moved to Southern California, where mostly blond-haired blue-eyed athletes in wealthy beach cities invented a game and became stars. Hermosa Beach was similar to Boulder, which was important because I'm better at everything when I feel at home. And if I was going to use fame and fortune to help bring an end to prejudice, I had to get a lot better at volleyball.

Breath

"It's all mental!" I lamented after playing poorly with my indoor team in Kansas. My ex-girlfriend, a violinist, nodded and made comparisons to defending first chair in orchestra. Our talk about the impact mental toughness has on performance was intense because in the back of our minds were her parents, so mentally small they couldn't see past the color of my skin. She was the first to give me a book on mental training for athletes.

~

The winter before Dane and I moved to Hermosa Beach my mom gave me the book Peak Performance, by Dr. Charles A. Garfield.

Dr. Garfield was a world class weightlifter in the 1970's and studied training techniques of top athletes around the world in the 1980's.

In 1976, the Russian (Soviet Union) Olympic team won more gold medals than any other country. The East Germans placed second. The U.S. placed third. The Soviet and East German success sparked controversy and many suspected drug use. In response, the Soviet weight lifting team reported on its success with, "mental training sessions."

Western cultures view the body more like a machine: X repetitions plus X weight equals X growth in speed and strength. Eastern cultures view the body more like a spirit: When an individual works to fulfill their highest purpose, they achieve spectacular results.

Soviets had long been allies with many Eastern cultures. Dr. Garfield describes their impact in the first chapter, Soviet Shamans in Milan, "Russian sports psychologists have been so highly esteemed that at least one has been awarded the venerated title of Academician ... The Russian public regards the Academician in much the same way that Americans regard an exceptional athlete or a war hero."

The Soviets studied Holocaust survivors and super-athletes for their ability to tap into "hidden reserves," that helped them survive and excel.

They also studied performance levels of athletes doing various ratios of physical to mental training. Group I: 100% physical. Group II: 75% physical, 25% mental. Group III: 50% physical, 50% mental. Group IV: 25% physical, 75% mental. Group IV, which spent 75% of their time training mentally, showed the greatest improvement.

Those results intrigued Dr. Garfield so he went to the Soviet Union to let coaches take him through a work-out and tell him more about their program.

~

Soviet coaches hooked Dr. Garfield up to machines that measured brain waves, cardiac activity, muscular activity and other body functions. Garfield was nervous, it had been years since he worked out with any kind of regularity. He hadn't been in the gym for months. In the last few years, he hadn't bench-pressed more than 280 pounds.

"What's the most he'd ever bench-pressed?" the coaches asked Dr. Garfield.

"365 pounds."

"How long would it take to get back into that kind of shape?"

"Nine to twelve months."

What's the most you could lift at this moment?

"300 pounds."

Soviet coaches asked Garfield to bench-press 300 pounds. Garfield was hesitant, but in all the excitement he did it. Soviet coaches then measured his height, weight, body fat percentage, metabolic rate and took a blood sample. They read instruments and analyzed information.

Next, the coaches helped Garfield into a deep state of relaxation. He laid down on his back and took deep breaths. He imagined his arms and legs becoming increasingly heavy and warm. Forty minutes later a tingling spread over Garfield's body and he felt fully awake and alert. They asked him to sit up, added 65 pounds to the bar, and told him to imagine lifting 365 pounds, "Approach the bar. Sit on the bench. Lie down. Hear the dull metallic ring as the bar tips and jangles the weights together. Breathe and vocalize like you normally would when working out. Confidently lift 365 pounds."

The monitoring equipment went haywire with Garfield's anxiety at the thought of benching 365 pounds. Again and again they talked him through confidently lifting the weight, "Breathe, zoom in and out of images imprinted in your mind. View yourself from above and the side. Look closely at your hands grasping the bar. Imagine how your muscles would feel completing the lift."

"Everything began to come together for me," Garfield writes, "Slowly and patiently ... I became convinced I could do it."

He bench-pressed 365 pounds.

"We calculate your present capabilities at somewhere between 345 and 395," the coaches said, "We chose 365 as a midway point. You no doubt could do more, maybe 395, but there are present physical limits that should be respected. You could tear a muscle or tendon. It doesn't make sense to chance it."

Garfield's first thought was to return to competition and challenge the world record. At least until the next day, when his aged joints assured him otherwise. Still, he reveled in the small miracle.

~

Dane and I could afford to live in Hermosa Beach thanks to a friend. Cheryl was a beach volleyball fan who graduated from Colorado State University, got an office job with the AVP and moved to 16th and Hermosa Ave. One block from the court most esteemed by locals, the location where one of the net's posts is a totem pole. I took that as a sign from our Native American ancestors, and we ended up sleeping in the living room of Cheryl's 800 sq. ft. apartment for five months.

Evenings were the best part of that long summer. A close second were the mornings, when I put on shorts, ate, grabbed a bag of balls, water bottle and walked a block to play in Hermosa's deep sand. But mostly I savored walking that block in the evening, to Tai Chi and meditate by the crashing waves and setting sun.

I fought depression all summer. I'd seen the emptiness death leaves since a classmate died in car accident in Jr. High. But hadn't understood the gravity until a year after Gail's death, when I still struggled to escape long quiet nights. My refuge was volleyball and the evening routine: the more sweat and attention I exerted, the better I'd sleep.

Constant reminders of my quest aided my focus.

The radio played responses to the acquittal of police officers who beat Rodney King and the riots that followed: 2Pac, "I Wonder If Heaven Got a Ghetto"; Off Spring, "L.A.P.D."; Dr. Dre, "The Days the Niggaz Took Over"; Ice Cube, "We Had to Tear This Muthafucka Up."

Driving through Los Angeles I was aware of borders running throughout the 500 sq. miles of asphalt and buildings. Just a few blocks separating the frighteningly poor from the terrifyingly rich. Where the wrong clothes could get me beaten or shot by street gangs. And the police.

All this madness fueled my fire. I gave 100% focus and energy to every chapter in Peak Performance: Sports Motivation Analysis, Unveiling Your Mission, Voluntary Relaxation, Mental Rehearsal, Athletic Poise, Letting Go.

~

In the first lesson, The Winner's Mind, Dr. Garfield writes about athletes who find "The Zone." A period of time when people run faster and longer, jump higher and farther, throw and shoot more accurately, and make uncanny decisions. Usually all with a sense of calm and ease.

"The Zone" isn't reserved for athletes. A WWII pilot improbably survived a mission. Injured and exhausted, the droning engine and sifting clouds put him in a dream-like state. When he started to give up, his dead grandfather appeared to give counsel and energy.

Some attribute such accomplishments to lock-jawed determination. However, the Soviets learned to tap into high levels of strength and power through "Rather subtle methods of breath control, mental concentration, and mind body unification, which they learned by mastering ancient meditation techniques."

I was reminded of the many times I made over 200 free throws in a row, or hit the volleyball on the lines all day long. Or listened to my breath and heartbeat on Independence Pass.

~

I was profoundly impacted by the lessons in Voluntary Relaxation: Exploring Relaxation and Tension, Breathing for Peak Performance, and Autogenic Training.

I loved the breathing techniques: Slowly fill the lungs to capacity. Hold the air in. Give thanks. When the body begs, slowly exhale. Squeeze every molecule from the lungs. Hold the air out. Give thanks. When the body begs, slowly inhale.

Dr. Garfield also writes about controlling the autonomic nervous system. He describes how scientists used sophisticated electronic equipment to find that "not only were yogis able to voluntarily alter their brain waves, heart rates, body temperatures and other metabolic processes … But the ability to voluntarily control these processes could be taught to others with little difficulty in a relatively short time."

Like most on the retreat with our cross country team in high school, I remembered, *who could raise and lower their temperature and heartrate.*

I especially enjoyed the Autogenic Training: Put on a Relaxation Mask, Create Heaviness, Create Warmth, Calm Your Heart, Create Warmth in Your Stomach, Cool Your Forehead. Each step has mantras: "My right arm is getting limp and heavy (Repeat six times). My right arm is getting heavier and heavier (Repeat four times). My right arm is completely heavy (Repeat six times). I feel supremely calm and relaxed (Repeat once)." I learned to warm, cool and relax my body from head to toe.

When meditating at Dane's parent's house in Chicago, I "softened" my eyes (blurring vision to help focus on air pouring through the nostrils, down the throat, into the lungs and out the mouth). Then a shadow appeared in the doorway. My heart beat harder and faster. I slowed my breath and I softened my eyes further. The figure stepped forward, touched my chest, filled me with warmth and told me to keep pursuing my dreams.

~

The writing exercises in <u>Peak Performance</u> included brainstorming, establishing long and short term goals, composing essays, drawing charts, and then regularly up-dating and revising. All of which altered the way I'd approach *everything* from then on. And I was ever more thankful for my mom's constant reminders, "Language isn't just reflective," she said again and again, "Language creates."

First, I wrote a list of moments when I felt a deep sense of satisfaction, fulfillment or joy. Then I circled three: Winning nationals with CU, First Motherlode tournament finals, and a moment with Gail. For each experience I wrote a title and sub-title in the middle of a clean sheet of paper. Then I pictured myself there, brainstormed words that came to mind and wrote them down: feelings, people, places, books, movies and more. I filled each page.

Finally, I reviewed all three pages, noted similarities and connections, then wrote a mission statement, "I'm blessed with privilege, talent and insight. With hard work and perseverance, I will be a pro beach volleyball star, and use my success and wisdom to help people."

~

Before Dane and I moved to Hermosa Beach, players had to move up the ranking system by winning in the main draw. A difficult task given the young talent and stubborn veterans who wanted a piece of the sky-rocketing prize money. When Dane and I got there, AVP qualifiers began a cumulative point system to earn membership. Dane and I decided to focus on the qualifying tour for several reasons. We'd have a year to get mentally and physically stronger, plus the top three finishers in qualifying tournaments were getting paid more than the last-place finishers in the main event. And most importantly, the top eight finishers at the end of the season received guaranteed entry into 18 tournaments the following summer.

My confidence soared when we won the first three out of four qualifying tournaments. I was getting faster and stronger. And though I was no stranger to making great plays at timely moments, <u>Peak Performance</u> had me making more of them.

With the room I have for mental and physical growth, I'm only a few years from world class.

~

Writing about your goals increases the chances that you will reach them. How do you see your setting? What are people doing and saying? What other things do you hear? What's the weather like? How do you and others feel? The more details you include, the better the odds.

In the last 1994 qualifying tournament I served three aces in a row, like in an essay I'd written five months earlier—*on a beach whose iron makes it darker and hotter than most, strong cross-court wind, two aces down the line at the weaker player, the third sharp cross-court, catching the better player off-guard because he was bitching at his partner*. Not every detail was the same, but the most important one was, Dane and I were the top team on the qualifying tour.

At the end of the 1994 season, I decided to move back to Colorado. I loved to coach and train in Boulder in the fall and winter. On my last night in Cheryl's apartment I went to my favorite spot of beach, watched the sun set, and meditated. Lesson six, Letting Go: Visualize the Event, Quiet Your Mind, Rid Yourself of Negative Thoughts, Focus on the Present. I was filled with light and warmth.

~

While I never worked harder at meditating than during that summer, I continued to study and practice breathing and relaxation. As a coach and teacher it often worked like magic. If my players or students were acting anxious, bored, or sassy, I'd take a few deep breaths while thinking about being confident, kind, or alert—and everyone's communication and energy improved.

Writing

Dane and I returned to Hermosa Beach in February 1995. The first apartment we looked at was the most affordable, but dozens of cockroaches were crawling in the closets and kitchen cabinets. The manager assured us they'd fumigate before we'd move in. We considered the millions in prize money and moved into a bug free apartment, closer to the beach. There's no shortage of reminders to get yourself a piece of the pie.

~

Eric Moore, my partner for the four Motherlode wins, introduced Dane and me to Bob Evans. Bob was a retired national ski team member turned agent who represented many skiers on the national team. Still, he wanted more work, especially in the summer when he had more free time. Dane and I were a perfect fit. Bob called not long after he started working for us. He used his ski team connections to help get us deals with Oakley Sunglasses.

Dane and I got into my ten-year old Volkswagen Jetta. I noticed that last night's wind took most of the smog with it and drew an extra deep breath. We rolled down the windows, nodded our heads to the beat of Cyprus Hill, "Insane in the Brain," merged onto the 405 south and rocketed through the warm bright air.

We parked next to a large white warehouse with the Oakley logo over the door. The lobby was white from tile floor to 30 ft. ceiling. Oakley banners hung on the walls and a long flight of black metal stairs led to offices on the second floor.

While waiting in the lobby to meet the volleyball rep, a man walked down the stairs with several foot-long cases (dozens of sunglasses) in his arms, wearing an Oakley jacket, hat, and a backpack clearly stuffed with more stuff. Dane's eyes grew wide, "I think that's Cecil Fielder [1990 and 1991 American League Home Run Champion]," he whispered.

Then our rep, George, took us on a tour. Walls were adorned with posters of Olympians, blueprints of lenses and frames, as well as awards and patents for performance and quality.

"I never dread coming to work," George said nodding and waving to most everyone, then added, "The casual attire shows how easygoing everyone is. Still, everyone gives 100%."

George also explained that Oakley was started by friends who were nationally competitive marksmen frustrated by how sunglasses distorted their vision. So they did some research, bought materials, set up equipment, and made sunglasses in their garage. Now, dozens of designs emerged from this massive warehouse, sold to sports enthusiasts world-wide.

A year later Oakley broke ground on a larger, custom-built warehouse—a polished steel fortress with two finishes. The atrium lobby had wings and chairs from a fighter jet, and a ten-foot steel logo matching the outer layer. A semi-circle hallway extended off the lobby with display-cases and pictures of stars wearing Oakley's. A full-sized wood-floor basketball court decorated with giant black and red logos. For special occasions, there's an amphitheater to host big name musicians.

At the plain white warehouse we sat at George's desk as he told us how he played basketball at Pepperdine University, but had to quit when a drunk driver nearly killed him.

"You learn who your friends are when you need someone to wipe your butt after going to the bathroom." He added, "I appreciate every step after having to learn to walk again. And I'm a big supporter of MADD (Mothers Against Drunk Driving)."

George said part of the reason they offered me a contract was my reputation. I occasionally worked out with the CU men's club team in the winter. A couple of those players were from Southern California and knew influential people at Oakley. I also played with and coached other junior club and high school teams. Apparently many thought I was a great player, coach, and teammate.

"When you sign with Oakley," George emphasized, "You're an Oakley man for life." Certain I would get better as a player and coach, I signed the contract.

~

In the long summer of 1995, as in 1994, I loved to get up, put on shorts, grab a bag of balls, and go play in the sand. But the best part of both summers came in the evening. In 1994 it was going to the beach to do Tai Chi and meditate. In 1995 it was going to read and write at a coffee shop by the pier.

I reaffirmed my mission on the AVP: "I'm blessed with privilege, talent and insight. With hard work and perseverance, I will be a pro beach volleyball star, and use my success and wisdom to help people." I read Dan Millman's, Inner Athlete, George Leonard's, The Ultimate Warrior, and Bob Klein's, Movements of Power.

I also read poetry.

I especially appreciated Langston Hughes' courage and honesty. Like what I wanted to say in Kansas, to the parents of my girlfriend and to the volleyball player's parents for wanting their daughter's relationship to end because he's black. "To Certain 'Brothers'" Hughes writes, "You sicken me with lies. With truthful lies. And with your pious faces. And your wide, out-stretched, mock-welcome, Christian hands."

Rumi's view on the eternal helped ease my struggles with death. "Don't Grieve: Anything you lose comes round in another form … God's joy moves from unmarked box to unmarked box. From cell to cell. As rainwater, down into flowerbed. As roses, up from ground."

Mary Oliver connected with my love for nature and language. Her poem "Stars" begins "Here in my head, language keeps making its tiny noises. How can I hope to be friends with the hard white stars, the yawning spaces between them, where nothing, ever, is spoken? What can we do but keep on breathing in and out, modest and willing, and in our places? *Listen, listen,* I'm forever saying, *listen to the river, to the hawk, to the hoof, to the mockingbird, to the jack-in-the-pulpit* … and come up with few words, like a gift."

By April I stopped reading and writing about being a better volleyball player. Instead, I read poetry and began writing a story about a bi-racial boy struggling to overcome a friend's death and find his identity. A book I'd hoped my volleyball fame and fortune would help sell.

~

I first met AVP pros Craig Moothart and Larry Mear at the Motherlode tournament.

Craig gave kind, honest advice about my strengths and weaknesses as a player. And once, while stretching my hamstrings, Craig walked up behind me, pulled my shoulders back, straightened my spine, and pushed on my back with his forearms. As he slowly counted to ten my chest dropped to my knees and my legs became warm, light, and powerful.

Larry was voted AVP sportsman of the year every year from 1989 through 1993. In 1991, Larry invited friend Mike Soucie and me to stay in his home in San Clemente. We road-tripped from Boulder and spent a few nights in his basement. One morning he trained and coached us.

I saw Larry at the Motherlode a decade later. Neither of us was playing. We discussed beach volleyball's rule changes: smaller court, point on every serve, a serve that hits the net is in play. Changes that divide volleyball enthusiasts to this day (though given the dumb luck involved with a serve that hits the net and drops for a point, most agree that one's a terrible rule).

"Well, they got to do something to make this shit exciting," Larry quipped.

That afternoon I fished a world class river, the Frying Pan. I waded in shallow and deep currents, watched the hatch, changed flies, nymphs, weights, and landed a few Browns and Bows. At dark I started back to my car and thought about Larry, Craig, and other kind people. I gave thanks with each careful step through the black water.

~

Few are as kind as AVP legend Mike Dodd: four-time defensive player of the year, three-time 'most inspirational,' two-time 'sportsman of the year with 62 tournament wins and a Silver medal from the 1996 Olympics in Atlanta.

Early in the 1995 season, the Mesa (Phoenix) Open, against a top seed, I made some great plays and critical errors. Dane and I lost. As I stewed over the mistakes Dodd sat beside me for the first of several times he reached out.

"You have potential," he said, "and should consider finding a different partner. This is a profession. Friendship can't get in the way of doing what's best for you."

Dodd had recently broken with long-time partner and friend Tim Hovland in order to play with budding star Mike Whitmarsh (with whom he won the Olympic silver medal).

After placing 17th or 25th in every tournament for the first nine tournaments, Dane suggested we find different partners. But the most valuable half of the season was starting, and I was not making plays I knew I could make. So I was certain Dane and I would succeed as soon as I got my game together.

Dane and I continued placing 17th or 25th and after 16 tournaments (in a fit of fear and poor communication), I decided to play with a different partner.

~

I was usually filled with rage when I played well. Like in a 9th place finish at the ATP (Association of Tennis Professionals) stadium in Indianapolis. Sand dumped two feet deep on courts that hosted champions like Andre Agassi and Pete Sampras. At night, under the lights, I was reminded of the 8 pm to 11 pm practices at CU. And the sand was hard-packed, more like indoors. I felt like a Silverback Gorilla lost in a display of power. Afterwards, Olympic Silver medalist Mike Whitmarsh said I looked like a wild tornado. I was really good when I felt like that, but people said I looked calm.

I'd never felt more relaxed than at the 1995 US Championships, my second tournament with new partner Burke Stefko. I'd again moved back to Boulder in late August because coaching at Fairview started and I liked to train in fall and winter in the foothills.

But there were other advantages to leaving LA. They came to mind each of the dozens of times I descended over LA's 500 square miles of pavement, pollution, and violently disputed borders. My soul screamed particularly loud coming in for the 1995 US Championships. LA's rush-hour gridlock traffic inspired scenes in my book. Hours sitting in corridors of smog. Then there's the environmental impact. To describe it, I looked in a thesaurus and found words like: imprudent, injudicious, and unviable.

Similar words could describe the socio-economic situation. Dane and I taught volleyball at an elementary school in a neighborhood in Watts: black, poor, steel bars covering bedroom windows, sand like gravel, many had never been to the beach. I was proof they could compete in a game dominated by blond hair and blue eyes. Still, of the 56 card-carrying members on the AVP, only three were black: me from Boulder; Dain Blanton from Laguna Beach; and Daniel Cardenas from Cuba (he defected when Cuba's national six-man indoor team flew through Miami). Mostly, the kids just enjoyed burying the equipment in the sand.

After landing in LA for the 1995 US Championships, my soul finally stopped screaming as I stepped from the plane and onto the jet-way. The warm heavy air reminded me the Pacific and deep sand beaches were near. So was Disneyland, The House of Blues, and The Museum of Tolerance (which, focusing on the Holocaust, demonstrates the horrors of unchecked prejudice and fueled ideas for my book). I felt light as I walked through the airport. Burke picked me up and we talked about how well we were going to play.

We finished 7th and hearing NBC announcers Chris Marlow and Paul Sunderland congratulate us on prime-time television added to our confidence for next summer, when beach volleyball would debut in the Olympics, in Atlanta.

~

I thought I'd finish my book by the end of the summer, but the three-hundred hand written pages were riddled with grammatical and structural flaws. It wasn't close. Nevertheless, I was convinced that if I split my time between volleyball and writing in a similar fashion the next summer, I could be successful at both.

"I can play that well consistently," I said to the Oakley rep after the US Championships adding, "I'm equally excited because my success on the court will benefit my work as a writer, coach, and peace activist."

"A lot of people think you can succeed," my rep responded, "But, if your motivation isn't out here," he gestured toward stadium court, Hermosa's fine deep sand, and the ocean rising and falling beneath the pier, "with opportunities to win millions, you should think about what you really want. Oakley supports you," he assured me, "I support you."

Reading

"Way to finally man up," friend and fellow competitor Nick Hannemann said after the 7th at the 1995 US Championships. Nick was right. Until then, my killer instinct had been missing. An aggression that had once surfaced in the previous summer, during an encounter in our living room with housemate Cheryl.

I was looking at a picture of Sinjin Smith on an AVP calendar, thinking about playing him and Ricci last summer, and the easy ball he hit that I shanked out of play. I scoffed, "I have no respect for Sinjin."

"How can you not respect Sinjin?" Cheryl asked.

Actually, I did respect his 129 pro tour wins, his 1990, 1991 and 1992 AVP defensive player of the year award, and 1989, 1990, 1991 and 1992 International tour championships.

I also met Sinjin at a barbeque in Boulder in 1990. My friend introduced us, and boasted about my being one of the best players in Colorado and "One of the nicest guys ever." Sinjin took a liking to me and asked if I would represent his clothing line, Side Out. He sent me shorts, shirts, hats and sweats the following week. My confidence, and regard for Sinjin, soared.

"While competing, especially against stars of the game," I explained to Cheryl, "disrespect keeps me from playing scared."

"You can compete against someone and still respect them," Cheryl argued.

"When Dane and I lost to Ricci and Sinjin 9–8 last summer," I tried to illustrate, "I spent most of that game thinking we should be kicking the shit out of their weak asses. Except in the end, when I thought about beating the great Sinjin—then I choked."

"Respect," Cheryl insisted, "is more important than winning."

"Sometimes contempt brings out my best."

I wish I had been able to express that creating genuine rage for my opponent gave me enormous pools of energy. An energy that could be channeled into skills. Which in turn would help me focus on pursuing my dreams rather than what it would mean to beat the 'Great Sinjin Smith.' Instead, we continued to argue.

"I'm surprised," Cheryl concluded and shook her head.

So be it, I thought.

~

Sinjin aside, however, the pro I most wanted to meet at the barbeque was Tim Hovland.

Known as The Hov, Tim is one of the most successful players in AVP history, winning 57 times. But his attitude made him infamous. He screamed at refs and players. Once, as he readied to serve, he turned, threw the ball at a fan and barked, "Shut the hell up when I serve!"

Before I got the nerve to introduce myself, a friend told me he saw The Hov leaving. I hustled to the driveway and saw him get into the back of a car, so I ran up, "You're the man Hov," I announced through the window, "I'm a huge fan. Love to watch you compete."

I next spoke with The Hov in 1993, my third AVP event in Belmar Beach, New Jersey. He and I bellied up to the bar at the same time during the player's party. Our eyes met and I gave him a nod hello. His brows furrowed and he strolled toward me, clearly drunk. He looked me up and down, poked me in the chest with his long finger and asked, "Do you want my job?"

For the first time in his career, The Hov was eliminated on the first day of the tournament. Baseball pitchers have "x" number of pitches before losing their mojo. Volleyball players also have "x" number of jumps. No matter how you breathe, relax, approach fast, and swing with everything you've got, the ball comes off your hand like you hit it with a giant wet sponge. Old Man Time waits for us all, and in the summer of 1993, the Hov was on the short list.

"Do you want my fucking job?" The Hov asked louder, poked harder, and brought his nose inches from mine.

"Yes," I answered.

"You can't have my fucking job!" Spit came off his lips. Another emphatic jab before people grabbed his shoulders and eased him back, "You can't have my fucking job!"

~

I loved volleyball for many reasons. My hard work was rewarded. People listened more closely, even when I didn't have anything interesting to say. And fortuitously, the AVP was growing. Started in 1984 as a player-run organization, the AVP promoted an obscure sport that gave away a quarter million dollars in prizes. A decade later the tour gave away millions and beach volleyball was the fastest growing game in America, televised all summer long.

Jose Cuervo was one of the tour's original sponsors. Cuervo hosted four tournaments that were touted as the tour's "Majors," like in pro golf and tennis. In 1988, Cuervo shocked media and fans by giving $50,000 to first place.

When AVP players saw that the first place share was three times second and twenty times eighth, which barely covered travel costs, they voted to balance the prize money. So Cuervo wrote checks to winners and winners wrote checks to other players.

In the early 1990's some top players became dissatisfied with the redistribution agreement and threatened to sue. Winners started keeping the money.

In 1996 Cuervo doubled 1st place to $100,000, six times 2nd's share, twenty times 8th's and one hundred times the share of 21st place finishers. Even in the newly-expanded field, that amount hardly covered what it cost last place finishers to attend and play.

Some players earned six and seven figures. Others jumped fences and slept on pool furniture.

Equity aside, the AVP's real problem was that most of the budget was given to prize money, while costs of setting up courts and stadiums in 25 cities throughout America put us deeper in debt every week.

It was suggested the AVP cut the number of teams in the main draw from 32 to 16. Then sponsor a separately-run minor league, like in professional basketball and baseball.

It was also suggested the wealthiest sacrifice to help grow roots. There was a lot of young talent from California. Dane and I were stars in Colorado, James Fellows from Maryland, Raul Papaleo from Puerto Rico, Henry Russell (one time AVP tournament winner) from Florida, and five-time winner Brent Doble from Michigan.

Neither side would budge, so we ignored the soaring debt.

~

By 1996 the excitement of traveling for work had worn off. Airports made me edgy. When I thought someone else was being an ass there's a good chance it was in my own head. Not to mention hours in the small seat breathing recycled air. Aside from Mike Dodd's advice to bring your own pillow and a few top ten finishes, I tolerated it because it provided ample opportunity to read.

I read James McBride, The Color of Water: A Black Man's Tribute to His White Mother. McBride grew up in Brooklyn's Red Hook projects— a black community. He knew his mom was different. When he asked she simply said, "I'm light skinned." Later he asked if he was black or white, "You're a human being," she snapped, "educate yourself or you'll be a nobody!" When McBride asked what color God was she replied, "God is the color of water."

McBride's mom taught her twelve children to transcend race and religion with unwavering discipline for school and church. Inspired, I used examples of my own mother's iron will and love in my book. I also thought my book would be a success because it illustrates how wealthy, white, liberals can be prejudiced too. The first step in overcoming 'divide and conquer,' is recognizing how people of all colors, religions, and political affiliations can be prejudiced.

I read Andrew L. Shapiro comparing the United States with 19 major industrial nations in, We're Number One: Where America Stands – And Falls – In the New World Order.

Number one in highest-paid athletes and last in teachers' salaries. *I thought about student-teaching in Kansas, Jon and Millie's extraordinary skill; the two black boys calling me a "Sorry excuse for a black man."*

Number one in big houses and number one in homelessness. *Coast to coast, multi-million dollar houses—millions of bath- and bedrooms rarely used.*

Number one in percentage of young people who say premarital sex should be avoided and number one in teenage pregnancies. *Our government (and others), must do more to feed, house, and educate children facing long odds.*

Number one in watching television, last in book titles published per capita. *I wished I'd fallen in love with reading sooner.*

~

Jonathan Kozol, in <u>Amazing Grace: The Lives of Children and the Conscience of a Nation</u>, speaks to life in the ghetto from children's perspective. From 1990 – 1994, Kozol interviewed and befriended children and families living in the South Bronx regularly experiencing hunger, disease, abuse, and murder. As well as hope. I cried and laughed. Toni Morrison wrote, "Beautiful and morally worthy … I thank you for the language of this book, its refusal to patronize … its insistence upon taking what [the children] say, feel and think seriously."

Shelby Steele's, <u>The Content of Our Character: A New Vision on Race in America</u> was hailed by The Los Angeles Times as, "The perfect voice of reason in a sea of hate." With chapters titled, "I'm Black, You're White, Who's Innocent? Race and Power in an Era of Blame," "Being Black and Feeling Blue: Black Hesitation on the Brink," "White Guilt," "The Recoloring of Campus Life: Student Racism, Academic Pluralism and the End of a Dream," and "The Memory of Enemies," Steele does a masterful job of calling out the good and bad in everybody.

~

A sub-plot in beach volleyball's inaugural Olympic year was the rift between the FIVB (International pro tour) and the AVP. Personal and business egos climaxed when both tours gave teams from the US a berth into the Olympics: two from the AVP; one from the FIVB. Because of schedule conflicts and being ranked through accumulated points, players had to choose between competing on the FIVB and the AVP. By rule, only a few teams from the US could compete on the FIVB. Besides, lofty travel expenses meant most couldn't afford to.

My fondest memories of Karch Kiraly (three-time NCAA DI national champion, three- time Olympic gold medalist, a record 147 AVP tour wins) began at a players meeting. We were debating the process to qualify for the 1996 Olympics in Atlanta.

"You shouldn't have to compete all over the world," Karch argued, "We should be like Track and Field, the best show up one weekend and the winners go." He pitched for America's (The Shinning City on the Hill) greatness. "Hard work, a clutch performance, and the underdog can represent our great country."

The easiest route for Karch to make it into the Olympics was through the FIVB. I knew he could afford the travel and avoid competing against the AVP's large talented field in a single tournament.

Sinjin Smith and Carl Henkel played the FIVB to get to the Olympics. I couldn't blame them for taking that route. Perhaps Sinjin's prolific carrier justified it. Still I, like many, felt bitter because Smith/Henkel became Olympians without having to compete against Karch Kiraly, Kent Steffes, Mike Dodd, Mike Whitmarsh, Randy Stoklos, Adam Johnson, Scott Ackatubby, Brent Frohoff, Ricci Luyties, and many more who could've beaten them on any given day.

Kiraly/Steffes met Smith/Henkel in the Olympic quarter finals. Kiraly/Steffes would beat Smith/Henkel nine times out of ten, but this being the Olympics, only one mattered. Adding to the drama was that Kiraly and Smith were decades-long partners and rivals from beaches that gave birth to the game. Each had over a hundred pro tour victories. Plus, the Olympics used FIVB ball and rules (slightly different from the AVP).

Smith/Henkel played great. I was reminded of many quarter and semi-final games during a Kiraly/Steffes record 13-tournament win streak with a supremacy that had some worried they were making the tour boring. Their opponents would be on fire: aces, stuff blocks, digs, beating Kiraly/Steffes 11–7 or 12 – 8 in a game to 15. Then, methodically and spectacularly, Kiraly/Steffes would come back and win.

After defeating Smith/Henkel in overtime, Karch turned to Mike Dodd and Mike Whitmarsh in the stands and struck a familiar victory pose: feet firmly planted, fists clenched, this time he yelled "AVP Baby!"

~

The AVP peaked in 1996: Olympic Gold and Silver; more tournaments, money, and media coverage than ever. Still, it was Thich Nhat Hahn who really got my attention.

Hahn was a Buddhist teacher, poet, and Zen master. He was chairman of the Vietnamese Buddhist Peace Delegation during the Vietnam War and nominated for the Nobel Peace Prize by Martin Luther King Jr. I read Hahn's, Be Still and Know: Reflections of Living Buddha and Living Christ, and reveled in the similarities he found between Christianity and Buddhism.

"No single tradition monopolizes the truth," Hahn begins, "we must glean the best values of all traditions and work together to remove the tensions between them. If we do, peace will have a chance."

Hahn's book made me think of Saturday at the 1994 qualifying tournament in Chicago. Dane and I, along with the top half of the bracket, played at North Beach, pristine sand surrounded by a beautiful park and high-end skyscrapers. Friends Mark Paaluhi and Nick Hannemann, along with the bottom half of the bracket, played a few miles south.

That night, in the player's hotel overlooking Lake Michigan, Nick and Mark told us they'd removed rocks and shards of glass from their courts all day. "But, it was worth it," they said, "The fans were incredible!" Then they showed us pictures. Group photos with a couple dozen black children (numbers we never saw on tour). Candid shots illustrating stories about their favorites.

Nick and Mark (both Samoan), had a certain confidence with being minority. Black eyes, wavy black hair, and like mine, their skin tanned quickly but took months to get really dark. Once, while in a dance club in Atlanta a guy called them half breeds. Nick and Marc looked at each other and burst with laughter, "Nope," they chimed, "100% Samoan. Stupid mother fucker!"

I laughed when they told me, but wished I could expose ignorance as easily. After a Colorado winter brought out the white in me, I went jogging down the beach in Boca Raton Florida and a stranger called me a half breed. I didn't respond. His words rang in my head until I did Tai Chi and pictured them pouring out the soles of my feet and into the ocean.

I took a lot of deep breaths in the South: confederate flags on capitol buildings and trucks, box row housing filled with minorities. Football fields filled with dark kids sprinting and bashing into each other for a virtually non-existent chance of getting out of poverty. Still, years of travel taught me the North isn't much different. Martin Luther King Jr. said he was never more afraid of racists than when in Chicago. The dark skinned and impoverished walk streets of gold amid luminous skyscrapers throughout America.

One of my favorite moments with Dane was in Chicago. We checked into the hotel and walked to a restaurant for dinner. We were struck and saddened by how many homeless people were in the streets. After taking our seats on the patio of an Italian restaurant, Dane motioned to a homeless gentlemen to come get some bread. I gestured that the manager or staff might be watching.

"So?" Dane said and handed the man our bread.

"Thank you, God bless." the man said and walked away.

"If while we practice," Hahn wrote in <u>Be Still and Know</u>, "We are not aware that the world is suffering, that children are dying of hunger, that social injustice is going on everywhere, we are not practicing mindfulness. We are just trying to escape."

~

I played with a variety of partners in 1996 and my improvements were modestly rewarded with a few 9th's and 13th's.

My shot at fame and fortune is now or never, I thought to begin 1997. And I used the evenings to write essays and goals for volleyball: shallow and deep sand, heavy winds, stifling heat, cold and rain, 9th or better in every tournament.

The first tournament was in Phoenix. I often played well in Arizona (the dry air reminds me of Colorado). In the round to see who gets 9th or better, the other team had game point 14-13. I swung for a side-out and slightly mishit the ball, sending it deeper in the court than I should have. Still, I saw the ball hit the line, making it quiver between two mounds of sand.

"Out," the ref called.

"That ball hit the line," I screamed, "That was in!"

The ref inspected the imprint the ball left in the sand and said, "Out."

"How could you not see the line move?!" I argued, "The fucking line moved!"

I fumed long after the game, mad at the ref for a bad call, and at myself for that and other plays I should have been making far more often.

A man walked up to me and said, "The ball was out."

I didn't respond warmly because the ball hit the line.

As he walked away, I thought he looked like Karch Kiraly's father, Dr. Lazlo Kiraly. I first saw Dr. Kiraly on T.V. during the 1988 Olympics in Seoul, cheering and waving a giant American flag from the upper deck of the arena. Commentators talked about him teaching Karch to play on the beach. He came across as the kind of guy who believes in luck, and that the harder you work, the more will come your way.

Whoever he was, I thought, *he just wants you to move on*.

The next five tournaments were in Florida.

~

In Miami, massive storms made the muggy air even more oppressive than usual. As I drove through the city I remembered the time I'd been there for a cultural awareness and leadership conference my senior year in high school.

One day we went to the Orange Bowl, took a boat tour of mansions with guest houses larger than most homes. We saw a street-side movie set where stars told jokes and crowds laughed, but my friends and I thought if we said the same things, in the same way, no one would've laughed. The other days we visited community centers for poor Haitian, Latino and African American neighborhoods, heard heart-breaking and soul-lifting stories. And felt the blazing sun and stifling humidity in fields with migrant farm-workers.

The AVP had new management and a first-class personal touch. Hospitality shuttles and services at airports and hotels. Volunteers reminisced and athletes sung the pride at post-game interviews, "We did our best" and "I couldn't have done it without my partner." I chuckled remembering how often I'd heard, "I made it happen" and "I fucking told you so."

I ate dinner, watched Sports Center, confirmed that the air conditioner would keep my room temperature at 64 degrees, and went to the players meeting. The conference room was plush and I was handed the richest bag of "swag" I'd ever received. "Swag" is free merchandise like clothing, watches, and top-shelf booze. I again marveled at how people who can afford stuff get stuff for free. And, like many who receive such perks, I gave clothes and watches to friends.

Swag aside, the players were buzzing because we were about to meet our new CEO. Jerry Solomon was a renowned sports agent who was going to help the AVP get an NFL or NBA-sized piece of the sports-entertainment pie. Fifty world class athletes were eager to meet Solomon and talk about "getting it done."

I thought about suggesting we give the swag to charity. There were deserving people in neighborhoods throughout Miami, and our generosity could ensure future profits. We'd be a model of success for businesses everywhere. But I figured that my suggestion and I would've received the same fate as the sports agent in the movie "Jerry Maguire."

Maguire founded an agency that grew into a giant. The bigger it got, the more greed and poor behavior he saw. From stars refusing to sign a kid's card because it's not the right brand, to dismissing an athlete's criminal behavior. The final straw came when one of Maguire's clients suffered his fourth concussion and while in the hospital, struggled to recognize his family. The player's son asked Maguire to tell his dad to take it easy. Maguire assured the boy his dad was tough.

"Fuck you," the boy responded.

That night Maguire had a crisis of conscience, wrote a manifesto and e-mailed it to everyone. A week later Maguire was fired for his rant promoting feel-good, lovey-dovey, idealistic "respect people and values more than money" nonsense.

~

Solomon started by thanking our sponsors for the swag. "This could be just the beginning," he explained, "happy sponsors are the key to success."

Then, Solomon used giant paper and markers to illustrate five different kinds of people who enjoy fitness and sports: 1) Weekend Warriors, 2) Semi-professionals, 3) Professionals, 4) Stars, 5) Super Stars.

"We need people to think our top athletes are Super Stars," Solomon emphasized, "better than human. Because when people think our stars are super human, masses will buy shorts, shirts and hats to join the fantasy and we'll add zeroes to our earnings."

"Better than human? Super human? I'm successful because I acknowledge and deal with fears and weaknesses. I want to represent being human."

~

Had I played up to speed with my partner in Miami we might have finished 9th or better. Instead, my partner carried us to one win and we finished 17th.   Though I'd never been as strong, fast, or skilled, I'd also never been as mentally and emotionally absent.

I reached my goal of 9th once over the next six weeks. The 13th and 17th place finishes weren't career-ending. But I also read Thich Nhat Hahn's, <u>Being Peace</u>.

"Suffering Is Not Enough," Hahn writes, "Life is filled with suffering, but it is also filled with many wonders, like the blue sky, the sunshine and the eyes of a baby. To suffer is not enough. We must also be in touch with the wonders of life. They are within us and all around us, everywhere, any time."

Plus I read Jon Krakaur's, <u>Into the Wild</u>, about a young man who graduated from college, gave his BMW and Trust Fund to charity, and traveled the country in a 1974 Dodge Dart. He worked odd jobs, made friends and learned to live simply while taking advantage of the nourishment and beauty in nature. My cautious nature was alarmed by how unfortunate circumstances in the Alaskan wilderness led to the young man's death. Still, in the middle of June, after 11 of 22 tournaments, I left the tour.

My timing was fortuitous because the AVP's financial bubble popped in July, and players received 10% of the scheduled prize money. By summer's end the AVP filed for bankruptcy and some players sued the hand that had fed them.

It was another bright day when I left L.A. for good. Driving east on I-15, I marveled at how quickly urban sprawl was replaced by desert.

Way to finally man up.

Breathing and Rising

PART III

It usually happens that
The more faithfully a person follows the inspirations he receives
The more does he experience new inspirations which
Ask increasingly more of him.

Joseph De Guibert

Breathing and Rising

Coaching

"To make sponsors happy," declared AVP CEO Jerry Solomon, "we have to give back. Like pro football, basketball and golf, which have excellent grass roots programs."

New in 1997, players were asked to coach clinics the day before tournaments. A month later Solomon seemed frustrated that players weren't more excited about doing clinics and other promotional work, "We have to connect with fans personally," he urged.

~

After three years (51 tournaments), the highest I'd been ranked was 32nd, and I was currently 48th. Which meant the clinics wouldn't pay me enough to cover the extra night in the hotel. Plus, my New Year's resolution was to finish the season in the top 20 or start a new career. I decided to spend the day before tournaments relaxing and hydrating, rather than standing in the hot sun. My renewed focus also meant I'd write about volleyball skills and goals, instead of the novel and children's books I'd been working on.

I started writing children's books because I'd developed writer's block over my novel's structure, grammar, and content that was often too dark. I thought writing children's books would help me simplify and lighten up. But I could still take on serious topics like Dr. Seuss in The Lorax, illustrating the stupidity of destroying our environment for money. Or The Butter Battle Book, on the catastrophic self-defeating potential in a nuclear arms race.

I wrote volleyball goals and essays until the third time Solomon pleaded for players to connect with fans and the player's response was silence. I was mad at the top players for not wanting to carry that load, especially because those same players justified receiving a huge percentage of prize money because the crowds came to see them. We'd come a long way from those early years of the tour, when top players were begging for opportunities to teach people about volleyball.

My frustration began to show. While I would start each writing session intending to write about volleyball, when the pen hit the page I wrote about other experiences. What appeared on the page was poetry and scenes for my book to help me deal with my struggles with race.

> *When I didn't laugh at a racial joke and someone thought I was angry, as opposed to just bored. And when my boredom led to frustration and anger. And when I faked a smile and changed the subject.*
>
> *When I tried to explain my love for rap music. "It's not always about violence and hate. Like the classics 'My Adidas,' 'Rapper's Delight,' and 'Basketball.' Though I do enjoy gangster rap from time to time," I confessed, "and judging by sales, suburban white kids love it as much as inner-city black kids."*
>
> *When people raved about my jumping ability, which meant they either saw me on one of the few days a year when I barely felt gravity. Or they couldn't see that I hit sharp angles because of impeccable timing, long arms, and a wrist snap that generates a lot of top spin. Or they confused me with one of the few dark-skinned players who really could jump.*

The most memorable encounter came in Baltimore, 1995. I mentioned it in an article for <u>Volleyball Colorado</u>, "Assignment AVP," part of a summer-long series I wrote about trying to make it on the tour. The conversation inspired a chapter in my novel.

> *I flew a "red eye" and checked into the hotel at 6 a.m. A room wasn't ready so I waited in a section of lounge chairs and coffee tables in the restaurant. Soon, a white man in a nice suit walked over from the bar and asked if we could talk.*
>
> *"Uh ... sure," I said and he sat, spine straight, shoulders relaxed.*
>
> *"I used to hate black people," he said after introducing himself and setting his double gin and tonic on the table. His tone was remorseful and apologetic so I listened.*

"My sister wants to marry a black man," he continued, "he's a great guy, but my dad and other family members are threatening to disown her."

"That's tough," I said.

"You have no idea," he went on, "the 'Good Old Boy' system is alive and well. Some businessmen will want nothing to do with me if she doesn't break up with him."

"Hate is so destructive," I consoled, "I'm biracial," I said because some don't see it, "my white mother and I are proof that love overcomes."

"What can I do?" he asked.

"I dated a girl with racist parents," I said, "Sometimes you can't do anything."

"It's not right," he said.

"In the end," I said, like my mom often advised, "The only behavior we can control is our own."

He bought me a drink and we talked sports.

Someone from the front desk told me my room was ready and we wished each other luck.

~

I regularly reread Hahn's book, <u>Being Peace</u>. My favorite chapter was, "The Heart of Practice", which begins, "Meditation is not to get out of society, to escape society, but to prepare for a reentry into society."

"When we go to a meditation center," Hahn continued, "we may have the impression that we leave everything behind—family, society, and all the complications involved in them—and come as an individual in order to practice and to search for peace. This is an illusion ..."

"All individuals are made of non-individual elements," Hahn explains further, "*sunshine* that nourishes wheat; *wheat* that nourishes bodies; *farmers* who harvest wheat; *bakers* who make bread. When *one* suffers, then *society* suffers. And, those who meditate not only seek solutions for themselves, but for everyone."

"I think that our society is a difficult place to live ..." Hahn added, "I know people in the Western world suffer a great deal psychologically, and that is why many have become Buddhists, practicing meditation in order to solve psychological problems."

"My practice helps me remain in society," Hahn concluded, "because I am aware that if I leave society, I will not be able to help change it. I hope those that are practicing ... succeed in keeping their feet on earth, staying in society. That is our hope for peace."

~

Before leaving the AVP, I was hired as head coach of Girls Volleyball at Fairview High School. I also planned to get a substitute teaching license. Though I'd given up my quest to use fame and fortune to create peace, helping kids enjoy physical activity, competition, and getting an education is a strong contribution towards peace. Plus, coaching and substitute teaching provided opportunities to write.

~

Hahn's book, Being Peace, reminded me of my experiences on Independence Pass: all things are connected; solitude and meditation help everyone; society is a hard place to live; and peace is created by those who nevertheless have the courage to keep their feet on earth and stay in society.

Between 1992 and 1997 I had to coach my team at Fairview on the Friday nights of Labor Day weekend and the Motherlode tournament. Each year I left Boulder around 9 pm and reached the top of Independence Pass around midnight.

In 1993, the year Gail died, there was a thick fog. Hearing my heart beat and breathing reminded me of a scene in the movie "Thunder Heart." Val Kilmer plays Ray Levoi, an FBI detective sent to a Sioux Indian reservation in the Badlands of South Dakota to investigate a rash of homicides. Ray is part Sioux and becomes torn between his duty as an FBI agent and a sense of duty to the Sioux Nation. In one scene, Ray has a spiritual experience while walking through thick fog. All we hear is his breathing and a heart beating. Afterwards, Ray speaks with a medicine man about his vision and Ray's allegiance towards the Sioux grows.

I grabbed my flashlight and walked into the fog and mist.

The sky was clear in 1994, 1995 and 1996—a dozen twinkling stars in every square foot of the midnight blue sky.

In 1996 I started up the rocky trail and turned off my flashlight because once my eyes adjusted, the moon lit the world like day. Each step felt light and powerful. Before long I stopped, sat and "softened" my eyes. I slowly inhaled – held the air in – gave thanks – slowly exhaled – held air out – gave thanks – slowly inhaled. After a few dozen breaths I focused my eyes on the rocks next to me. Peaks and valleys in the lichen, bellflowers and tussock grass—treeless peaks that span the horizon.

I wasn't surprised when I saw a man walking from the west, cutting his own path over the rolling mountain. I knew he was Native American. And that he wanted to talk.

~

Before turning 20, the only time I woke up early and with a clear mind was after a good dream, before going skiing and camping, or in elementary school, when I got up at 5:30 am on Saturday mornings to watch "The Lone Ranger." The world was dark except for the glow of our T.V. I'd use pillows to make a lounge chair in the middle of the living room. And while I liked the masked man, I liked Tonto more.

Time and again Tonto went to town, got his ass kicked figuring out what was going on, but made it back to give the Lone Ranger details about how to take the bad guys out. I just wished Tonto armed himself better and brought more friends the first time he went to town.

Tonto inspired me to pay attention to Native Americans. I love how they used every part of an animal: meat, tendons, intestines, bones, skin and marrow, respecting all that God creates. And in my admiration for Native American culture, I developed a passion for nature and looking for connections between mountains, rivers, lakes, plants, animals, and people.

I also feel close to Native Americans because I don't want to argue about degrees of horror. Whether your home was stolen and culture eradicated, or you're stolen from home and made a slave, or are dragged from your homes and hauled off in cattle cars, people like us, who get treated as subhuman, need to stick together.

~

The Native American on Independence Pass steadily approached.

"Greetings!" he said then sat across from me, eyes smiling, "I have seen you before. Our pilgrimages have coincided over the last few years. You shouldn't feel so alone," he continued, "You're my brother. My People's brother. All humanity, all things are family."

We sat silently for a moment.

"Learn more about your Native ancestors," he suggested then stood up, "time to get to the sweet-river," he said striding toward the Arkansas and concluded without turning around, "that river has the tastiest trout!"

I felt warm and my heartbeat and breath were steady and strong as I drove into Aspen and won the second of four straight Motherlode titles with Eric Moore.

While it'd be another seven years before I'd do a serious research project, my mom regularly gave me books with Native American stories and quotes. One favorite is of a medicine man teaching children.

"Inside everyone," the medicine man explained, "a good wolf and a bad wolf are always fighting for control."

"Which one will win?" the children anxiously asked.

"Whichever one you feed," the medicine man answered.

~

I was excited to run Fairview's volleyball program, teaching team-work, goal setting, and mental training, in addition to the technical, and physical skills. Also, to substitute teach and make connections in a district where it's difficult to get a permanent teaching job. But most importantly, after having lived in Kansas, L.A., and traveled coast to coast, I knew Boulder was home.

On the drive back to Colorado my girlfriend and I drove through Utah and stopped for a two day hike down Zion Canyon. At the trailhead, a foot-wide stream cuts a two foot ditch. At the bottom, 300 ft. rock walls rise straight from the edges of a 20 ft. wide river. The ten mile descent featured waterfalls, trees rooted in rock, and a 15 foot long log laying 10 feet above ground, wedged between canyon walls by a flood.

We camped on a small beach between the main river and a tributary and watched a million shades of darkness slowly reveal a million stars. Before going to sleep I took deep breaths and fell into a deep state of relaxation. Then I dreamed a Native American man walked out of the canyon walls. "Your friend at Gail's funeral was right," he told me, "you can find those who have died in the earth, rivers and sky."

In July and August I also communed with the ancient spires, cliffs, arches, and dwellings in Utah's Bryce Canyon and Canyon Lands; with the geysers, waterfalls, and jagged peaks in Wyoming's Yellowstone and the Grand Tetons. As always, my pilgrimages came back to the most spiritual place I've known, Rocky Mountain National Park. 45 minutes from Boulder; and thanks to my German family's effort to re-live vacations in the Swiss Alps, a drive my family has made ever since I can remember.

~

In Boulder the plains begin their steep ascent to majestic heights: sweet smell of pine, aspen and sage; columbines, paintbrush and sunflowers blush azure, crimson, and gold; rivers and lakes filled with brown, rainbow, and greenback trout; elk, cougars, and black bears roam; hawks and eagles soar; and seasons cycle like the Phoenix burns and rises.

Some plan to stay in Boulder for months and end up staying for life, mostly because of the picturesque mountains and 300 days of sun a year: running, cycling, skiing, golf, hiking, back-backing, camping, fishing, the list goes on. Locals call the phenomenon "Chief Niwot's curse."

Niwot, chief of the Southern Arapaho, was born in Boulder in 1825. In 1858, he said, "People seeing the beauty of this valley will want to stay, and their staying will be the undoing of the beauty." The 'curse' first struck me while on break from college in Kansas. The monotonous drive across muggy plains vanished as soon as I crested Boulder valley's eastridge to gaze at the massive foothills aptly named Flatirons and the snowy peaks framing the western edge of town.

~

I coached summer volleyball camps at the University of Colorado for years. In 1999 we ate at Cheyenne-Arapaho Hall amid displays commemorating the tenth anniversary of the Hall being renamed.

Originally the Hall had been named after David H. Nichols, a Boulder resident and Speaker of the House in the late 1880's. Nichols supported bringing the University to Boulder and was said to have made a midnight ride to beat the deadline and deliver funds needed to establish the University in Boulder. The Regents honored Nichols in 1961.

Many protested honoring Nichols because of his participation in the Sand Creek massacre. In 1969, a petition to rename the hall had been submitted and denied. In the 1980's, students held Friday vigils in protest of the name. In 1987, Chancellor Corbridge asked Professor Limerick to research and report on Nichols' military service. Limerick found Captain Nichols' company kill[ed] ... twenty-five or thirty fleeing or surrendering Indians at Sand Creek. And, though Nichols worked to bring the University to Boulder, there was no evidence of a "midnight" ride. Limerick advised to change the name.

I was grateful for Nichols' work to bring the University to Boulder. I loved going to football games on hot, frozen, and perfect fall Saturday afternoons throughout my childhood. I completed my education and got a teacher's license there. I won a National Championship with my CU team. I also took graduate level courses and attended annual lectures and panels, including the Conference on World Affairs.

Still, I'm glad they renamed the Hall. Because I spent two decades in Boulder's schools, had long bragged about being struck by a 'curse,' and was finally learning that Chief Niwot of the Arapaho and Chief Black Kettle of the Cheyenne were extraordinary leaders.

~

Niwot was a gifted linguist, learning English and other Native languages as a child. As Chief, he led his people to war against the Shoshone, Utes and Pawnee. He also valued business and regularly campaigned for peace through fair and open commerce—with whites especially. He knew more would be coming.

In the early 1860's, the Sioux declared war on the US. Niwot feared mistaken identity when neighboring tribes raided and murdered settlers. So in spring 1864, he and Black Kettle called a meeting to reassure US officials that their people were peaceful. They would camp at Sand Creek in the fall. And as agreed, Niwot flew the American flag as a sign of truce.

"… the massacre lasted six to eight hours … I tell you Ned, it was hard to see little children on their knees have their brains beat out by men professing to be civilized" Captain Silas Soule observed.

It's hard for me to fathom the blinders Theodore Roosevelt had on when he declared, "[The Sand Creek Massacre was] as righteous and beneficial a deed as ever took place on the frontier."

On the other hand, when Black Kettle met with US treaty officials a year later, it was clear to me that his actions still aligned with his beliefs. "Although the troops have struck us," he said, "we throw it all behind and are glad to meet you in peace and friendship."

~

As a coach, I yelled at referees to fire up my team, slow the pace of the game, or to urge the ref to make better calls. I almost always held them to high standards (though it should be noted I wasn't nearly as vocal if the calls went our way).

During the most memorable dispute, the first illegal contact was called a "lift." The ball hit my player on the fleshy part of her forearms, nearer her elbows, so it rebounded softly. Still, after she initially misjudged the serve and positioned her feet poorly, she adjusted her torso and pressed her shoulders and forearms as one platform: the ball didn't come to rest; changed directions once; and went to the setter. I stood up and told the ref his call was too tight.

He called another "lift" on a pass that rebounded more crisply. I stood and waved. Then, he called a lift on a good set. I stood and waved emphatically. He told me to sit down.

When he called another lift on another good set I jumped up and yelled, "What are you doing?!"

He gave me a yellow card, a warning that if I interrupted again I'd get a red card, which would cost us a point.

Another bad call and the rest of the match was a blur. When the final whistle blew I walked straight toward the ref (the only time I didn't line up with my team and shake our opponents' hands at the end of a match).

"We have to talk," I said to him.

He walked right past me. I followed and tapped his shoulder. He kept going. By the time he got behind the benches I'd stepped in front of him.

"I have powerful friends," he said.

"Do you think we handled the ball that poorly?" I fired back, "Or, that they handled the ball that much better?"

"I mean it," he reiterated, "I have powerful friends."

"My players deserved better," I said and walked away barking, "Unbelievable! Get a clue!"

That week the governing body for Colorado's high school sports suspended me for one match for having touched a ref.

One of my player's parents was a lawyer with three kids that loved a variety of sports. He'd watched coaches and parents go after referees and umpires for over a decade. "I saw the whole thing," he said, "This ruling is ridiculous. You didn't do a thing." and concluded, "If you want to fight this, just give me the word."

"No," I said because I did touch the ref. Besides, the punishment— sitting in the stands for the first match at the state play-off District Tournament that Saturday—had little chance of impacting our goals. We had time to prepare. I trusted my assistants. And my team would do well at districts even if they had to coach themselves (besides, there was even a chance they'd actually benefit from my not being there). I sat in the stands for the first match and barely moved, so the CHSAA representative sent to observe wouldn't think I was sending signals. We qualified for the Regional tournament.

A year later a ref came up to me in a parking lot, "You have a bad reputation," he began, "but your players are polite, work hard, and enjoy playing for you." Then he added, "I tell other refs I see a quality, passionate young coach who we can learn from."

"Thanks," I said, "it's not always about the officiating. When my team is sluggish they might pick it up if they see me fighting for them. And other times, well, I just expect a lot from myself, my players, and the refs. But I'll work on communicating more positively."

~

My fourth year as head coach, the father of a junior was furious she was cut from the Junior Varsity team. He'd invested in years of summer camps and club volleyball, and those coaches spoke highly of his daughter's skills. We reviewed our evaluations. She was a fine player, but in her position, we had others who were better. She became team manager.

Her father did some research and found that the district was out of compliance with Title IX. He filed a lawsuit, which meant the next year all Boulder Valley schools could no longer make cuts in volleyball. We had to accommodate every girl that tried out. Which also meant head coaches spent more time hiring coaches, scheduling practices, matches, referees, and just having to be in the gym. Other coaches goaded me, "You should've kept that girl."

Part of me agreed. Still, we made close calls at tryouts, turning away players who, over the next few years, may well develop better than the player we chose. I was certain a player from one of those teams would contribute to my Varsity team one day. Also, and more importantly, it was cool that more people were enjoying volleyball.

Dave Blessing (my coach at CU), coached our cross-town rivals Boulder High. Dave gave me great advice that included dealing with refs more positively, and that I should get parents to write letters of recommendations because in a couple of years there will be a new set of parents that may not like me or my coaching. His words and actions always focused on his players' best interest. He wrote letters to district administration advocating for girls' volleyball coaches to get paid the same as boys' football, because the work-load was the same.

Colorado High School Girls Volleyball lost a lot when Blessing stepped down, but everyone understood his wanting to have more time with his wife and five kids. Plus, as he noted, his timing was fortuitous because after years of contending for state titles (winning one), there was a severe drop in talent at Boulder High and Boulder's club volleyball program.

Men's collegiate club volleyball is an opportunity for late bloomers and athletes disinterested in mainstream sports (similar to many of my teammates' and my own experience at CU). But girls club volleyball finds the biggest, strongest and fastest and grooms them early (like feeder programs in boys basketball and football). Great athletes can compete, but most kids can't keep up without the repetitions in the eight months outside the high school season.

Club volleyball is costly, and the better the club, the more time and money it costs. This rift was most obvious in the first round of the state tournament, when schools with players on club teams (mostly from wealthy communities), crushed teams without club players. It was also evident at the top, where some of the best players ended up on the same high school teams, even though they lived in different districts.

When Boulder High won State, most of their players played together on Boulder's top club team. One of their key middle hitters was from Winter Park (60 miles west of Boulder).

Smokey Hill, in Denver and our league, was the best team in Colorado for two years. Their coach and most players were part of Front Range volleyball club (widely regarded as the top club in the state, recruiting Denver and beyond). When we played in Smokey's gym, we warmed up with balls marked Front Range 18's—their club team's practice balls.

There must be some fancy paperwork on that roster. But who am I to judge where someone calls home. Plus, their coach saved the school money by not buying practice balls. And if I coached those kids eight months a year, I'd want them touching the dull thud in a club-sanctioned ball, as opposed to the lively bounce in high school's balls. Not to mention that a parent's success should provide opportunities for their children. I respect the hard work their coaches and girls put in. And the state finals were usually competitive. Still in the end, I don't really like paperwork. Making players stay in their home district wouldn't hurt the quality of play much and, above all, would make more athletes better.

Smokey was pushed by Lewis Palmer (from Colorado Springs, city with Colorado's second largest talent pool). Many of the same players competed for two years. Though after Smokey beat Palmer in most meetings, including back-to-back state finals, it was clear Palmer's players were a little small. And Smokey had one of the best setters in the nation.

~

I stopped coaching in 2003. Little things began to bother me. Like how my players and my "success" depended on club volleyball (an extension of our society's haves and have nots). Then there was the mother who was critical of me and my program. She talked with a coach at another school and was impressed with him and how they often won their league.

But their league is weak! Every year at the State tournament, fifth and sixth from our league trounce the number one and two from theirs. Her daughter could transfer to where her skills would fall further behind, or stay among friends, compete against the best, and learn from someone with over a decade of experience as a professional player and coach.

"I'm thinking about transferring my daughter," she said.

Good riddance, I thought and came way too close to saying.

~

Still, most of the frustration and anger that drove me from coaching came from elsewhere. A year teaching literacy at two Boulder Valley elementary schools. Two years earning an MFA and coaching the CU men's club team. But the two things that most influenced my decision to leave coaching were September 11 and the invasion of Iraq.

Halfway through the 2003 season at Fairview, I knew recruiting and crafty paper work in high school girls-volleyball, or any volleyball, wasn't how I wanted to spend my time. And though I could find ways to coach without having to do much of either, volleyball was too small a pond for the kinds of fish I was after.

Soldiers

In elementary school I dreamed I was a fast and strong medieval knight who battled for years, became a hero, was injured and suffered three long days and nights before dying. Jr. and Sr. High school brought American Revolution and Civil War types of dreams. The advances in weapons made heroics less frequent, though injury and death were still long and brutal. Movies like "Apocalypse Now," "Platoon," and "Full Metal Jacket" brought machine guns, artillery and napalm. Heroics were virtually non-existent. And mercifully, death came more quickly, though each dream ended the same. I begin my last breath, then wake in a cold sweat.

~

In my twenties my biannual war dreams were stark reminders of how fortunate I was to be a pro beach volleyball player rather than fighting in Iraq, Bosnia, Kuwait, Somalia, Liberia, Central African Republic, or Cambodia. After each dream I was more determined to use fame and fortune to combat dictatorships, racists, sexists, classists, all prejudices.

After the inequality and injustice I saw during my four years in LA and traveling coast to coast 25 weekends a year, I wanted a "war" more than ever. I could've used my new levels of energy and focus to endure the mundane drills, physical pain, and other sacrifices it takes to be a world class athlete. Which is why part of me will never forgive myself for leaving the AVP and a chance to be the best. And why most of me still knows that committing more time and energy to peacemaking was the right choice.

~

A year after leaving the AVP I saw the movie, "The Thin Red Line." I was instantly captivated by the powerful examples of war's contrasts: chaos and boredom, confidence and fear, love and hate – all leading to the destruction of minds and bodies.

In the opening scene a camera pans: a moss-covered alligator slips into black water; sunlight streams through canopies of broad dark green leaves; tree trunks slowly wrap, swallowing other trees. "What's this war at the heart of Nature?" The narrator asks, "Why does Nature vie with itself? The land contend with the sea. Is there an avenging power in Nature? Not one power, but two?"

I reveled in the truth about nature's beauty and harsh reality. Then I longed to see the answer the young narrator would find, because I don't think nature is at war with itself. The wolf pack and herd of caribou aren't enemies: they need each other to survive. And while it's clear those in a war fight to survive, declarations of war aren't always simply about survival. Especially with the weapons used in modern-day warfare. "Going to war" is more about killing—eliminating the "enemy" in order to meet perceived needs, which makes war a uniquely human endeavor.

~

The second scene is of US Army Private Robert Witt living with natives in a small Melanesian village in the South Pacific. Witt had gone AWOL from C Company. The Army soon tracked him down.

"What is this?" 1st Sgt. Edward Welsh asks Witt in the brig of a battleship cruiser, "The fourth time you've gone AWOL? Don't you think it's time you wise up? Stop being such a punk recruit? I mean, if you're ever gonna?"

"Well," Witt responds, "We can't all be smart."

"That's true," Welsh replies, "look at you ... Fact is you can't take straight duty in my Company ... so I'm assigning you to stretcher bearer."

"I can take anything you dish out," Witt says, "I'm twice the man you are."

"In this world," Welsh states after a long stare, "a man, himself, is nothin. And there ain't no world but this one."

"You're wrong there Top," Witt says, "I seen another world. Sometimes I think it was just my imagination."

"Well, then you're seeing things I never will," Welsh counters, "We're living in a world that's blowing itself to hell as fast as everybody can arrange it. In a situation like that all a man can do is shut his eyes and let nothing touch him. Look out for himself."

Witt's looking out for himself by going AWOL and Welsh can't see life without war, I thought after the third time watching. *This might be the darkest scene in the film.*

~

Another front runner for darkest scene is the initial assault on an Island in the South Pacific. No movie has replicated the physical horror I saw and felt in my war dreams. Still, "The Thin Red Line" does capture the agony of severed limbs and charred bodies. Also how the last moments for many are filled with anger and regret. And how strength and speed might make heroes when soldiers use swords, but physical gifts mean little in the age of machine guns and artillery.

After landing and hiking inland, C Company reaches the front line: a ridge at the bottom of a steep hill protected by five bunkered machine guns and mortar launchers. At first light, C Company attacks with a platoon and reserve. Bullets and mortars rip the soldiers and hillside apart. Two platoons and reserves sit behind the ridge, listening.

A Sargent who led the assault sprints back and dives behind the ridge. A dozen soldiers watch as the Sgt. rips a hand full of grass and tosses it, "That's us. That's us. I lost all 12. I lost all 12," he says, eyes twitching, "I told them what to do and gave them a push. I don't know who is in charge here, but don't let 'em go! Don't let 'em go! Ok. I'm outa here. I'm outta here. I'm outta here. Move feet. Move. Move. Move."

But he doesn't move and soldiers around him tell him to take it easy. "I'm movin', I'm movin'," the Sgt. barks but he remains still.

A soldier puts his hand on the Sgt.'s shoulder and takes his rifle.

"Don't touch ... Don't touch," the Sgt. warns, "Ok. Ok. I'm outta here."

The soldier removes his hand and points to the rear of the line.

Sometimes you're better off not surviving.

~

The carnage continued with a soldier getting shot in the stomach. Holding his intestines in his hands he stumbles back towards the ridge, then falls and screams. Two platoons and a reserve 10 paces away.

"He'd be dead before we could get him to a surgeon," a doctor says to the Captain, "but I could give him a morphine shot and maybe leave him a few for himself."

"Could you give them to him all at once?" the Captain asks.

The Doctor scrambles over the ridge, weaves through enemy fire, kneels beside the soldier, reaches into his belt, and gets shot through the heart.

The soldier screams.

C Company listens.

Sgt. Welsh drops his gear and sprints over the ridge. Bullets fly.

Welsh picks up the soldier.

"Fuck you," the soldier cries and squirms from Welsh's arms, "Fuck you. I'm dying. I'm dying."

Welsh, still taking fire, digs through the dead doctor's belt and lays a few morphine shots beside the soldier. They look into each other's eyes.

"Bye Sgt.," the soldier says.

"Bye kid," Welsh says and sprints back behind the ridge.

"I saw the whole thing through the glasses," Captain Staros says, "I want you to know I'm going to mention you in orders tomorrow. I'm going to recommend you for the Silver Star. It was the most courageous thing ..."

"Captain, if you say one more word to thank me," Welsh interrupts, "I'm going to knock you right in the teeth. If you mention me in your orders I'll resign my rating so fast and leave you here to run this busted up outfit by yourself. You don't understand?" Welsh asks in response to his Captain's look of surprise, "Property. The whole fucking thing is about property."

Most soldiers do the "right thing, which is mortifying when you also consider that humanity has spent thousands of years murdering, enslaving, robbing and raping each other. The Greek tragedian Aeschylus in fifth century B.C., and the many who have analyzed war had it right: Truth is the first casualty.

~

While on leave from the front line, Witt visits the village he was living in at the beginning of the movie, but gets a different reception. No one shakes his hand or speaks to him. He sees villagers shout at and shove each other—young and old with fevers and spots. Witt returns to C Company.

"Who you making trouble for today?" Welsh asks Witt when he returned.

"What do you mean?" Witt asks.

"Isn't that what you like to do? Turn left when they say go right," Welsh persists, "Why are you such a trouble maker?"

"You care about me don't you Sgt.?" Witt responds, "I always felt like you did. Why you always make yourself out like a rock? One day I can come up and talk to you, and the next day, it's like we never met."

"You ever get lonely?" Witt asks after a moment of silence.

"Only around people," Welsh replies.

Only around people," Witt repeats thoughtfully.

"You still believing in the light are you?" Welsh asks, "How do you do that? You're a magician to me."

"I still see a spark in you," Witt concludes.

Like Witt, I see a spark, and like Welsh, I often feel most alone when surrounded by people.

~

I feel lonely for many reasons. Mostly because I'm not comfortable with many generally accepted norms. I rarely like to make small talk about the weather or material possessions (especially if they're expensive). I'm easily aggravated by those who boast of American rags-to-riches stories.

I know "class" doesn't always determine a child's success, but even the hardest worker would be a fool to turn down upper-class odds. Plus, those in a position of privilege often continue to say and do things to keep the odds in their favor.

Another reason I feel lonely is because I think communism and socialism—the redistribution of wealth—are good ideas. But to be clear, I think greedy crooks come in all flavors: communist, socialist, and capitalist. So I don't really care what someone calls themselves, I just want to do business with those who can see beyond their own profit margins and keep other peoples' best interests in mind too.

Still, most of my seclusion is rooted in America's original sins.

I'm easily angered when people dismiss our Founding Father's ignorance as a product of the time, as opposed to a major flaw in personal and institutional character. I don't think their transgressions should define them. Still, their offenses were slavery, theft, murder, and rape. *They should've known better!* A lot can be learned by critically examining how and why intelligent, compassionate people kept themselves and others in the dark.

I also get angry over how white Americans reconciled the Civil War with Jim Crow and the KKK. And "educated" people wrote books portraying Robert E. Lee as a hero (found in libraries and offices of congressmen today). Crushing the unlawful John Smith up-rising and nearly defeating an army superior in numbers and resources may make Lee a model for battle acumen and courage. But Lee's lack of insight and courage for four million enslaved people, plus his prolific career murdering abolitionists of all colors, always has and always will disqualify Lee from being my hero. Though it's also worth noting that I think Lee lived up to America's highest ideals: because after losing, he embraced the results to create a stronger union. And then encouraged the South's most bitter to do the same.

~

"The Thin Red Line" illustrates many depths of insanity created by war.

"All they sacrifice for me," thought the Lieutenant Colonel who ordered C Company to lead the assault on five bunkered machine guns, "Poured out like water on the ground."

In a triage by a river turned red, screams from soldiers with mutilated legs and arms are muted (smart, considering nothing can replicate those cries, and coming close would turn most audiences away). "Maybe all men got one big soul," the narrator asks, "Who everybody is a part of. All faces of the same man. One big self. Everyone looking for salvation by himself. Each like a coal drawn from the fire."

While on leave most of C Company gets drunk for each other, for those who can't, and to forget the bloodshed. "War don't ennoble men," the narrator says as two US soldiers fight while dozens circle and cheer, "It turns them into dogs. Poisons the soul."

~

"That's how white people do you," a few on the black half of my family said after watching yet another news report of white racist's acts of terrorism against blacks. They also talked about love and appreciation for my mom and Oma. So while it didn't sound right, I understood what they meant.

I learned that violence has a lasting impact. Language has limitations. And if I don't see a light in others, it's probably because I'm not looking.

~

Witt looked for a light until the end.

C Company is reinforced and ordered back to the front line. Their new, inexperienced Captain marches them deep into enemy territory. They take position in a river surrounded by thick jungle and echoing through the trees they hear Japanese commanders shouting orders, gunfire, screams, and Japanese commanders shouting more orders—the enemy is closing in. The Captain's second in command begs for him to order their retreat. Instead, the Captain orders the platoon to hold their position and for Privates Fife and Jones to scout ahead.

"I'll go," Witt says to the Captain.

"You don't have to go [Witt]," the Captain says, "two have already volunteered."

"No. No. I want to go," Witt explains, "in case something bad happens. But, I want you to know I think it's a bad idea. If they come down that straight they're going to knock our position to pieces. "Witt, Jones and Fife run into a reinforced elite platoon a few bends up river. While retreating they get spotted, take fire, and Jones gets hit. All three take cover behind large tree roots along the bank of the river.

"One of us has to go back and warn the others. One of us has to stay here and hold them off," Witt says to Fife before clarifying, "I'll hold them off."

Fife retreats. Witt pushes Jones into a swift current that he can ride back to the platoon, then jumps up on the bank, runs, shouts, and draws the Japanese into the jungle. Taking fire, Witt sprints over a ridge and into a clearing where he is quickly surrounded by six Japanese soldiers, rifles cocked and aimed. Witt stops, arms to his sides, rifle in one hand. A Japanese soldier orders Witt to drop his rifle.

Witt desperately looks for a way out.

"I was scared of the death I'd seen in her," Witt thinks of his mother dying of cancer when he was young, "I didn't see nothin' upliftin' about her goin' to see God … And, I wondered how it'd be when I died. How it'd be knowing this was going to be the last breath I ever took."

"Drop your rifle," the Japanese soldier screams again.

Finally, Witt's face and shoulders relax.

I've often replayed that moment (you'd miss it if you sneezed). It's the climax. Witt understands that war would always rule his life, as Sgt. Welsh put it, "There ain't no world but this one." Seeing no way out from the institution that kills many who would otherwise benefit all humanity, Witt slowly raises his rifle and gets shot through the heart.

~

I enjoyed parts of my war dreams. I felt empowered, using all my skill and focus to help protect family, friends, and ideas I hold most dear. Like in elementary school, when I was a knight with superhero-like powers. Or in the three dreams I had shortly after: being accepted to Naropa in January 2001, September 11 2001, and our invasion of Iraq in spring 2003. In each, I was a sniper in the mountains of Austria, 1944.

Great snipers like to watch, listen, and disappear into enemy territory. We breathe and gather adrenalin into a steady flow that feeds our minds and bodies. We climb walls, trees, and cliffs, forge rivers and sewers, sleep in tall grass and dark alleys, savor nourishment in insects and rotting food, and understand that targets must be exterminated—like Hitler.

In my last dream I assassinated six high ranking officers. During one mission, hundreds of enemy troops doubled back through my position. I spent eight hours in a hollow log, a night in a tree, and scaled a cliff. Back in camp soldiers started to whisper, "He's one of the invincible." Still, in the end, like in almost all my war dreams, there's one too many pair of eyes.

Enemy soldiers spot me, yell, and shoot. I sprint along buildings, a tree line and drop to one knee. Breathe. Aim. Squeeze. The target falls. "The kill that springs me," I think and run. I reach the river, a platoon of friendlies not far beyond. But scorching heat in early spring made where I had crossed three days ago impassable. I sprint downstream, scan for a place to cross, see the tip of a rifle and flash—my chest burns—I begin my last breath.

I sit upright, cold and drenched in sweat. It takes a moment to realize I'm in bed. I find a dry spot on my pillow, lay back, take deep breaths, slow my heart, and warm my feet. Then I think of American soldiers stationed throughout the world, risking everything.

Americans who are living comfortably need to work as hard as those on the front-lines. More Americans must be dedicated to ending violence. And as Jesus, MLK Jr., Gandhi and many more have taught, nonviolence is more than refraining from assaulting others. It's learning to respect their humanity.

I renewed my vow be the best soldier for peace that I could be.

Excellence

Greatness comes to those who relax. Not the "Nap after Thanksgiving Turkey" kind of relaxed, but the fully alert kind. As an athlete, I practiced breathing and Tai Chi to get stronger, faster, make better decisions, and win. I practiced while coaching, teaching, and earning an MFA because others benefited too. Like magic, when I relaxed, classmates, players, students, and co-workers would sit up straighter, walk taller, and communicate better.

I often found it easier to relax when teamed with talent, like our indoor National Championship team at CU, qualifying for the AVP with Nick, winning the Motherlode with Eric. The most talented teams I've coached were my first year as girls head coach at Fairview, and my first year as men's head coach at the University of Colorado.

~

At Fairview, ten of twelve players were seniors, all had experience playing club, and only three were clear starters. Which meant a lot of players had a good argument as to why they should be starting. I worried available playing time, or lack thereof, would hurt morale.

"Athletes improve most when they give 100% on every play," I emphasized at the beginning the year, "which makes the depth on our team an advantage."

"Every team spends 80% of their time competing against themselves and 20% against others," I emphasized. "So if we give 100% in every practice and celebrate everyone even though only 6 can play, then by the end of our short three and a half-month season, each of you and our team as a whole, will improve more than any in the state and we'll become state champions."

I learned that while it's nice to have good speeches about teamwork, the best way to keep morale high is to speak regularly with each player about personalized and concrete expectations and rewards.

State play-offs consisted of three tournaments played on three consecutive weekends, Districts, Regionals, and State. We won our District and Regional tournaments. Eight teams made the final State tournament and were arranged into two "pools" of four. Each team plays the other three teams in their pool. The two teams with the best record "break pool" and compete in the semi-finals. Losers played for third. Winners play for the championship.

Cherry Creek, Boulder High and Coronado were in our pool. Cherry Creek and Boulder were also in our league and during league play, we beat Cherry Creek while Boulder beat us.

In the first round at State we beat Cherry Creek. In the second round we played Coronado, who served tough, played scrappy, and forced us into costly errors and a loss. Then, we scouted the Boulder vs Coronado match and took the bus back to Boulder.

Early the next morning we met at Fairview, made the 45 minute commute, had a team meeting, warmed-up, played sluggish, lost to Boulder, and finished 5th.

Cherry Creek and Boulder broke pool, won their semi-final matches, and played in the championship. Cherry Creek won.

A few nights later I dreamed I hadn't worried about saving money. That we had stayed in a hotel in Denver instead of going back to Boulder. Had eaten dinner, hung out, went to bed early, and eaten breakfast before a short commute. We came out firing and remained composed when Boulder played well. I woke up before seeing if we won, but we were glowing.

~

My first year with the CU men's program, the National Championships were in Kansas City. We stopped at a truck stop an hour into a nine hour road trip because a blizzard had closed I-70. Six hours later state patrol announced I-70 wouldn't open until morning, about the time of our first match. But east bound I-80 through Nebraska was open so we drove north, then east, then south. We arrived at our hotel with just enough time to check in, eat, and get to our 8 am match.

Having your team sleep while riding in a van the night before the biggest tournament of the year should be unnerving, but I felt calm. I played 14 players that day. Everyone played well. A few were exceptional. We comfortably won our matches.

I used most of our roster and everyone's great play continued on the second and third day. In the Championship match we played a team that had beaten us a few times that season. We won the first game in a best of three match and took an early lead in the second game. Then, our opponents played better and we grew quiet and hesitant. We lost in three games.

A few nights later I dreamed I developed more offensive plays for L.V. He was our best hitter whom I subbed out of the back row for better ball control to provide opportunities for our other excellent middle. But, L.V. had the kind of fire power that could light up our team and the crowd. After losing two points in the middle of the second game I looked down the bench, "Get ready L.V." After losing the next point I called for a substitution, "Now's the time," I said, "Pound the fucking thing." Then turned to our setter, "Set him every ball."

~

In 1999 I was a literacy teacher for Kindergarten, 1st, 2nd, and 3rd graders in Boulder Valley School District. I was hired by the principal at CrestView Elementary, but before school began, half my hours were given to Lafayette Elementary, 15 miles east of Boulder. While I liked many aspects of teaching at both schools, the most personally rewarding was helping to lead CrestView's Peer Mediation Program.

CrestView's fifth grade teachers nominated a few students who agreed to be trained and spend a couple lunch recesses a week on the playground helping resolve conflicts over games, equipment, bullying, etc. Training included a few after-school sessions and an overnight retreat in the library. With stories, worksheets and roleplaying, we taught them that conflict arises between everyone: family, friends, classmates, co-workers, neighbors, and strangers. And conflict can lead to positive change when handled properly. We also taught guidelines. All parties must: Agree there's a problem; Remain calm; Tell your side of the story; Listen to the other side; Suggest solutions and agree on one; If they can't stay calm or agree, go to a teacher.

Peer mediators walked the playground in green vests and with clipboards, pencils and sheets to guide and record the peacemaking process. On Fridays we met and reviewed what went well and what they could've done better. I've always thought kids were great problem-solvers and I became even more convinced. At the end of the year our principal asked me to speak at the all school assembly.

"Everyone at CrestView: principals, teachers, paras, janitors ... everyone is thankful to our mediators," I said before passing out certificates, "mediators sacrificed their own time to help students solve conflict and have more fun on the playground. And having fewer discipline issues to deal with, staff could focus on getting other important work done."

"When I think of us entering this new century, and the conflicts between different nationalities, cultures, races, and religions around the world, our mediators give me hope. Because by the end of the year, students solved conflicts using the mediation process without mediators. And 1st and 2nd graders said they wanted to wear the green vest in 5th grade."

~

Lafayette had among the highest population of minorities and poor in the District. At the beginning of the year, a few teachers and I were sent to the computer room to dust and examine a truckload of old computers and disks that had been sent over from a warehouse. Many didn't work. We erred on the side of caution while deciding how blurry monitors could be before damaging the student's eyes. We worked all morning and ended up with 15 machines of various makes, models, and usefulness. A larger pile had to go back.

That afternoon, with a wealthier and whiter population at CrestView, I taught in the tech room with 25 new Apple computers. And next to the mail boxes in the teacher's lounge, the art teacher opened a letter and yelped with delight because when the PTA decided to give P.E. $500, they felt they had to do the same for Art. I was especially struck because CrestView does not rank among Boulder's schools with the most privileged population, but it clearly had parents who were rich enough to contribute more.

~

One advantage to being a literacy teacher is the chance to learn from other teachers.

One male teacher I worked with at Lafayette was sharply criticized by many. He emphasized hands-on learning, minimal seat time, collaboration, flexible curriculum and schedule, personal and peer evaluations. I'd always been drawn to such learning environments. High energy boys and second language learners did well in his classroom.

Other teachers had more rigid schedules and seat work: worksheets; reading based lessons; standardized tests for high stakes. And while most of Creekside's students did well in that environment, one smart, high-energy boy struggled.

The boy was bombarded with "Stop that," "Sit down," and "Be quiet." Then he'd sit, shoulders hunched, brows furrowed and huffing short breaths.

"I've seen you do one very important thing," I told him at a recess in late fall, "something many great athletes do."

"What?" he asked.

"Breathe," I said. "I practiced breathing when I was pro athlete. A lot of pros do. Because when you really want to win, or think the ref made a bad a call, or your teacher tells you to sit crisscross apple sauce, breathing helps you stay calm and make good decisions. The key is to take long slow breaths," I demonstrated and we practiced a few, "Next time you feel really frustrated, focus and take three deep breaths."

"I'll try," he said.

His mother approached me in the parking lot near the end of the year. She had come from a meeting with his teacher and the principal.

"They made him sound completely out of control," she said.

"He doesn't like to sit but he likes to learn," I said, "and the way he makes connections can get off topic. But that's also a sign of good humor."

"I struggle with his active body and mind too," she said, "but they said I should transfer him to a different school."

"You should keep setting goals," I encouraged, "But after teaching in Kansas, five years as a teacher's assistant and substitute, and this year at CrestView and Lafayette, I think he's a good-natured, smart kid. I wouldn't be overly concerned."

"Thank you," she said, voice filled with relief.

~

Years later I saw a BVSD principal featured in a local T.V. news story. She had earned a degree and learned that aspects of a traditional classroom, like lots of seat work, reading-based lessons, and constant quiet, aren't the best learning environment for many boys. And she was helping teachers implement strategies for boys throughout the district.

A step. But I still questioned how much things would change. *One woman takes classes to learn how to teach boys. While my teammate and I, with life-long, first-hand understanding of what suits boys, have our professionalism constantly questioned. I guess BVSD needs a woman to take some classes about hiring and celebrating male teachers.*

~

I had other concerns that year too. First was having to commute to Lafayette. Early in the year I met with an assistant superintendent to explain that one of my weaknesses is paper work and planning. So when CrestView hired me, I moved into an apartment a few blocks away, so I could spend more time on lessons and evaluations. And while I liked Lafayette, it hurt my professional goals to be driving an hour a day.

"Before signing the contract," I explained, "I wished I had understood I worked for the district, and might not teach at the school that hired me."

"Moving teachers isn't something we like to do," the assistant superintendent explained, "but it's hard to predict enrollment and sometimes we have to."

"I get that," I said, my heart beating faster, feeling a misunderstanding building, "and the drive won't keep me from fulfilling my duties. But, I could do a lot for my students and myself with an hour a day for a year. If I'm going to drive every day I might choose to sub and be guaranteed time to write my own curriculum in evenings and other days off."

The assistant superintendent insisted the District wouldn't want to be more transparent in the teacher contract because, "The best teachers might not apply."

Yah, yah, I thought, but pressed that people are better off when everyone understands the bottom line in their signed agreement.

"Right," I blurted after going back and forth a couple times, "it's fucking silly to talk about the Truth."

I know I have a short fuse when it comes to administrators that dismiss transparency. But my cussing surprised me: usually I just sulk away in silence. We wrapped up the meeting and I vowed not to cuss in a meeting like that again.

In the spring, I debated whether or not to speak with the assistant superintendent about the inequality I saw in the district. Like Lafayette Elementary students learning on, and their teachers saddled with setting up and maintaining, outdated equipment. And the male teacher who was overly criticized. And the smart, funny boy who was asked to leave. And the stranger on Pearl Street who called me a nigger. And the woman who clutched her purse. And the police who followed me.

"The District," I'd conclude, "needs to do a lot more to alleviate the inequities minorities experience in Boulder."

But my heart and mind race when talking to administrators and sitting in chairs that cost way too much considering how many students go to school hungry. Plus, even though I vowed not to cuss again, the f-bomb had slipped out last time, and the odds were pretty good she'd parrot what BVSD administrators have said for forty years, "We're deeply concerned about minorities feeling alienated, and are doing what we can to make our District a more welcoming community." I decided not to risk it.

I gave my students my best until the last bell, then focused on my own education: The Artists Way Workbook by Julia Cameron, A Thomas Merton Reader by Thomas P McDonnell, and core readings for a week-long MA short intensive titled, Creating Peaceable Schools, at Lesley College in Cambridge, Massachusetts.

~

I took that course in June. Dozens of workshop leaders, keynote presenters, panelists, and staff guided hundreds of principals, teachers, assistants, and other educators in small and large groups. It was just what I needed.

Opening speakers talked about what to do to create peaceable schools, including: Celebrate diversity; find resources, not deficits, in others; discuss root causes of violence and conflict; collaborate on solutions. "Differences don't cause problems," the speaker stressed, "Problems arise when we attach negative values to differences. And when we ignore differences."

"When everyone's an individual," the speaker continued, "the dominant group thinks their experience is neutral. For example, many whites think, 'Why do we have to talk about race?' 'Why can't we all just be individuals?' and 'I don't think of myself as having a race.' While many of color assert, 'I have to focus on my group identity until you finally see, acknowledge and respect me. The stereotyping of my group strips away my individuality.'"

Yes! It hit me with a rush, *people who don't want to talk about race dismiss how I've been impacted: my ex-girlfriend's racist parents, strangers who call me nigger, women who cross the street, police who follow me, regular acts of terror around the nation. But if I bring it up, many will say I'm just playing the race card.*

I sat upright. Alert. Ready to take notes and find ways to help people overcome the prejudice we inherited from our complex and painful histories.

~

In the first keynote, Roots of Violence: Establishing a Peaceable Community, Dr. Ulric Johnson and Cathy Hoffman talked about their conflicts with family, friends, and neighbors. They also pointed out that they had been victim, bully, and silent witness throughout their lives. They said most people play all three roles at one time or another, then asked us to remember times in which we'd been a victim, bully, and silent witness.

"Stereotypes guide our thoughts," Dr. Johnson began the next lesson, "like grooves on a record guiding a needle to play the same old songs."

"Take out a piece of paper," Hoffman continued, "and write down the first ten descriptive words that come to mind when we ask you to describe various stereotypes, such as 'black,' 'white,' 'liberal,' 'conservative.' Don't censor yourself—*smart, weak, loud, poor, beautiful*—write the first words that come to mind."

Dr. Johnson listed stereotypes, pausing between each so we could write our reactions. Then, we reviewed our lists and noted which were positive or negative. On my lists, liberals received seven positive words, while conservatives received just three.

Next, we introduced ourselves to the person next to us, and shared why we used certain words to describe certain stereotypes.

> *Brilliant exercise. Help people recognize that some describe black men as "tardy," "uneducated," and "impulsive," while others use "flexible," "street-smart," and "decisive."*

My partner and I also noticed it was hard to come up with words for some stereotypes. And some words could be positive or negative. We also both regretted how many negative words we used to describe others. For a gay man I wrote *weak*, and wasn't thinking positively when I wrote *feminine* and *emotional*. We finished by sharing accounts of friends and family who used racist and sexist language.

In closing, Dr. Johnson and Hoffman asked audience members to share the stories behind their lists. We heard about prejudice, kindness, hatred, and love. The audience regularly nodded and shook their heads with empathy. We were reflecting on being bullies, victims, and silent witnesses. We were also looking for retribution. Exactly what was due; because justice is what makes peace possible.

~

"The only time schools are peaceful is at 3 am," Alfie Kohn said to begin his keynote titled, From Compliance to Community.

Kohn described how discipline is found on a continuum, from negative to positive. Negative reinforcement such as hitting, timeout, and exclusion, can suppress children's desire to be creative, ask questions, and make mistakes. Positive reinforcement such as compensation, rewards and, bathing with praise, can give students the impression they won't succeed on their own and those in authority don't trust them.

"Students learn from positive and negative feedback," Kohn emphasized, "Great teachers understand their student's needs and artfully complicate their lives using both."

~

In the weeks after school ended, I second-guessed quitting my literacy position in order to substitute teach and write. But I knew I'd made the right decision at the conference when panelists described how corporations have targeted profits in public education and had begun a campaign to devalue and disempower teachers and their unions. Then I read my poetry during an open mic. Two older women praised my writing and offered advice.

"Remember," the black woman said, "White people want *you* to think *you* are crazy."

"Keep writing," the white woman said, "just go somewhere and write, write, write."

~

My step dad (sociology professor who started The University of Colorado peace and conflict studies program and made it possible for me to attend the Peaceable Schools Conference), gave me, <u>On Writing Well: An informational guide to writing nonfiction</u>, by William Zinsser.

Zinsser begins with seven "Principles." In the first principal, The Transaction, he describes being on a panel with another writer. The audience was made up of student newspaper editors, English teachers and parents, all eager to learn about the secrets and glamor in writing.

"What was it like to be a writer?" an audience member asked.

"It was tremendous fun," Zinsser's fellow panelist exhorted, "The words just flowed. It was easy."

"Writing isn't easy and it isn't fun," Zinsser said confirming what I discovered trying to finish my first novel and children's books, "It's hard and lonely, and the words seldom just flow."

"Is it important to rewrite?" another audience member asked.

"Absolutely not," the other panelist said, "Let it all hang out, and whatever form the sentences take will reflect the writer at his most natural."

"Rewriting is the essence of writing," Zinsser emphasized, "professional writers rewrite their sentences repeatedly, and then rewrite what they have rewritten ... E. B. White and James Thurber rewrote their pieces eight or nine times."

"What do you do on days when it isn't going well?" another in the audience asked.

The other panelist said he stopped writing and put the work aside for a day when it would go better.

"The professional writer must establish a daily schedule and stick to it," Zinsser explained, "writing is a craft, not an art, and the man who runs away from his craft because he lacks inspiration is fooling himself. He is also going broke."

"Do you use symbolism in your writing?" a student asked.

"I love symbols," the other panelist exclaimed.

"Not if I can help it," Zinsser said reaffirming what I've always disliked most about reading and writing, "I have an unbroken record of missing the deeper meaning in any story, play or movie, and as for dance and mime, I have never had even a remote notion of what is being conveyed."

"This," Zinsser summarizes, "is the personal transaction that's at the heart of good nonfiction writing. Out of it come two of the most important qualities that this book will go in search of: humanity and warmth."

I was thrilled to read the rest of Zinsser's book. After the novel I wrote while on the pro tour ended in six years of writer's block, I was looking for tools.

If I want to follow my step-dad's example—a life dedicated to peace—I need to get better at speaking and writing about my own and other people's humanity and warmth.

~

Fall 2000 I applied to the Jack Kerouac School of Writing and Poetics graduate program at Naropa University. I went back to school full time in June 2001.

Peacemaker

"The shame of this generation will not be the small number of extremists who bombed and terrorized, but those who stood silently by and did nothing to stop it." MLK Jr. expressed in words what I imagine blacks had said about whites for the last twelve generations.

I also thought many Americans in my generation would experience a similar shame after George W. Bush's presidency. My concern began when many said they liked W. Bush because he seemed like the kind of guy they could have a beer with. W. Bush reminded me of the kind of guy hooked on America's sense of being exceptional. The kind I saw a lot of in Kansas. We were friendly but had no reasons to be friends.

Then came September 11. The attack enabled President Bush to create The Patriot Act, which dismantled constitutional rights to privacy and in less than two years led to a declaration of war.

Bush also created No Child Left Behind, a bill mandating testing, unobtainable goals, school choice, closing public schools, disempowering teachers, racial and cultural segregation, hiding declining graduation rates, and paving the way for private corporations to profit in the education market. All while our government fails to address unemployment, drug addiction, poverty, disease, hunger, and the resulting despair.

~

I studied ancient and contemporary poetry, prose, and essays. Chomsky, Mandela, and The Dalai Lama were favorites. I went to rallies, presentations, and workshops; collaborated on writing and other projects with students and professionals from around the world; practiced meditation, Tai Chi, and painting. I published chap books, greeting cards, and read my poetry to crowds ranging from 10 to 150.

I saw a peace activist speak at CU. Flags flew throughout the court yard, Israeli on one half, Palestinian on the other. There was a Palestinian woman holding a sign in one hand and a young child in the other. A man tried to grab the sign from the woman's hand but she wouldn't let go. The man twisted and yanked. The woman barely hung on to the child. People quickly closed in to separate them. I watched the man make his way through the crowd towards his friends, my heart pounding, urging me to march, close in and grab him, shake some sense into him. *Seriously—a woman carrying a child!?*

Then the activist started to share. Israelis booed and hissed as Palestinians cheered and clapped. As the activist continued, some Israelis who had hissed applauded, while some Palestinians who had applauded hissed.

Brilliant! Sensitive. Aware, forthright. Everybody's been hurt… everybody could be more respectful and kind.

Afterwards people huddled in groups with hard stares and loud conversations, "They're animals," and "[the speaker] is a fucking idiot!"

I walked away knowing I wanted to be like the speaker—except for the engagements on podiums and death threats.

~

My concerns over President Bush's leadership grew when he talked about invading Iraq to "get" Saddam Hussein. A dictator who Bush's father helped empower and who commanded a military we helped arm and train.

I was skeptical because 15 of the 19 terrorists on 9/11 were from Saudi Arabia. I became a cynic when I learned the canisters General Colin Powell said could be used to enrich uranium were only poor configurations for the process. And I lost all faith in our government when a host of other evidence the US presented was totally discredited by inspectors who had been monitoring Iraq for years. "Saddam," the international experts said again and again, "does *not* have WMD's."

Nevertheless, dozens of TV channels, months of 24/7 news cycles, and the best reporters presented "proof" provided by our best intelligence agencies. The relentless message was, "Saddam *does* have WMD's … It's not a question of if, but when he will use them. Preemptive war is necessary!"

Late 2002 I signed up with MoveOn.org to collect signatures and be a spokesman. Early 2003 a group of twenty, students, moms, dads, veterans, teachers, and business people met at the office of Congressman Mark Udall. We all crammed into a small room with a large desk. The congressman was busy, so we spoke to his assistant.

After introductions I spoke about our petition's demands: Do *not* invade Iraq until we research, have debates, and make plans to address the following:

First, Saddam is a charismatic leader with significant power and resources. He's also a sworn enemy of Osama Bin Laden and the Taliban. Ousting Saddam will leave a power vacuum that could destabilize the region. How will we keep terrorists from gaining power in Iraq and neighboring countries?

Second, After the initial "Shock and Awe" invasion kills tens of thousands of innocent Iraqis (conservative estimates), what will we say and do to convince surviving young Iraqis that they should join us, instead of the terrorists?

Third, What accounts for the discrepancy between White House's estimated cost of the war, $50 - $100 million, and that of other experts, $450 - $500 million?

Fourth, Our Veteran Affairs services are already stretched too thin. Before going to war, we need to budget more resources and build more infrastructure for the VA.

Finally, Tens of millions of people world-wide – presidents, professors, priests, CEO's, teachers, athletes, musicians, chefs, waiters, janitors and more – DO NOT think we will be greeted as liberators, and have spoken, chanted, and screamed in protest.

Then many who squeezed into that little room shared their own experiences: veterans from two wars; US citizens who immigrated from Europe and Africa; non-violent peace activists (one who started with MLK Jr. and another who refused to have more regrets). They spoke of love for our country, the devastating costs of war, and their belief in other people and the political process.

Then I read a few comments and quotes from the petition.

"All of us," I concluded, "the twenty who took time out of our busy schedules to be here, and the five thousand who signed this petition, recognize that there are good reasons to remove a man like Saddam from power. We are also thankful for soldiers who are willing to risk everything in order to protect us from dictators like him. But war is only half the journey to peace. And right now, is a time for diplomacy."

Udall's assistant assured us that the congressman shared our concerns.

~

Throughout graduate school I felt like Captain Willard in the hotel in Saigon at the beginning of "Apocalypse Now." Awaiting a mission in the relative comfort of my Boulder home while my opponents gain strength in their single-minded pursuits.

AVP stars Dain Blanton and Eric Fonoimoana won gold at the 2000 Olympics in Sydney Australia. A fortuitous turn of events since they wouldn't even have qualified if they hadn't partnered and finished in the top three of the last few international tournaments.

Both Dain and Eric were in elementary school when they first dreamed of standing atop a podium and singing our National Anthem. They instantly had great chemistry and pulled off an improbable run that concluded with beating a superb Brazilian team in the Olympic finals.

Dain is the first African American to win on the AVP. Eric is the first Samoan. Each has the work ethic preached by many minority parents for generations: People *will* judge you unfairly, so shut your mouth, work twice as hard as everyone else, and prove beyond any doubt that you're the best person for the job.

In the years following gold in Sydney, Dain and Eric created foundations and programs to get kids to the beach: sun, sand, and teamwork. They gave speeches and used personal income to finance volleyball and academic programs.

Dain's and Eric's success reminded me of what I'd given up, especially leading up to the 2004 Olympics. I was 33. It would have been my ninth year as a pro, when experience makes up for losses in youthful explosiveness. I'd have mastered breathing and efficiency like Sinjin Smith, Mike Dodd, and Todd Rogers (Olympic Gold medalist in 2008). Though not the best athletes, they were highly skilled and had the will to pass and kill every serve. Of course, they partnered with Randy Stoklos, Mike Whitmarsh, and Phil Dahlhouser, three of the best blockers ever. So it would've taken the right partner, but I could've been among the best in Athens, Greece.

Instead, I felt I wasn't very good at either poetry or beach volleyball. And I was about to receive a degree most employers don't care about, trying to get people to talk about things they don't want, or even think we need to talk about.

Then President Bush landed on an aircraft carrier, "Mission Accomplished!"

Really!? No WMD's; No Bin Laden or Saddam; Swaths of Baghdad in rubble; Car bombings becoming routine; Iraqis marching in streets and demanding that we leave.

"Never give up on a dream," Eric said when summarizing his and Dain's improbable run to Olympic Gold, "Never give up on a dream."

~

I wrote a letter to the Colorado Daily newspaper: "The Goals of Peacemakers are Clear."

"In response to 'The Left is Wrong Again.'" I began, "I would like to address the great number of letters from pro-war-makers who assume the goal of a peace activist is to do nothing about oppressive regimes such as the ones in Afghanistan and Iraq. I am a student of the leaders Gandhi, Martin Luther King Jr., Jesus, Buddha, and many more. Gandhi won the independence of a nation. The Emancipation Proclamation was lost in Jim Crow and Segregation for 100 years, until MLK Jr. used nonviolence to inspire the Civil Rights act. Jesus said we cannot justify killing anyone – ever. Buddha's sentiments as well.

American policy does nothing against, and in fact has aided oppressive regimes throughout our world … All empirical regimes throughout human history have done these things. The number of quotes from President Bush that sound exactly like Stalin (or any of this world's most oppressive dictators) is startling. 'You're either with us or against us,' and 'The axis of evil,' are soundbites while our government changes our Bill of Rights.

Many peace activists agree with war-makers… sacrifice must be made. Peace activists simply wonder if we sent tens of thousands of disciplined, well-trained men and women, along with billions of dollars in equipment and resources to help educate and build, as opposed to shoot and blow up, whether people wouldn't be inspired and able to liberate themselves.

Understanding this level of human potential and action is the only way to peace. Some seem to believe peace is a matter of proving others right or wrong. In fact, peace is a matter of being with the effort, creativity, and willingness to produce an environment that supports everyone."

~

A friend gave me Sam Hamill's book, <u>Poets Against the War</u>. Hamill authored thirteen volumes of original poetry, three collections of essays, twenty-four volumes translated from ancient Chinese, Japanese, Greek, Latin and Estonian, received more than a dozen fellowships and awards. He was also invited to the White House by First Lady Laura Bush.

Sam asked poet-friends to write, "For the conscience of our country," in opposition to Bush's 'Shock and Awe' attack on Baghdad. Sam received 11,000 responses in 30 days. It turned into a movement. Never had so many poets from around the world, organized so many days of poetry to protest a war. Sam and two dozen friends, writers and editors sorted through the 11,000 offerings, picked 262, and dedicated the book to First Lady Laura Bush.

Robert Pinsky, United States Poet Laureate from 1997-2000 wrote:

Dear Mrs. Bush,

Thank you for your invitation to the White House event ...
However, to my regret, I must decline to attend.

Specifically, I mistrust the president's contention that we must
invade Iraq preemptively, in defiance of important allies, and contrary
to the processes of international law. He asks us to trust him that this
extraordinary, violent and uncertain plan is in our interest ...

To participate in a poetry symposium that speaks of "the" American
voice, in the house of authority I mistrust, on the verge of a
questionable war, is impossible – the more so when I remember the
candid, rebellious, individualistic voices of Dickinson, Whitman,
Langston Hughes.

I salute your intentions, and I hope a time may come when we will
again be able to honor such great ancestors, wholeheartedly, together,
at the White House.

"And when our critics on the right," Sam wrote in the introduction,
"suggest that poetry might somehow divorce itself from politics, we say,
'Read the Greeks, read the classical Chinese; tell it to Dante, Chaucer,
Milton or Longfellow ... Tell it to Garcia Lorca, to Joseph Brodsky or to
the Chinese poets living in exile in our country today.' The voice of
dissenting poets is unwelcome at this White House, but it has been and
will be heard."

~

At Naropa, like many places in Boulder, people were generally open,
thoughtful, and kind. Still, even with the best intentions, it's hard to do
inclusion right.

~

Fall 2002 I took the class, Documentary in Poetry. I was excited to
finally heed the advice the spirit on Independence Pass had given me, and
spend a semester researching and writing about Chief Joseph of the Nez
Perce. Joseph is best known for saying, "I will fight forever no more," and
like Chief Niwot of the Southern Arapaho, he worked tirelessly for peace
while their people and culture were being eradicated.

For centuries Joseph's tribe was known as the Numipu. Then French explorers called them the Nez Perce because some Numipu had pierced noses. I found two translations for Numipu, We People and Real People. So I titled my documentary, <u>We Real People</u>.

The text alternates between poetry and prose. The poetry tells Chief Joseph's story from 1830 to 1878, highlighting Numipu traditions and how they tried to deal with overwhelming numbers of invaders, including liars, thieves, and murderers. One section of prose illustrates the dates and details of conflict and treaties between the Numipu and the US. Another prose section comments on how imperialism continues to spread ignorance, fear, greed, and violence. Illustrating how 'divide and conquer' will work until the day all minorities stand together and for each other.

I open with MLK Jr. "One day we must come to see that peace is not merely a distant goal that we seek, but a means by which we arrive at that goal. We must pursue peaceful ends through peaceful means."

My professor called my documentary a powerful sermon. He was also impressed with how I knew exactly what I wanted write about and my thorough research. Everyone said they enjoyed getting to know me and giving feedback. They appreciated the documentary. One classmate was certain my work would be published.

~

Spring 2003 I took a class on transcending borders of identity. Nationality, religion, race, gender, sexuality. We wrote to rattle doors – strike nerves – transform.

That spring the US also invaded Iraq. In my horror, I wrote a poem that blasted war-makers. I'd written similar rants numerous times. Like in 1999, after two bullied students brought guns into Columbine High School and killed twelve people. I'd feel guilty after writing such rants, because I also knew that throughout human history soldiers have made peace possible. So then I had a ceremony to burn my rant, forgiving myself and all those who throw stones with language.

I drove my 'Shock and Awe' rant up Flagstaff Mountain: two narrow lanes, steep switch backs, and a dozen pull-outs that overlook the city of

Boulder to the east, and valleys rising to the 12,000 to 14,000 foot peaks in the west. I perched on a rock facing west, watched the sun set, and took out a lighter. Then I thought about my class on transcending borders of identity, and instead of burning my rant, I decided to share.

I titled the rant, <u>Creators,</u> and like most of my writing, open with a quote, "The world has achieved brilliance without conscience. Ours is a world of nuclear giants and ethical infants." – Omar Bradley.

"Creators slung us way back, into the bowels and shit," I began, "Here I stand and breathe encased by fear – Weapons of mass destruction – Marines – Taliban – Total dedication to annihilate life – For the preservation of life? FUCK VIOLENCE! Stop it! Stop playing the game!" The poem continues for six pages of fuck this and that, name calling, and mocking questions. Writing it felt great. Burning it would've felt good too.

The feedback I received was the same, "Defense mechanisms going up," "Overstated," "Turns me off," "Offensive."

I know rants can be offensive and get defensive responses. Still, I was in liberal Boulder, hyper-liberal Naropa University, and in a class about challenging borders of identity. Classmates had had months to get to know me. A few were in my Documentary in Poetry class, which meant they spent a semester with me, learning I was a student of Gandhi and MLK Jr. and giving me feedback on my 53-page tribute to nonviolence that our professor called "a powerful sermon." I was hurt and angry when no one responded, "Yes, violence blossoms from injustice," or "True, it's not 'peaceful' when we can park nuclear submarines on each-others shores," or perhaps give me a little credit and grace, like, "Right on brother, just let it all out."

I told my classmates I was just venting—an exercise I do from time to time. They said they thought it might have been something like that, and given our pre-emptive strike on a sovereign nation, agreed that some anger was warranted.

~

At a graduation barbeque I was talking with the classmate who thought my documentary on the Nez Perce would be published, yet was initially unnerved by my rant. Then a stranger joined our conversation.

After a while the stranger said something so common I don't remember what it was. Like about how black people don't like the outdoors. Or I must've been an incredible jumper to play pro ball. Or I should be really, really proud of earning a Master's Degree.

My classmate took offense and told the guy he was being ignorant and insensitive. I liked that she noticed. Sometimes I just want to be a guy who loves to backpack and fish. Or just the hard working intelligent athlete who, naturally, earned an advanced degree.

The stranger winced as if my classmate had hooked him; the barbs sunk deep. His eyes darted for a way out. He didn't mean any harm. If alone, he and I might have laughed and carried on over my love for the outdoors vs. many black people's disdain for it. Or that I wasn't really a high flyer, even if I had days when I soared and I was world-class quick side to side. Or as a black man raised by a single white mom, we *should* be damn proud.

Potentially, it was a teachable moment. We could've talked about how to navigate the many layers of meaning and intention of language in explosive topics. But a graduation barbeque with a stranger wasn't, as is so often the case, the time or place.

"No worries," I interrupted the silence. Then changed the subject.

Revolution

It's hard to move forward drudging up guilt and other hard feelings, I thought before starting my thesis on poetry and social change, *Still, the most frightening thing about what happened in America over the last 400 years, is that our social hierarchies are not unique. That's how people have treated each other all over the world for millennia.*

My 33 years as a mixed race, first generation free black American male, raised by a mother and grandmother from Germany taught me that if people are going to come together, we have to reconcile the different messages, values, and loyalties that come from having different heroes.

~

My thesis begins with a Hopi elder.

"You have been telling the people that this is the Eleventh Hour, now you must go back and tell the people that this is the Hour. And there are some things to be considered: Where are you living? What are you doing? What are your relationships? Are you in right relation? Where is your water? Know your garden. It is time to speak your Truth. Create your community. Be good to each other. And do not look outside yourself for the leader."

"There is a river flowing now very fast," the Elder continues, "It is so great and swift that there are those who will be afraid. They will try to hold on to the shore. They will feel they are torn apart and will suffer greatly. Know the river has its destination. The Elders say we must let go of the shore, push off into the middle of the river, keep our eyes open, and our heads above water. And I say see who is in there with you and celebrate."

"At this time in history we are to take nothing personally," the Elder emphasizes, "least of all ourselves. For the moment that we do our spiritual growth and journey comes to a halt. The time for the lone world is over. Gather yourselves! Banish the word struggle from your attitude and your vocabulary. All that we do now must be done in a sacred manner and in celebration," the Elder concludes, "We are the ones we've been waiting for."

The first part of my thesis is 64 pages of original poetry that relate my experiences and faith in nonviolence.

Part two, in 35 pages, describes the impact poetic language has had on social change in America from 1600 to 2000. I begin with a quote by Henry S. Haskins, "Treat the other man's faith gently, it is all he has to believe with."

~

I quoted Chiefs Seattle and Joseph because their views transcend economics and race. They remind me that I'm human. A part of all things.

"How can you buy or sell the sky?" Chief Seattle responded to President Franklin Pierce's request to buy their land in the 1850's, "The idea is strange to us. If we do not own the freshness of the air and sparkle of the water, how can you buy them? Every part of this earth is sacred to my people; every shining pine needle; every sandy shore; and every mist in the dark woods. Every clearing and every humming insect is holy in the memory and experience of my people. The sap which courses through the trees carries the memories of the Red man. So when the Great Chief in Washington sends word that he wishes to buy our land, he asks much of us ..."

"How can any man sell the earth?" Chief Joseph asked President Andrew Johnson, "We do not own earth, water or air. We are a part of all things. I wish to be a free man who lives and thrives with land where I was born. And my father's fathers and my mother's mothers were born, in the beginning of time."

~

In the 1800's, most white poets and playwrights ignored the horrors of slavery. Black authors like Armand Lanuss, Pierre Dalcour and Victor Sejour mostly ignored slavery too. But thankfully, other black authors like

Phillis Wheatley, George Moses Horton, and Frances E. W. Harper had the courage to speak out and write.

Harper was born in 1825, educated in Baltimore, worked for the Underground Railroad, Anti-Slavery Society of Maine and wrote, "The Sale: Young girls were there, defenseless in their wretchedness, whose stifled sobs of deep despair revealed their anguish and distress. And mothers stood with streaming eyes and saw their dearest child sold. Unheeded rose their bitter cries while tyrants bartered them for gold. Ye may not know how desolate, are bosoms widely forced to part, and how a dull and heavy weight will press the life—drops from the heart."

In 1852, whites asked Frederick Douglas to help celebrate the Fourth of July by giving a speech. I imagined Douglas went home, had a shot of whiskey and wrote "You Must Be the Dumbest Mother Fuckers on the Planet." Then had another shot and crossed that out.

Instead, Douglas asked the almost all-white crowd, "What to the Slave Is the Fourth of July? The sunlight that brought life and healing to you, has brought stripes and death to me. This Fourth of July is yours, not mine. You may rejoice, I must mourn … Fellow citizens, above your national, tumultuous joy I hear the mournful wail of millions. To forget them, to pass lightly over their wrongs, and to chime in with the popular theme, would be treason most scandalous and shocking and would make me reproach before God and the world."

"To side with the right, against the wrong," Douglas poured it on, "with the weak against the strong, and with the oppressed against the oppressor! Here lies the merit, and the one which, of all others, seems unfashionable in our day."

~

Langston Hughes (1901–1967) wrote, "I know you washwoman," to celebrate millions of black women who remain unheralded, though they were the backbone of everything that turned out right. "I know how you send your children to school, even college. You work and help your man when times are hard. Build your house up from the wash-tub and call it home. Raise your churches from white suds for the service of the Holy

God. And I've seen you singing, wash-woman … Singing, hanging, white clothes on long lines in the sun-shine. And I've seen you in church on Sunday morning singing, praising your Jesus, because some day you're going to sit on the right hand of the Son of God and forget you ever were a wash-woman. And the aching back and the bundles of clothes will be unremembered then. Yes, I've seen you singing."

~

In the 1970's June Jordan asked, "Tell me something, what you think would happen if every time they kill a black boy, then we kill a cop? 18 cops in order to subdue one man. 18 strangled him to death in the ensuing scuffle (don't you idolize the diction of the powerful: *subdue* and *scuffle,* my oh my) and that the murder, that the killing of Arthur Miller on a Brooklyn street was just a 'Justifiable accident' again (again). People been having accidents all over the globe so long I reckon the only suitable insurance is a gun. I'm saying war is not to understand or rerun, war is to be fought and won."

~

"The railroads were the first large industrial users of the water belonging to the land and people," Simon Ortiz wrote in the 1980's, because our government has never stopped lying to Native Americans, "they found it easy enough to get, they simply took it. Choice Aacqumeh lands … the railroads took Navajo people's land too … it was easy enough to disregard the farming livelihood that was taken away."

~

Rapper Tupac Shakur was aware of how 'divide and conquer' devastated him and his community. In his rap, "Only God Can Judge Me," he illustrates how most people who get caught in cycles of violence, actually want out, "Is it a crime to fight for what is mine? I been trapped since birth – cautious 'cuz I'm cursed – fantasies of my family in the hearse – and they say it's the white man I should fear, but it's my own kind doing all the kill'n here – and all my memories, of seeing brothers bleed, and everybody grieves, but still nobody sees – recollect your thoughts don't get caught up in the mix, 'cuz the media's full of dirty tricks ... I'd rather die like a man, than live like a coward – there's a ghetto up in heaven and it's say'n, Black Power – is what we scream when we dream in a paranoid state, and our fate is a lifetime of hate."

~

The heart of my thesis focuses on MLK Jr. Nonviolence is not just refraining from attacking others, but learning to like them. A struggle poignantly illustrated in MLK Jr.'s famous "I Have a Dream" speech, "This sweltering summer of the Negro's legitimate discontent will not pass until there is an invigorating autumn of freedom and equality. The whirlwinds of revolt will continue to shake the foundation of our nation until the bright day of justice emerges. We must forever conduct our struggle on the high plane of dignity and discipline. We must not allow our creative protest to degenerate into physical violence. Again and again we must rise to the majestic heights of meeting physical force with soul force. Some of you have come from areas where your quest for freedom left you battered by the storms of persecution and staggered by the winds of police brutality. You have been the veterans of creative suffering. Continue to work with the faith that unearned suffering is redemptive."

~

But it is Chief Seattle who speaks to the soul of my thesis. A voice I hear most clearly in the mountains. Reminding me to work hard, and show love and respect for all things.

Spring of 2003 I went backpacking to unplug for a couple nights. I started up the 7 mile trail to Crystal Lake in Rocky Mountain National Park at 8 am. Dark clouds hung low and rain was forecast (I love to play in the rain—volleyball, golf, fish—whatever). A mile up the trail fog thickened and visibility shrunk to ten feet. A mile later the fog quickly lifted and rain fell out of the sky like out of a faucet. I was soaked before I could drop my bag, zip the pocket, pull out and put on my poncho. A mile later I saw a grove of pine and aspen thick enough to stop most of the downpour, so I sat and had some water and cashews.

The sun was approaching its peak but it was dark. And aside from rain crashing off everything, it was quiet and still.

This storm isn't going anywhere, I thought, then remembered the steep parts of the next couple of miles to the lake. So when I saw a pad of leaves and needles well above where rain would gather and run, I set up my tent, got on dry clothes, lounged in the thermo-chair, drank rum from the flask and read, <u>The Enlightened Heart: An Anthology of Sacred Poetry</u>: Book of Psalms, Upanishads, Bhagavad Gita, Francis of Assisi, Rumi, Dante, Kabir, Shakespeare, Basho, Blake, Whitman, Dickenson, Yeats, Rilke. I highlighted Lao-tzu:

"Some say that my teaching is nonsense. Others call it lofty but impractical. But to those who have looked inside themselves, this nonsense makes perfect sense. And to those who put it into practice, this loftiness has roots that go deep. I have just three things to teach: simplicity; patience; compassion. These three are your greatest treasures. Simple in actions and in thoughts, you return to the source of being. Patient with both friends and enemies, you accord with the way things are. Compassionate toward yourself, you reconcile all beings in the world."

The storm stuck around, for 48 hours. I ate and went to the bathroom in various degrees of a downpour. Though dark and wet it was surprisingly warm, so whenever I left the tent I didn't bother with my poncho and headed out with just the same wet socks, shorts, t-shirt, and hat.

On the way to fish the lake I stopped under a large pine. Ate hard salami, spray cheese, crackers, and a hand full of soft toffees. Again too lazy to hike the final stretch, I fished a tiny creek with no fish—casting and presenting on small flows and eddies that were challenging targets—stayed sharp for the shrewd 18-22 inchers that lurk in larger rivers.

I spent the afternoon in the tent reading Rumi, "Out beyond ideas of wrong-doing and right-doing, there is a field. I'll meet you there. When the soul lies down in that grass, the world is too full to talk about. Ideas, language, even the phrase *each other*, doesn't make sense."

The rain hammered harder and the temperature dropped. I pictured the clouds growing thousands of feet straight up, releasing millions more gallons of ice towards earth. I had a good buzz from the rum, was warm in my sleeping bag, and fell asleep.

I dreamed I spent the afternoon and evening in a teepee with Chiefs Niwot, Joseph, and Seattle.

It started snowing mid-day and by nightfall twelve inches covered everything while huge flakes were still pouring down. Fire made the teepee warm. We enjoyed tobacco, buffalo jerky, and ice cold water fresh from the river.

"I spoke plainly to the US government too" Chief Seattle said, "I wrote a letter that said 'One thing we know, which the white man may one day discover, our God is the same God. He is the God of man and his compassion is equal for the red man and the white. This earth is precious to Him and to harm the earth is to heap contempt on its Creator ... Continue to contaminate your own bed and you will one night suffocate in your own waste. If we sell our land, love it as we've loved it ... Hold in your mind the memory of the land as it is when you take it. And preserve it for your children and love it – as God loves us all. One thing we know, our God is the same God. This earth is precious to Him. Even the white man cannot be exempt from the common destiny. We may be brothers after all. We shall see ...'"

We nodded, smiled, ate, drank and basked in the brilliant fire.

I woke up alert and energized, like after a flying dream. I vowed to help people understand that between paradoxes in language, and being taught a violent history filled with greed, jealousy, lust, guilt, and vengeance, we all speak and act with prejudice.

Still, if we can be honest, apologize, and forgive, we can learn how to help each other pursue what makes us happy.

Poetry

Fall of 2003 I parked in front of a Jefferson County school and panicked.

What am I going to do if the kids don't get it or don't care? I felt like throwing up, *How much good can a poetry workshop do? What if my curriculum gets exposed for the peace loving, liberal propaganda that it is? The teacher hadn't paid me yet, I could just drive away.*
    Two years, a crap load of effort and money to earn that MFA just to come up with this curriculum.

I took a few deep breaths and the nausea went away. Then I gathered my notes, book of large pad of butcher paper, tape, brand new box of colored markers, and walked into the school to give my first Poetry to Celebrate Life workshop.

The teacher greeted me with a huge smile. We met golfing that summer.

"I was born and raised in Boulder," I said walking down the first fairway.

Then we noted how few natives are still around, "Especially black ones," she added with a smile.

I thought about how the few minorities who are able to come to Boulder, quickly end up leaving. They get tired of the innuendos and having to answer questions on behalf of all minorities again and again. Each incident is innocent enough, but the frequency drips on the forehead like a form of water torture.

"Yah," I chuckled, "I'm a strange bird."

She laughed.

"I taught K - 3rd grade literacy in BVSD for a year," I answered walking up the second fairway, "and have been getting a Master's degree in writing for the last two."

"I teach 3ʳᵈ grade," she replied, "I love teaching."

"Yah, I love working with kids, too," I said, "I'm head coach of girls-volleyball at Fairview, substitute K - 12 in BVSD, and am looking for ways to teach the poetry workshops I developed."

We talked throughout the round. Walking off the 18ᵗʰ green she asked if I'd do a workshop with her class in the fall adding, "I have grant money to pay you."

~

While watching NFL football in 2002 I saw a story on Pat Tillman, an undersized overachieving defensive safety for the Arizona Cardinals. Tillman was troubled by 9/11 and felt a moral obligation to fight al-Qaeda and the Taliban. So he walked away from a $3.6 million contract to enlist in the United States Army.

I felt connected to Tillman. We were both in our prime and left opportunities to play a game we loved. I imagined Tillman cleaned out his locker and thought, "Way to man up," like I did when driving out of L.A. Still, leaving the NFL, Tillman gave up a lot more money and prestige than I did. Plus, he left for a war zone. So I vowed to work harder.

~

"Stereotype is one word made with two words," I began and wrote *stereotype* in black across the top of the first page of butcher paper.

Then I drew a blue vertical line down the middle of the paper and wrote *stereo* across the top of the left half. And *type* across the top on the right.

"*Stereo*, is having multiple speakers hooked up to the same radio; each speaker playing the same song," I said, then drew four black speakers and red lines to show them blasting.

"*Type*, is a group of people or things with the same traits and/or characteristics. For example," I said and drew stick figures to illustrate, "some like long hair and dresses; some like short hair, suits and ties; some dunk basketballs; others play guitar; some love to read."

"*Stereotype*," I said and wrote along the bottom of the page, "is an assumption about people based on them having similar interests, traits and/or characteristics."

"Boys can be stereotyped," I said as I tore off the first page and taped it to the white board. Then I drew a blue horizontal line across the middle of the clean page, wrote *boys* in black in the middle of the top half and asked, "What do boys like?"

A few students raised their hands. "Football," one said.

"Excellent," I replied and wrote *football* in purple in the top half and asked, "What else do boys like?' A dozen hands shot up and I wrote: *cars, soccer, video games, baseball, basketball, comic books, recess,* and *snakes.*

"I've taught and coached kids for a decade and have known a lot of boys who like," I said as I used my green marker to circle: *football, basketball, cars, recess.*

"Girls can be stereotyped," I said and wrote in black in the middle of the bottom half under the boys cluster and asked, "What do girls like?"

I wrote in purple: *dolls, dancing, school, dresses, make-up, shopping,* and *volleyball.*

But as the list grew, students started to object, "Some girls don't like to shop," one girl spoke up. "Yah," said a boy, "Some boys don't like snakes."

"Good, I'm glad you're also noticing how," I replied tearing the brainstorm from the pad, taping it to the white board, then writing in red at the top of a clean sheet of paper and saying "Stereotypes are wrong!"

"Some boys don't like recess, video games, or sports," I further detailed, "Some girls don't like make-up, dolls, or dancing."

"Look," I continued, "we stereotype for good reasons," and pointed to the boys cluster and the words circled in green, "After a decade as a coach and teacher I've inspired a lot of boys with lessons and rewards having to do with sports, cars, and recess. Still, when stereotypes refer to hundreds of millions of people, like boys, girls, blacks, whites, Latinos, Europeans, or Africans—*millions* will not fit the mold."

"Not only do stereotypes cause us to judge *millions* of people incorrectly," I continued, "stereotypes make it hard to celebrate one of humanity's greatest gifts," I said and then wrote in purple in the middle of the page, "Everyone is unique!"

"There never has been, nor will there ever be another," I said and gestured towards students reading the name tags on their desks, "Nick, Stephanie, or Jasmine. Everyone in this class is one-of-a-kind. Each of you has your own strengths, weaknesses, fears, hopes and dreams."

"240 years ago America's Founding Fathers wrote The Declaration of Independence," I summarized part one of the workshop. And at the bottom of my paper underneath "Stereotypes are wrong!" and "Everyone is unique!" I wrote in black: "We hold these truths to be self-evident; all people are created equal and are endowed with unalienable rights—like the pursuit of happiness."

~

Pat Tillman was killed in Afghanistan on April 22, 2004. When I first heard that I thought about all he gave up: family, friends, pro football, and money. I wondered how his family and friends were dealing with the long, dark, grief-filled nights. And how easily modern weapons snuff out the fastest, toughest, and smartest. Then I wrote a poem berating war-makers.

That evening I drove up Flagstaff Mountain, watched the sun set over the 14,000 thousand foot peak, burned my rant, and meditated, "For Tillman," was my mantra as I renewed my efforts to be a soldier for peace.

~

"Think of a time when you were happy," I began part two of my workshop, "maybe a celebration with family and friends. Maybe you were alone. Maybe you were in a special place. Or received an award, or some other good news."

"One of my happiest moments was at a swimming pool in Boulder," I said, then wrote in the middle of a clean sheet, "Scott Carpenter Swimming Pool: First jump off the high-dive."

"Now, pick a moment when you were happy," I continued, "and write a title in the middle of your paper."

"Next you're going to close your eyes, take a few breaths and picture yourself there," I went on, "Who was with you? What were people doing and saying? What was in your surroundings? How did you feel? Was it sunny; snowing; raining? What did you smell?"

"*Scared*," I said and wrote next to my title as an example, "*nervous, excited, confident, Motherlode, Florida,*" I kept going, "*popsicles, lotion, chlorine ...*"

"Keep writing until the entire page is full. Don't stop to think of the perfect word, write down whatever comes to mind."

"For example," I pointed out, "After, *confident* I wrote, *Motherlode*. That's a Pro/Am volleyball tournament that happens every Labor Day weekend in Aspen. 600 teams, professionals and Olympic athletes from throughout North America come to play. And I won that tournament four times."

"Then I wrote, *Florida*. Because in one Motherlode final, I served four aces and other great serves that led to easy points in a dominant 15-5 win. Which reminded me of being in Florida, doing a drill and serving 20 balls in a row when the stand-out pro beach volleyball veteran I was training with said he'd never seen anyone serve that well."

"Also, don't worry about making sure each word is spelled correctly," I added, "There is a time to worry about spelling, but it's not now. Think about the meaning, sound it out, make a good guess, and start writing the next word that comes to mind."

The room was silent. Students brainstormed and wrote. I walked around:

"How did you *feel* at your recital?"

"What were the crazy Denver Bronco fans wearing?"

"*Enthusiastic*, great word!"

"Three minutes," I finally announced. "If you've filled the page keep going on the back. Next, I'm going to show you how to turn your cluster of words into a poem."

~

Jon Krakauer wrote, <u>Where Men Win Glory: The Odyssey of Pat Tillman</u>. He also wrote: <u>Into Thin Air</u>, <u>Under the Banner of Heaven</u>, and <u>Into the Wild</u> (part of what inspired me to leave pro volleyball). I identify with Krakauer's observations on the beauty and peril in human- and mother-nature.

"It's amazing the turns one's life can take," Tillman wrote in his diary on July 28, 2002, "In my life there have been a number [like leaving the NFL for the Army]… But on top of my list, as odd as this sounds, a diving catch I made in the 11-12 all-stars was a take-off point. I excelled the rest of the tournament and gained incredible confidence. It sounds tacky but it was big."

~

"You can change the title later," I continued part two of the workshop, "but I'm having you start with "What I want is _____," because I agree with The Declaration of Independence." Then I walked to the white board and pointed at the words as I read, "We hold these truths to be self-evident that all people are created equal and are endowed with unalienable rights—like the pursuit of happiness."

"Writing about what you want can help you achieve it," I further explained, "When I wanted to be a professional beach volleyball player I wrote clusters, statements, and essays on goals and skills. Then reviewed my writing and rewrote—reviewed and rewrote—reviewed and rewrote. Again and again I painted a clearer picture. Told a better story."

"What I Want," I said and wrote as the title at the top of a clean sheet, "Is To Jump Off the High Dive."

"Sometimes," I said, "I like to start a poem like I'm filming with a camera and simply describe what I see in the lens. I could also choose words from my cluster to begin. But today I'm going to describe the pool through my camera, looking from an airplane," then wrote.

From an airplane
The pool looks like an L
Short leg is the deep end
Two spring boards and a high dive

"Now, I'll describe more of what I see as my camera zooms in," I went on, "and add how I felt."

It's a long climb – first time
Up the wet steps of the high dive
Goose bumps grow as I ascend
Each step closer to freezing – petrified

"Back to what I saw and some of what I heard," I said and wrote,

But I keep shuffling in the long slow line
Finally, the boy in front of me steps to edge
Jumps and disappears
"Cannon baaaaalll" – sploosh!

"Then end with feelings and a final shot with the camera,"

I step weakly to the edge
Look for my landing and jump
Pointed toes – straight legs and back – Splash!
Swim to the edge and start the long climb
Back to the top.

~

In <u>Where Men Win Glory</u>, I wasn't shocked to read that most of the two dozen soldiers on site thought Tillman's own platoon had fired the fatal shots. Or that the Army kept this information from Tillman's wife, family and the American public for five weeks following his death. Or that President Bush repeatedly invoked Tillman to promote his administration's foreign policy. Or that long after Tillman's nationally televised memorial service, the Army told his closest relatives that Tillman had "probably" been killed by friendly fire.

I also wasn't shocked to read the first American soldier killed in Afghanistan died of friendly fire as well. A radio man was reading coordinates for their bombing target when the batteries in the device died. Quickly, he replaced the batteries and read the coordinates. Seconds later the bombs fell. Tragically, when he put the new batteries in the device the coordinates were reset, so that instead of reading their target's coordinates, he read his own.

Friendly fire; civilians caught in crossfire; city blocks turned into infernos, I remembered Civil War hero General William T. Sherman saying, "War is cruelty. There is no use trying to reform it, the crueler it is, the sooner it will be over ... War is at best barbarism, its glory all moonshine." Still, Sherman regularly condemned the media to make sure the whole truth was not told too often. "I hate newspapermen. They come into camp and pick up their camp rumors and print them as facts. I regard them as spies, which in fact, they are."

And 140 years later, the national spotlight shines on only parts of Tillman's story.

~

"One of the reasons I love poetry," I told the 3rd graders in my first workshop, "is that you don't have to follow so many rules like spelling, grammar, and punctuation. Still, even poetry has guidelines for delivering messages that are more clear and powerful."

"Line Breaks are like periods," I wrote and said, "Use them to signal a complete thought, idea or picture. Like the first four lines in my poem," I pointed and read, *"From an airplane; the pool looks like an L; short leg is the deep end; two diving boards and a high dive."*

"Details make writing interesting," I pointed again, "instead of 'I step to the edge,' I wrote, 'I step *weakly* to the edge.' Instead of "Up the steps," I wrote, 'Up the *wet* steps ....' And after jumping, I make a more detailed picture by adding, *pointed toes – straight legs and back.*"

"Word choice also makes writing interesting. So rather than adding more words, choose a different word for a more accurate description. I used two words to describe jumping into a pool – *sploosh* for the boy in front of me because it sounds far away – *splash* for me because it's more in your face. I used *freezing* and *petrified* to describe how difficult it was for me to move. You can also find new and interesting words in a thesaurus. It's like a dictionary and under *frozen* and *petrified* you'll find words like *solid* and *fossilized*."

"Rhythm gives a poem depth and feeling," I wrote and said, "Length of lines and syllables affect the rhythm. So does rhyme and alliteration."

"Rhyme is using words that end with the same sounds," I continued, "Rhyming helps the reader anticipate so sentences roll off the tongue. There's one rhyme in my poem, 'It's a long climb – first time.' Rhyming is fun to read but difficult to write," I warned, "My poetry rarely rhymes. Even Dr. Seuss, one of the best of all time, makes up a ton of words."

"Alliteration means using words that start with the same sounds. I don't have it in my poem, but an example is, "Sally sells sea shells by the sea shore."

"Now it's time for you to write," I announced, "Don't get stuck trying to make your poem perfect right away—it won't be. All great writers revise and I'll talk more about that important work later. But for now, look at your title and cluster of words, picture yourself there, take a few deep breaths and start writing. Don't stop writing for long. If you get stuck, find a word in your cluster or camera and start writing."

~

"The right-wing harridan Ann Coulter," Krakauer wrote in <u>Where Men Win Glory</u>, "claimed [Tillman] as an exemplar of Republican political values. The left-wing editorial cartoonist Ted Rall denigrated him in a four-panel comic strip as an 'idiot' who joined the Army to 'kill Arabs.' Neither Coulter nor Rall had any idea what motivated Pat Tillman. Beyond his family and small circle of close friends," Krakauer asserted, "few people did."

Pat enlisted with his younger brother Kevin. When their uncle and Pat's agent were unable to talk them out of it, Pat's parents set up an intervention with Pat's wife Marie and her family.

"Okay!" Marie's sister recalled Pat opening the discussion, "Tell me whatever you want to tell me! Throw it out there, and I'll respond as best I can. Bring it on!"

"Pat believed," Marie told Krakauer, "that everybody had a right to tell him what they thought and to try and talk him out of it."

The conversation began orderly, with Pat's mother bringing up her fear of her boys getting hurt or killed. Pat and Kevin insisted that wasn't going to happen.

When it was clear fear of personal injury and death wouldn't convince the two to abandon their plans the group turned to Marie.

"But I didn't feel like I needed to answer to anyone, not even our families," Marie told Krakauer. "It was between Pat and me. I understood why he was doing it, and I supported him. Our conversations about how this decision came about were really nobody's business."

Marie's father appealed to Pat's economic rationale, pointing out that Pat would be leaving at the peak of his career, and the peak of his market value as a player. He might not even be able to return to the NFL. "Pat countered that he would be away from football for only three years," Krakauer wrote, "and would probably have no trouble playing again."

"The emphasis on the financial downside pushed Pat's mother over the edge," Krakauer continued, "'Why are you talking about money?!' she exclaimed, 'this isn't about money! Pat and Kevin could get killed!' She began to sob ... She reminded them that the current commander in chief of the nation's Armed Forces was not a man who inspired trust or confidence. Then, as her emotions got the better of her, she asked everyone to leave."

"Pat cared a lot about the people around him," Marie assured Krakauer, "He didn't hurt people on purpose. It killed him that it hurt his mom or hurt me. That was very, very difficult for him to handle. But he had to do what he thought was right."

~

I walked around the 3rd grade classroom and checked in with each student, "I see students want to be lawyers, teachers, doctors, scientists, pro-athletes, and hang out with friends," I announced, "everyone has chosen excellent topics."

I also gave individual feedback.

"I like how your line breaks emphasize the *ocean* and *sea turtles*."

"Great details, I can really picture your back yard."

"Fantastic rhyming (every workshop seemed to have one with the gift)."

I checked the time, gave them a three minute warning to wrap up, and took a moment to enjoy that we'd gone an hour and the students were still engaged.

"Excellent work," I announced, "everyone is off to a great start, but this is just a first draft. To make your poem more powerful, you'll need to revise. Tomorrow or next week, you might remember important details, learn new words or skills, or decide to take something out. The clearer the picture, the better the story—the greater the chance your dreams will come true."

"I'm with you just for today," I continued, "but, your teacher is going to help you revise and said she'll send me copies of your final drafts. I look forward to reading them. But we still have about ten minutes and I was hoping some of you would like to share."

"It's important to read your poetry aloud for two reasons," I emphasized, "First, because having the courage to stand up and tell others your dreams, like writing them down, increases the chances they'll come true. Second, when others tell us what makes them happy, we learn ways to appreciate, respect, and celebrate them."

~

Tillman did have quality leaders, made good friends, and excelled as a soldier. But it wasn't always easy for him.

"The first indication that it might prove difficult for Pat to adapt to the Army's hidebound ways," Krakauer wrote, "occurred when Pat, Kevin, and several other recruits lined up before an especially abrasive master sergeant who began shouting contradictory orders at them before they'd signed any documents committing to enlist. Pat felt compelled to point out to the master sergeant, 'Hey, you're confusing everybody. Besides, you're treating us like assholes, and we haven't even signed up to be treated like assholes yet' ... [The Sergeant] jumped down Pat's throat. Unintimidated, Pat yelled right back at him, and the two men came close to exchanging blows ... Still, Pat and Kevin signed on."

"Pat had been introspective since childhood," Krakauer continued, "but the Army seemed to make him even more so. 'What kind of man will I become?' [Tillman asked in his journal], 'Will people see me as an honest man, hard-working man, family man, a good man? Can I become the man I envision? Is vision and follow-through enough? How important is talent and blind luck? ... There are no true answers, just shades of grey, coincidence and circumstance."

"Sometimes, I'm overwhelmed with an injection of intense sorrow that is difficult to control," Tillman also wrote, "An intense need to be close to Marie, surrounded by her touch, smell, sound, beauty, and ease ... Just when I think my emotions have flat-lined they rear their ugly head. Yesterday, from out of nowhere, I got so fucking mad/upset/sad that I was having trouble maintaining my cool. It only lasted a short while but it was strong and surprised me. All I wanted was to squeeze Marie, tell her how much I care, give her back all that I've taken ..."

"You know what we did today?" Tillman's struggles continued, "We fucking sat in our platoon area all day. For four hours we cleaned weapons, for another three or so we sat with our rucksacks taking inventory and collecting our linens. It may have been the most unproductive day of my life. This place is fucking tired."

"Often I am so disgusted with the people I'm surrounded with that my heart fills with hate." Tillman vented, "I've been exposed to an element of people that can be worse than any I've encountered, including in Juvenile Hall. They're resentful, ungrateful, lazy, weak, and unvirtuous, as often as not. They bicker, complain, lie, tell tall tales, mope and grumble incessantly …"

"Illegal as hell," Tillman wrote of the Iraq war.

"My heart goes out to those who will suffer," he continued in a tent in a desert 35 miles outside Iraq when 'Shock and Awe' began, "Whatever your politics, whatever you believe is right or wrong, the fact is most of those who will feel the wrath of this ordeal want nothing more than to live peacefully."

~

When I asked the 3rd grade class who wanted to share I got the usual ratio: a few hands would shoot up even if strapped to a 200 pound dumbbell; a few would not if strapped to a rocket. And one went up … down … up … down … until we talked her into it.

"Everyone gives the person who shares a round of applause," I emphasized, "I'm not saying you have to like everyone's poetry equally, it usually works out that you'll think some are better than others; be as loud as you want for them. But even if you don't understand someone's poetry, they deserve a hand for showing the courage it takes to share."

Most students received the standard applause. A couple received boisterous laughs and cheers. All sat down – back straight – chin up.

"It's ok that some didn't share today," I said, "but I hope everyone shares a final draft. And it's most important," I emphasized, "that you listen for ways to respect and celebrate each other."

"That's our time," I concluded, "Thanks for being a part of my first ever Poetry to Celebrate Life workshop. I had fun. I hope you did too."

An hour and fifteen minutes after starting, I gathered my markers, tape, and paper, went to the other 3rd grade classroom and gave them the same lesson.

~

On the day Tillman was killed, his patrol was divided into two teams. When fighting echoed down the canyon from one team's position, "Tillman sprang into action," Krakauer wrote, "'Pat was like a freight

227

train,' said Private Josey Boatright recalling how Tillman sprinted past him."

"O'Neal! On me! O'Neal! Stay on me!" Tillman commanded, "Let's go help our boys."

"And he started moving," O'Neal testified, "And wherever he went, I went."

An Afghan soldier named Syed Farhad joined Tillman and O'Neal and they took position over-looking the mouth of the canyon—steep incline—barren except for a few boulders.

"Minutes later two vehicles came speeding out of the canyon and stopped ninety yards beneath the boulders," Krakauer continued, "Several Rangers climbed out of a Humvee and gazed up toward Tillman and O'Neal, who waved to let their buddies know they were up there and had them covered. It appeared as though Serial Two had escaped the ambush and everything was copacetic. And then, without warning, hundreds of bullets began to pulverize the slope around Tillman, O'Neal and Farhad."

A Ranger armed with a machine gun that fires ten-round bursts testified that he "identified two sets of arms straight up,' through the scope of his weapon, 'I saw the arms waving, but didn't think they were trying to signal a cease-fire.' So he pulled the trigger again and sprayed them with another ten-round burst."

Despite corroborated testimony, there remains a cloud of mystery over Tillman's death, "The Associated Press," Krakauer wrote, "published an article reporting that the Navy pathologist who performed Tillman's autopsy testified that the forensic evidence indicated Tillman had been shot three times in the head from a distance of thirty-five feet or less."

Tillman had become a good soldier—but even the best training can't overcome the confusion of ideas and loyalties that are part of war.

~

Chaplin and Army Captain Jeff Struecker held a meeting for soldiers struggling with Tillman's death. Struecker, famous for surviving the firefight depicted in the best-selling book and movie <u>Black Hawk Down</u>, said it really helped him to talk about what happened, instead of carrying it around inside.

"I didn't know what the long-term effects would be," said former Ranger Mel Ward, friend of Tillman who attended Struecker's meetings, "You see these old guys on the History Channel talking about being in World War II. A guy will still be bawling over some friend that died sixty years earlier. I don't want to be that guy. So I talked about what happened, my little piece of it. Others did too."

"Ward didn't judge any of the other soldiers, even the shooters—not initially," Krakauer continued, "But then he heard that some of them may have gotten together and changed their stories between the first investigation and the second, 'Friendly fire happens,' Ward says, 'But if someone has lied or changed their story, they can fucking hang. I don't care who they are. If you are going to lie and cover up what happened to someone who gave their life, who believed so firmly in the importance of coming over here that he left his wife without a husband—then you deserve to fucking swing.'"

"If I had been killed that day," Ward explained part of why he didn't reenlist, "and it had not suited the Army to disclose to my wife the manner in which I died, nobody would ever know what really happened because I'm not famous. I'm not Pat. It wouldn't have been a news story. For the rest of her life, my wife would think I was killed by whatever bullshit story they decided to make up. They'd write up a couple of medals like they did for him, and that would be it."

Thus it has always been, and always will be, Krakauer lamented in the prologue. In war, truth is the first casualty.

Mostly because the reality is too devastating to speak and write about. Healing requires finding a path forward. My poetry curriculum is a powerful tool to teach people to be honest about their experiences.

~

I received a package from the 3rd grade classes in October 2003. Beautifully written final drafts with illustrations. The packet included a pleasant surprise: thank you letters.

Nick wrote: "I had fun with you. My favorite part was when we did poetry. We had really fun! It was a blast together. It was the greatest time in my life. I want you to come to school with me every day. It was fantastic."

Birva wrote: "Thank you for coming to our class. I enjoyed it a lot. What I learned is that if girls are popular, then it doesn't mean that boys aren't popular. We really appreciate you. I learned a lot of new things."

Jasmine wrote: "Thank you for coming to our class room today. We enjoyed the company. You are a great man. I hope you can come again another day. I learned that some people like some things more than other people."

I decided to put more time and energy into the workshops.

Focus

I listened to and read conservative media regularly from 2000 through 2003. The way they attacked liberals made it hard, but I was searching for common ground. I stopped in 2003. I still felt that some liberal views should be criticized and those who do so aren't bad people. But as the horror of September 11 and dust of 'Shock and Awe' settled, I felt the rhetoric in conservative media was making everyone overly fearful, angry, and judgmental. Or more importantly, I knew their rhetoric was making me overly fearful, angry, and judgmental.

~

I considered developing Poetry to Celebrate Life curriculum for high school and college level students. Looking for age appropriate material and having heard that President Bush read it, I picked up the New York Times bestseller, Bias: CBS Insider Exposes How the Media Distorts the News, by Bernard Goldberg. Goldberg was a reporter and producer for CBS News for 28 years and won seven Emmy Awards. He'd also written op-eds for the New York Times, Wall Street Journal, and Washington Post.

"A must read," says a quote from The Wall Street Journal on the cover, "[Goldberg's] case is airtight."

After the introduction and first chapter I agreed that Bias is a must read. But was alarmed that the WSJ called his case "airtight." It was frightening to see how easily people justify treating others unfairly just because they've been treated unfairly.

~

"They Think You're a Traitor," Goldberg emphasizes in bold, "I have it on good authority that my liberal friends in the news media, who account for about 98 percent of all my friends in the news media, are planning a big party to congratulate me for writing this book ... media stars will make speeches thanking me for actually saying what they either can't or won't ... they'll thank me for agreeing with Roger Ailes of Fox News that the media divides Americans into two groups – moderates and right-wing nuts."

Goldberg writes two more paragraphs describing the honors he expects to receive from his liberal friends until he clarifies that the date for his ceremony is set for, "exactly three days after hell freezes over."

"Okay, maybe that's too harsh." Goldberg continues, still in bold, "Maybe, in a cheap attempt to be funny, I'm maligning and stereotyping the media elites as a bunch of powerful arrogant, thin-skinned celebrity journalists who can dish it out, which they routinely do on their newscasts, but can't take it. Except I don't think so ..."

Goldberg begins his book with four paragraphs of biting sarcasm, I noted. *What an ass.*

"What made writing this book so hard," Goldberg claims two paragraphs later, "was that I was writing about people I have known for many years, people who are or were once my friends. It's not easy telling you that Dan Rather whom I have worked with and genuinely like for most of my adult life, really is two very different people; while one Dan is funny and generous, the other is ruthless and unforgiving."

First, I agree with the media stars. Unlike Goldberg's assertion, "Reasonable" and "civilized" people do not kill to show killing is wrong; do not bitch about 40 years of affirmative action after 400 years of slavery and segregation; do not hesitate to give LBGTQ people equal rights; and do not tell women what to do with their bodies and lives.

Second, these networks are not liberal extremists. Any liberal extremist knows the networks don't spend near enough time covering the need for reparations: race, gender, and class. Or addressing how everyone benefits with free, quality, education and health care. Or recognizing how expanded welfare could provide young under-educated women options besides getting pregnant or needing abortions. Or considering the potential benefits of investment in infrastructure and rehabilitation in prisons, drug addiction and mental health facilities.

Third, anyone who describes his friends of thirty years as "arrogant" and "thin skinned," and then calls one of his closest funny/generous and ruthless/unforgiving, is bound to be in the running for hypocrite of the year.

This book is destined for the compost. Except, it's a New York Times best seller, so I'll at least finish the introduction.

~

Naropa, graduates were given the opportunity to share with faculty, staff, classmates and their families on graduation weekend.

"First," I began, "I'd like to thank my mom, Oma, and step-dad. They gave me the financial and emotional support that made attending Naropa possible."

"I'd also like to thank the Naropa community: classmates, professors and other faculty. I would never have received this educational experience in Kansas (where I got my BA), or many colleges and universities across the nation. Thanks to Naropa's deliberate, outspoken commitment to mindfulness, compassion and diversity, I pursued and developed a curriculum I wish I'd been taught as a bi-racial boy who is identified as black and raised by white women in a white community."

"Still, the Naropa community must remember it's in Boulder Colorado," I warned, "And, our government just embarked on one of the most extensive propaganda campaigns in history to label entire nations of dark-skinned people "evil," and start a "preemptive" war. And while I know most in Naropa's community disagree with the White House administration's narrow world views and military aggression, no one is immune to spreading stereotypes and fear. Especially in a town where minorities feel alienated, a place White Supremacists might like to call home, and the wealthy boast of progress while the market drives out the poor."

I continued, "I was accepted into the, Jack Kerouac School of Disembodied Poetics, but knew little about Kerouac or Beat Poetry, and often felt excluded. Classmates and professors spoke about how being a starving artist and out of the American mainstream made them 'down-to-earth', but they could be as judgmental as athletes earning millions in sports entertainment. I'm grateful for Naropa because it's the most open and thoughtful school I've attended. But remember," I concluded, "even the best can get better."

~

"When Peter Jennings," Goldberg continues, "was asked about liberal bias on Larry King Live, [Jennings] said, 'I think bias is very largely in the eye of the beholder.' This might offend the two or three conservative friends I have, but I think Peter is right, except that instead of saying '*very largely*' he could have left it as '*sometimes*'. Because some people who complain about liberal bias think Al Roker the weatherman is out to get conservatives just because he forecasts rain on the Fourth of July. And others who say they want the news without bias really mean they want it without *liberal* bias."

> *Bias **is** largely in the eye of the beholder. Not just because some conservatives blame Al Roker for bad weather, but because some liberals think the evening news isn't liberal. A liberal news network doesn't just show MLK Jr.'s* I Have a Dream *speech. A liberal network shows MLK. Jr.'s speech on the need for a living wage, the social and economic impacts of war.*

"[Poverty is] a second evil," MLK Jr. said at his 1964 Nobel Peace Prize address, "There is nothing new about poverty. What is new, however, is that we have the resources to get rid of it ... The time has come for an all-out world war against poverty ... The rich nations must use their vast resources of wealth to develop the underdeveloped, school the unschooled, and feed the unfed. Ultimately a great nation is a compassionate nation. No individual or nation can be great if it does not have a concern for 'the least of these.'"

> *A liberal network shows how the next revolution of love and kindness has the potential to end poverty.*

~

"It's important to know, too," Goldberg continues, "that there isn't a well-orchestrated, vast left-wing conspiracy in America's newsrooms. The bitter truth, as we'll see, is arguably worse … Even though I attack liberal *bias*, not liberal *values*, I will be portrayed by some of my old friends as a right-wing ideologue."

No shit. After the first four spiteful paragraphs, a sentence in the middle of page four about not wanting to attack liberal values still amounts to slander. Spoon feeding headlines like – The Bitter Truth: Liberal News Worse Than Vast Left Wing Conspiracy, *to right wing propagandists who have been preaching America's decline since liberals marched for civil rights.*

~

Still, having grown up in Boulder, I understood Goldberg's frustration with liberals who only talk the talk.

Though I've been graced with people who have done so throughout my life, liberals who walk the walk aren't easy to find. Which is part of why I jumped at the chance to leave Boulder and be a beach volleyball star in Southern California. And why, after hearing conservative born-again Christian football coach Bill McCartney, I thought I was destined to succeed.

"White guys don't get it. White guys are stupid," Coach McCartney sounded like a racist to bring attention to a common problem, "They don't see that they have advantages. I think the white man needs to know that he's responsible for the repression of the black man. He's held him down, pinned him down. He's benefited at his expense. Most white people try to excuse themselves as not having any bias. Truth of the matter is that all of us have benefited in different ways, whether we knowingly partake or not, and we need to put that right up front."

McCartney also praised CU's Black Studies professor Dr. Wil Miles, for guiding him and his players on how to deal with subtle and blatant forms of bias and racism. McCartney and players said Dr. Miles was essential to their family atmosphere and winning a national championship. And McCartney improved awareness on campus, and in Boulder's Police and City Council.

Over the years I looked to McCartney for inspiration. In 1994 McCartney resigned from CU football to run the "Promise Keepers," a deeply conservative Christian organization for men. "Promise Keepers" preached what they called traditional families, spiritual, moral and sexual purity, and commitment to their interpretation of Biblical values. While they bridged divides between some people and beliefs, they also deeply broadened divisions by narrowly defining the roles for LGBQT individuals and women.

In 1997 "Promise Keepers" held a march on the National Mall in Washington with 600,000 to 800,000 men in attendance. I was unnerved by the growing conservative voice in our nation that (intentionally and unintentionally) created more power for privileged white heterosexual men. I felt relieved that membership declined after 1997. And when McCartney retired in 2003, I hoped he'd personally continue to work at bridging racial divides.

Still, with the success of conservative talk radio, FOX News, success of groups like "Focus on the Family", plus the election of G.W. Bush followed by his policies 'Shock and Awe', The Patriot Act, and No Child Left Behind, I felt there was an all-out assault on liberal thought and values.

~

"I also suspect I will hear my name linked to the words 'disgruntled former employee' and 'vindictive,'" Goldberg emphasizes, "Let me state the following without any fear whatsoever that I might be wrong: Anyone who writes a book to be vindictive is almost certainly insane ... Staring at a blank page on a computer screen for hours and hours and hours is not the most efficient way to be vindictive. It seems to me that staring at the TV set for a couple of seconds and blowing a raspberry at the anchorman would take care of any vindictive feelings one might have."

I know it's difficult to write a book. I've also felt satisfaction in rude gestures and respect Goldberg for having won seven Emmys. But I know someone is full of shit if they have no fear of being wrong when they write that "blowing raspberries takes care of vindictive feelings," and only insane people get revenge through writing. First, blowing raspberries wasn't nearly as satisfying as pounding volleyballs. Second, and most importantly, when it comes to history, news, education, and the law, the sweetest revenge goes to those who write.

"I am not a traitor, nor am I the enemy," Goldberg writes a few paragraphs later, "And neither are the millions of Americans who agree with me. The enemy is arrogance. And I'm afraid it's on the other side of the camera."

Maybe Bias is satire, like the publication The Onion.

~

I developed a knack for substitute teaching. It's the art of letting students get away with a few things while keeping the room in order and getting work done. As I developed a rapport, students gave teachers positive feedback about me and from K-6 classrooms, to K-12 PE, Art, and special education, I was repeatedly asked to work in many of the same classes.

My Poetry to Celebrate Life workshops were well received in after-school programs in Boulder and Longmont. I also had an excellent grant writing tutor, and after receiving grants in Boulder and Thompson Valley school districts, dared to think getting grants was easy.

~

The first chapter of Bias is titled, "The News Mafia." And Goldberg likens the CBS News "Family" to The Sopranos, and Dan Rather to Tony Soprano and The Godfather.

Goldberg explains that he first got on the wrong side of the CBS "Family" when executives asked what he thought about Washington correspondent Eric Enberg's report on presidential candidate Steve Forbes and Forbes' flat tax proposal.

"[Dan] Rather introduced Engberg's piece with the standard stuff," Goldberg illustrates, "How it would 'look beyond the promises to the substance' of the Forbes flat tax. Television news anchors enjoy using words like 'substance,' mostly because a half-hour newscast (about twenty-one minutes after commercials) has so little of it."

True, most major news networks don't commit the resources and time it takes to deliver the in-depth reporting we need to understand and solve problems.

"Engberg's voice covered pictures of Steve Forbes on the campaign trail," Goldberg continues, "Forbes pitches his flat-tax scheme as an economic elixir good for everything that ails us."

"Scheme? Elixir?" Goldberg wonders, "What the hell kind of language is that? These were words that conjured up images of con artists, like Doctor Feel-Good selling worthless junk out of the back of his wagon."

I reread the table of contents. Titles begin, "The News Mafia," which made me think of cutting the head off a horse and cement shoes. There's also, "Mugged by 'The Dan'," "The Emperor Is Naked," and "Where Thieves and Pimps Run Free."

Now that's how to conjure up images! Still, Goldberg was right about the flat tax story being one-sided. Engberg could have found economists to support the flat tax. And TV journalists often framed their stories like the New York Times and Washington Post – where most think flat taxes enrich the rich and burden the poor.

"Should a journalistic enterprise like CBS News," Goldberg asks, "which claims to stand for fairness and objectivity – allow words like 'scheme' and 'wacky' in what is supposed to be a straight news story?"

"Scheme" and "wacky" should definitely be used sparingly, and never when a successful businessman who is a legitimate presidential candidate shares ideas on how to solve problems.

~

"I told Fager [CBS producer] I had been complaining privately about bias at CBS News for years," Goldberg explains the beginning of his end with CBS on page 26, "I told Fager I was going to write about it, and then maybe he and the other people who decide what gets on the air would listen."

I feel you Goldberg. It sucks when you tell a painful truth and powerful people spin the narrative to screw you over.

But my sudden empathy for Goldberg gave me pause, so I re-read. On page five, Goldberg derides media star Tom Brokaw for his reaction to Goldberg's nationally published articles, "And that, to [Tom] constitutes a 'feud,' which strikes me as a convenient way to avoid an inconvenient subject that [media stars] don't especially like to talk about or, for that matter, think too deeply about."

"Feud" is among the least dismissive words you'll hear when you challenge a colleague's professional integrity in two nationally published articles, I thought, *besides, now, on page 26, Goldberg lets us in on how he's been complaining for years. Bias is like The Onion,* I laughed.

I reread the cover: bold black print labeled Bias, CURRENT EVENTS/MEDIA. Bright red print quotes the Wall Street Journal, "His case is airtight."

Then I thought about the many who praised Goldberg and the many who condemned him—echo chambers of partial stories and half-truths.

I felt a chill.

Power

Chapter two, "Mugged by The Dan," starts with Goldberg calling Dan Rather to warn him about the Wall Street Journal article that Dan probably, "won't be ecstatic about."

"Bernie," Dan responds, "we were friends yesterday, we're friends today, and we'll be friends tomorrow."

As Goldberg describes the article Dan becomes, "… viscerally angry."

"Angry I was expecting," Goldberg claims, "What came next, I wasn't … Rather's voice started quavering, and he told me how in his younger days he had signed up to serve his country—not once but twice!"

"What the hell did that have to do with anything?" Goldberg questioned before answering, "then it hit me: somehow, Dan Rather, red, white, and blue American, Texan, ex-marine-and-damn-proud-of-it, thought that if I believed the *CBS Evening News* … tilted left then I must be suggesting that it's just a short hop from being a liberal to being … *an unpatriotic American!* Sure it's crazy, but why else would he tell me that he signed up with the marines, twice?"

Some conservatives do think liberals are unpatriotic Americans. Being born and raised among conservatives in Texas, Dan's afraid of how some will likely react to Goldberg's language. And if you want to defend your credibility after being accused of being too liberal in Texas, boast of your military service. Dan was defensive but surely not "crazy."

~

"When Heyward [president of CBS] called me," Goldberg explains further fall-out from the WSJ article, "It was obvious that steam was coming out of his ears. What I had done, he told me, was 'an act of disloyalty' and 'a betrayal of trust.'"

"'I understand how you feel,' I told him, trying to defuse a bad situation," Goldberg writes, "'But I didn't say anything in the piece about how even you, [Heyward], have agreed with me about the liberal bias.'"

Goldberg's comment failed to calm Heyward, instead he went "ballistic" and screamed, "That would have been *like raping my wife and kidnapping my kids!*"

"If there was an instant when I knew just how dark things would get," Goldberg explained, this was it. This one, frantic statement—*That would be like raping my wife and kidnapping my kids*—told me everything I needed to know about the magnitude of my sin."

"Writing an op-ed was like raping his wife and kidnapping his kids!" Goldberg pours it on, "Criticizing, publically what I saw as bias in network news was *like raping his wife and kidnapping his kids.*"

"This is how self-centered the media elites can be," Goldberg begins the next paragraph (longest in the chapter) generalizing the "media elites," writing "These are people who ... These are people who ... These are people who ..." and concluding, "because [they think] taking on the media is like *raping their wives and kidnapping their kids!*"

Goldberg and his editors condemn the "liberal" media for using words like "scheme" and "elixir," which conjure up "images of con-artists ... selling worthless junk out of the back of a wagon." But they take one out-burst by one man to imply all "media elites" think challenging their ideas is an assault and go on to write in italics "raping their wives and kidnapping their kids," four times in three paragraphs. Images! Images! Images! Images!

I'm still amazed I didn't rip <u>Bias</u> apart and throw it in the compost. But I decided to take it seriously because some praised Goldberg. Colleagues and Americans from coast to coast wrote things like:

"In the future, if you have any derogatory remarks to make about CBS News or one of your co-workers ... I hope you'll do the same thing again."

"I wish to join with so many other Americans in thanking you for raising such a very important issue. I find it incredible that Andrew

Heyward ... chooses to treat you as the issue rather than the liberal bias of the media elites."

"Liberal bias among the television networks has done something that market forces could not have engendered, the revitalization of radio. Rush Limbaugh would never have become the success he has if the firm of Rather, Brokaw, and Jennings had done its job. Instead, they failed.'"

"Those of us outside the media have been aware for years of the liberal bias that is so pervasive. That's why the 'alternative media' audience has grown and the so called 'mainstream' media audience is shrinking."

Keep searching, I thought taking deep breaths, *there's got to be some common ground.*

~

I received grants to conduct week-long workshops with classes at three elementary schools in Boulder: CrestView, Flatirons, and Columbine. I began to marvel at the relative ease of my work. Kids get excited about recognizing the problems with using stereotypes, hearing and reading good writing, and writing and speaking about what makes them happy. I also began to hear a compliment I'd hear regularly for the next four years (mostly during my three years teaching 5th grade at Creekside Elementary), "You just explain things in a way that makes sense."

Mike wrote – <u>What I Want is Music</u>:
    What I want is more music in the world
    With guitar, base, piano and drums

    Tuning is refuge, tuning is key
    Without tuning your music will sound horribly

    On guitar, the electric amplifier and soft acoustic
    On their string they wander stray and they play

    On the drum
    The boom the bang and the clang

On the piano, the soft keys play
While you are the one who listens and sways

All this means nothing to some
But to others it is most fun

What I want is to make music
Yes, you need fingers, picks and drumsticks

But to make true music
You need to start from the heart.

Sasha wrote – Moonlight Hiking:
Late one night
In the cool fall breeze
By the moonlight
Me and my dad
Go for a hike
On Flagstaff mountain
Lots of rocks and
Warm sweaters and jackets
I
Feel calm yet excited
Saying
"Let's go over here and
Let's climb that rock"
I hope we will go again!

Mallory wrote – Saint Louis Cardinals Win:
Watching the baseball game
Eating hotdogs and ice cream

Hot
Sweaty afternoon

People
Soda and peanuts

Mommy, Payton, Mallory and me
Cheering
Clapping

GO Larry Walker
Hit a home run!

Yah
Saint Louis Cardinals win!!

Traffic like a stampede
Honk! Honk!

~

Goldberg begins chapter four, Identity Politics, describing his family's humble beginnings in a Bronx neighborhood that was, "widely seen as one of the most rundown slums in all of America, a national symbol of urban decay."

"My parents had to cash in a small insurance policy to get me started in college," Goldberg continues, "Rutgers University in New Brunswick, New Jersey ... like most of us on campus in the 1960's I was liberal on all the big issues. I was an especially big fan of Lyndon Johnson's Great Society."

"Martin Luther King," Goldberg writes, "is one of the two or three greatest and most courageous Americans of the twentieth century." Adding that he, "didn't vote for Reagan either time. But ... vote[d] for McGovern—twice," is pro-choice, and "for gay rights, too."

If Goldberg had begun Bias detailing how he thought the most reasonable and civilized views were liberal, I would've recognized

Bias as less of an attack on liberal views, and more of a call for journalistic integrity.

"I'm still against racial discrimination," Goldberg continues, "But I'm against it even when its targets are white people. So while I'm for what we like to call affirmative action when that means reaching out to bring more minorities into the process, I'm against affirmative action when it means racial preferences, which in the real world is what affirmative action is usually about. Why should the children of Jesse Jackson or Colin Powell or Diana Ross get some kind of racial preferences when they apply to college or go out for a job, but no 'affirmative action' is given to the child of a white Anglo-Saxon Protestant coal miner from West Virginia?"

Giving all people of color opportunities is a sure way to bring diversity into the process. And like I told my college roommates a decade ago, I'll pay higher taxes if they provide Affirmative Action for more minorities of race, class, gender, religion, any. That way more Americans are better educated, with better chances of becoming employed, productive, and happy citizens.

"I'm also 100 percent against sex discrimination," Goldberg continues by suggesting women may be getting the upper hand on men, "just as I was when the modern women's movement began in the 1960's and early 1970's. But these days I see an awful lot of sexism masquerading as feminism. Which means I'm against sex discrimination even when it's aimed at men, whether it's called affirmative action or anything else."

Of course some feminists are sexist. And as Goldberg correctly pointed out, some of the reasons women earn 75 cents for every dollar men earn, aren't due to sexism. Still, until men get sexually assaulted as often as women; occupy as few positions of leadership and power; and have to wear shoes that ruin feet, knees, and hips to be sexy, we shouldn't spend too much time worrying about Goldberg's "awful lot of sexism masquerading as feminism."

"I think welfare is absolutely necessary for some people," Goldberg continues, "but I also think it's wrecked the lives of far too many Americans who have gotten hooked on it."

At least Goldberg didn't use the term "Welfare Queen." Even though millions of women have earned being called a "Queen," it's still misleading to label the impoverished with titles of the extraordinarily wealthy. But Corporate America can be seen as royalty, making "Welfare Kings" a much more accurate term. Being "Hooked," as if on crack cocaine or the Holy Spirit, really only describes women who would delight in raising children in neighborhoods that often resemble hell.

"If all that makes me a neoconservative, fine," Goldberg laments, "But I see myself as an old-fashioned liberal. I'm a liberal the way liberals used to be."

Don't make liberals out to be extinct! I thought getting angry again, *many liberals have, and continue to make significant contributions toward positive change. We work to spread love because love overcomes.*

~

A few students in each workshop wrote about kindness and peace.

Sarah wrote – I Want Everyone to Give:
    Give to a friend or a teacher, mom or dad
    Give them a friend, make them belong
    Make them feel safe, give a gift
    Like a game or book on Christmas or birthdays
    No matter when
    On a cold winter night people are freezing
    So give them a blanket or sweater
    And make them feel better
    Make them feel right

Bake a cake, bake some brownies
To give to a friend
Hoping you all will just give!

Margery wrote – <u>I Want to Paint</u>:
    I want to be a professional painter who can
    Paint families of different cultures

    I would paint the end of all wars
    So we could all be joyful with each other
    And dance all kinds of dances: ballet; jazz; hip hop

    What I want is to paint happiness in the world
    With Iraqis, Asians, Mexicans ... I could go on and on

    I'd paint every skin color and mix them into one color
    So we could all be equal

    And be one whole world, with no groups
    Or enemies that could start a war

    What I want is to be a professional painter
    Who can paint families of different cultures!

~

In chapter five, "How Bill Clinton Cured Homelessness," Goldberg quotes Philip Terzian, an official in President Jimmy Carter's administration who authored an article about the drop in homelessness news stories after Reagan left the White House.

"In 1988 when the 'heartless republican' Reagan was in the White House," Terzian wrote, "the New York Times ran fifty stories on the homeless, including five on page one. But a decade later, in 1998, when the 'compassionate Democrat' Clinton was in charge the Times ran only ten homeless stories, and none on page one. In 1990, when George Bush was president, there were seventy-one homeless stories on the ABC CBS,

NBC, and CNN evening newscasts. But in 1995, when Bill Clinton was in the White House, the number had gone down to just nine!"

That's more than I would've guessed, but not by much. It's appalling how President Clinton wasn't held accountable for contributing to poverty and homelessness. With NAFTA shipping jobs over-seas, the war on drugs, addiction on the rise, and the 'three strikes you're out' policy in full force, he fiscally and emotionally devastated families across the US.

But, I would have criticized Clinton more if conservatives had not, in the name of smaller government and lower taxes, legislated like Clinton on steroids: greed in Capitalism reigns like a god; defund rehabilitation programs of every kind; intensify a "war on drugs" that's already incarcerating poor and minority in mass; and privatized education, healthcare and prisons—for profit.

"I choose to believe," Goldberg sarcastically concludes, "it was not CNN's way of suggesting now that a conservative Republican is president Reagan-era misery will soon be back with us in full force. Instead I choose to believe homelessness really is a thing of the past ... the media would never play politics with poor homeless people. I choose to believe that Bill Clinton really did end homelessness and that the end of homelessness is good news. Fantastic news. I choose to believe it is too-good-to-be-true news."

Sure, network news was wrong for its lopsided reporting. And as Goldberg also pointed out, for not reporting on how increases in poverty and homelessness were connected to addiction, mental health, and greedy capitalists. They were also wrong for misrepresenting the homeless population by showing clean cut, blond-haired, blue eyed people (even though research shows Americans give more when those in need don't have dark eyes, hair and skin).

Still, after yet another sarcastic conclusion, I imagined smacking Goldberg in the back of the head, like a father correcting a son for saying "fuck" at the dinner table.

~

I didn't always feel that way about <u>Bias</u>. I loved how Goldberg pointed out that most liberals deciding what programs to air, were out to please most conservatives.

"CBS, NBC, ABC, and Fox," Goldberg claims, "represent a cadre of like-minded Moguls—the Titans of Television—the people who shape our pop culture by deciding what gets on the prime-time TV schedule and what doesn't. As far as the NAACP was concerned, these white liberals were behaving like a gang of rednecks decked out in Armanis who might as well have been fronting for David Duke."

"NAACP president Kweisi Mfume said [in response to the networks' fall schedules]" Goldberg continues, "The TV business was 'the most segregated industry in the United States.' Other civil rights leaders accused the Moguls of whitewashing, even ethnic purification."

"Advertisers like white Audiences," Goldberg quotes Black Entertainment Television network mogul Robert Johnson, "They have more money to spend. If I'm a network executive, who's probably white … and I'm going to launch a show that I think advertisers will like because it will deliver a white audience that the advertisers value more, I'm not going to go and try to do something risky and creative with black people and white people.'"

It's good to know the networks weren't ignoring minorities because of their skin color—but the end-result is the same. Conservatives dismiss minorities while liberals pretend to give us a voice. Another phase of 'divide and conquer'. And while Goldberg throws plenty of gasoline on the fire, he also reports valuable statistics that show both white liberals and white conservatives often do a poor job representing minorities.

Goldberg also highlighted the Nielsen Media Research of March 29 – June 27, 1999. He found evidence to support why the market dictates programing. The top five programs blacks watched were: "The Steve Harvey Show," "For Your Love," "The Jamie Foxx Show," "P.J's," and "Walker, Texas Ranger." Among whites, those ranked 150th, 145th, 145th, 108th, and 50th. The top programs whites watched were: "Frasier," "ER," "Friends," "Veronica's Closet," and "Will and Grace." While among blacks, these ranked 105th, 22nd, 102nd, 92nd, and 112th.

It's me walking into Bethany College's cafeteria all over again, still choosing to sit at tables filled with whites, I thought after noting that I watched Frazier, Friends and ER, and didn't watch Steve Harvey, For Your Love, or Jamie Foxx.

I decided to go on a run to blow off some steam. When I reached the overlook I spotted my high school, the sand volleyball courts.

Why am I always running? Desperate to prove that walls are built in the womb, when we first hear certain voices, languages, stories, and perspectives. Divisions that grow morning, noon, and night – day after day.
Bringing different worlds together isn't easy, I decided, *though the mountains and my mom often did. Run back down like a warrior. And be yourself.*

~

My workshops improved student's Language Arts skills, but I especially liked how they gave students a voice. With a soft spot for underdogs and outcasts, these were two favorites.

Steve wrote – <u>What I Want is to Control my ADHD</u>:
A pencil dropped, voices
In the hall, a kid trips
Then he falls.

My mind overloads, I can't
Focus. I wish that I could with
A quick hocus-pocus

Swinging my feet, twirling a
Pencil, messing around with some
Other utensil

A kid is mean to me, I
Yell because I'm mad, all the
While I feel somewhat sad

Swinging my fists, yelling
Real loud, I feel great anger, my
Minds in a cloud

Now I'm in trouble, the office
My place, an expression of gloom
And sadness on my face.

Reggie wrote a two page essay (excerpt) – I Want an Eternal Peace:
When your soul talks you don't hear it, you feel it, like a cool summer breeze flowing through your heart and mind … Please, let my suffering end! I don't know this cruel world! I see my most beloved friend being struck down again and again and there is nothing I can do! Why God Why?! … And I know you have an endless ocean of love for him, and I pray you will listen. And I send one message to the rest of the creatures in the universe, in heaven and earth. Remember to believe. And listen.

~

Goldberg begins the chapter, How About a Media that Reflects America, by commenting, "Peter Johnson, who writes a TV column in USA Today, wrote that many of [Goldbergs] colleagues dismissed him as dead wrong, an ingrate, a nut, or all of the above … The bad news was that the anti-Christ, Rush Limbaugh, and the other conservative elites, had come riding to [Goldberg's] defense."

"[Goldberg is] in trouble for nothing more than calling it like it is," Limbaugh said, "Here's a guy who says what I would venture 70 percent of the American people agree with—that the press is liberal—and he's in huge trouble."

"Yes. And it got a lot huger after Limbaugh's testimonial," Goldberg goes on, "I didn't want to become a darling of conservatives. Sure, I was a critic of the networks' leftward tilt just as they were, but I wasn't part of some right-wing cabal ... The fact is, I would have loved to get some support from the Left ..."

Really? It's not rocket science, Goldberg. Include a few paragraphs (maybe chapters) about Limbaugh being at least as hateful and divisive as some in the "liberal" networks. Like in 1993, when Limbaugh said: "Let the unskilled jobs that take absolutely no knowledge whatsoever to do—let stupid and unskilled Mexicans do that work." Or 1994, when he said "Women should not be allowed on juries where the accused is a stud," and, "When a gay person turns his back on you, it is anything but an insult; it's an invitation." Or 1995, before getting charged for using illegal prescription drugs and getting off with a short stint in rehab, "Too many whites are getting away with drug use. The answer is to go out and find the ones who are getting away with it, convict them and send them up the river too."

Goldberg goes on by citing examples of liberals who sounded as narrow-minded and hurtful as Limbaugh. Roxanne Russell, CBS Washington bureau correspondent, "nonchalantly referred to this conservative activist as 'Gary Bauer, the little nut from the Christian group.'" Ted Turner, CNN Washington bureau, once said Christianity was a religion "for losers," and when he came across women with ash on their forehead said, "At first I thought you were in the [Seattle] earthquake, but I realized you're just Jesus freaks."

CBS failed miserably when neither Russell nor the executives thought to run a correction. But it's cool that Turner apologized for being, "thoughtless."

"An affirmative action plan for conservative journalists might bring some real diversity to the newsroom," Goldberg concludes, "News executives are always saying we need our staffs to look more like the real America. How about if those reporters and editors and executives also thought just a little more like the real America? And shared a little more of *their* values? And brought just a little more of *their* perspective to the job? Nahhhh! It's definitely too crazy! The journalists who love affirmative action would hate it."

This liberal would love it! Right along with an affirmative action plan for all minorities in employment and programing. We need more opportunities for people to find common ground. I'd also love it if Beck, Goldberg, Limbaugh, Rather, Jennings, Hannity, Brokaw, The Wall Street Journal, and CBS—all were as critical of themselves as they are of others.

~

In 2005, I applied for more grants than in 2004, but received fewer. Still, I spoke with Elementary, Jr. and High school teachers and lined up workshops to do while substitute teaching and in after-school programs. Students continued to create great poetry and thank me. But I grew tired of bouncing around. I thought of student teaching in Kansas, my cooperating teachers. John saying, "Remember, I'm having dinner with your dad on Friday." Then the student confesses, apologizes, and promises to do better. And Millie running to the home of the student who skipped out on a test. She finds him hiding in the basement and brings him back to school.

Great teachers are a part of the community!

Boulder is my community. So I vowed to get a job teaching in BVSD fall 2006. I would make my workshop the foundation of a diverse and compassionate community that excels in academics.

Because the best chance America has of overcoming our deeply rooted conflicts is to educate children.

PART IV

Human Kindness has never weakened the stamina
Or softened the fiber of a free people.
A nation does not have to be cruel to be tough.

Franklin D. Roosevelt

Breathing and Rising

Teacher

Summer of 2006, I signed a one year contract to teach 5th grade at Creekside Elementary. Elementary school curriculum is basic, but it does include the subjects Reading, Writing, Math, Social Studies, Science and others. Plus, in order to shelter instruction that accommodates strengths and weakness in individual students, there's all the planning, grading, and record keeping (my greatest nemesis). I knew this job would be physically, emotionally, and mentally exhausting. I was prepared to work as hard as ever.

In the spring of 2007, Dave Blessing (my volleyball coach at CU in 1993, now photography teacher at Boulder High School), told me BHS's Art teacher was retiring and encouraged me to apply. Considering my skills and love for art, the lighter grading and paperwork, plus that I came highly recommended by everyone in BHS's art department after subbing for each regularly over the last few years, there was a good chance I could land the job.

I told my principal and my teammate in the other 5th grade class that I was considering applying for the position. They encouraged me to do what's best for me.

I reviewed my evaluation. Evaluations contain five Standards, each with criteria that are graded on a scale of one to four: One – Does not meet district standard; Two – Partially meets standard; Three – Meets standard; Four – Exceeds standard.

I was initially alarmed by my evaluation because in the first Standard, "The teacher shall demonstrate knowledge of subject matter and effective instructional skill," there are five criteria. I only "met" standards in one. And "partially" met standards in four.

"Why would a teacher who only partially meets standards in so many criteria be asked to return?" I asked my principal.

"Mastering the spectrum of knowledge and skills required in teaching is difficult," my principal explained, "so teachers don't have to meet all standards immediately. Some teachers take many years to meet all criteria."

I liked our principal. She was an eight-year Veteran. And though some staff complained she was soft on discipline, discipline is my strength, and the community seemed to otherwise thrive. Also, the other 5th grade teacher and staff were extremely helpful with organization, planning, and lessons. I knew I'd get better at managing paper work, standards, and curriculum, as well as assessing and serving needs in all my students; and above all, I loved Creekside's diverse population. We were the home school for an international population attending CU, so our students spoke dozens of languages. We also housed Title IX and special education programs. But the best part of the year came not long after winter break, when some students told me they hated Language Arts coming in to 5th grade, but now they love it. And some who began the year loving Language Arts said they loved it more.

I decided not to apply for the art position and instead stick with fulfilling my dream of being an elementary classroom teacher.

~

My second year of teaching, the other 5th grade teacher and staff were again very helpful. And again, many students thanked me for giving them a new love for language arts. But what stood out was how the curriculum and grade level were perfect for me. A bi-racial American man who is identified as black. A teacher who has worked to excel in Language Arts, Social Studies, and positive leadership. And who is required to teach a curriculum that covers 200 years of tumultuous American history, to the grade that all the other students in the school look up to.

To begin the year I taught the US Constitution and Bill of Rights. Then we debated and wrote a Bill of Rights to govern our class for the year, which also reinforced my Poetry to Celebrate Life workshop in Language Arts. This made for a powerful foundation for us to read, write, speak, listen, and learn how to honor individuals.

For Slavery, I highlighted Founding Fathers who profited from institutional power, showing how even good people can make bad decisions. Students wrote a slave journal to explore dynamic experiences and language. I announced (with exasperating regularity given the looks on my students' faces) that they were fortunate to get an education and need to work hard because some people, whether they're slave owners or not, take advantage of the less educated. I'd conclude like my supervising teacher in Kansas, "Being educated," Millie would say while making eye contact with everyone, "gives you the best chance of doing what you want."

I taught that the Civil War started for many reasons, but the North won because Lincoln promised to abolish slavery, a cause two million whites and four million blacks were willing to kill and die for (which should debunk the whole "slaves were happy" theory, unless you're complimenting slaves for the courage, faith, and love it takes to find happiness in hell). I emphasized that family, friends, and neighbors signed up to kill each other, and more Americans died than in all other wars combined. I highlighted many voices, including the Southerners who opposed slavery and died in Sherman's scorched earth campaign (similar to my German family opposing Hitler only to be killed by American bombs). I made a point of racist Southerners and Northerners creating terror through the KKK and Jim Crow. I connected the 13th Amendment to my student's 1st, 2nd, and polished drafts. And while their polished drafts would be their best work and receive a grade, they handled criticism better knowing even our Founding Father's writing needed to be revised.

For the Civil Rights movement I featured Martin Luther King Jr. saying that the shame of their generation wasn't the hateful 10 percent, but the silent majority. And how our Constitution received another important revision once some of the majority did speak up. I emphasized nonviolence as more than avoiding physical fights, but learning to like others—which served as a powerful conclusion to what I'd been teaching all year with the district's bully prevention, and my poetry workshops.

At the end of the year students chose their favorite writing genre from a unit we did that year: poetry; essay; report; magazine; short story; journal; skit. Then they wrote, shared, and celebrated. Each walked taller after their applause for bravery. And a few got the kind of applause that's more like an eruption, and boosts people into the stars.

~

I also made improvements in my evaluation that year.

In the first Standard, I "met" standards in two of four criteria I had only "partially" met the previous year. "Curtis," the Veteran wrote, "you have continued to improve both your understanding of the fifth grade standards and expectations as well as your skill in instructing our very diverse student population ... you have demonstrated an increased awareness of intentional instruction, knowing the students' performance levels and addressing their needs more specifically ... You have worked very hard to give your students more timely and direct feedback about their work ... and I see you are feeling more organized about your record keeping of grades and performance."

There are four other Standards on the evaluation. II – Teachers shall demonstrate Competency in valuing and promoting understanding of diversity. III – Effective management of the learning environment. IV – Commitment to education as a profession. V – Effective interpersonal skills.

Of the 13 criteria in those four standards, I "met" standards in 7 (having raised two from "partially met" last year). I "exceeded" standards in the other 6 criteria (having raised three: Demonstrates a commitment to educating his students; Commitment to ongoing professional growth; Interacts with students in order to build supportive relationships). Which meant I exceeded district standards on one third of my evaluation.

Considering my resume and decision not to apply for the Boulder High Art position, I had proven my commitment to Creekside and elementary education. I should've been given credit for exceeding those standards last year.

The purpose of the evaluation was stated on the cover. "To serve as a basis for improvement of instruction; to enhance the implementation of programs of curriculum; to serve as a measure of professional growth and development; to measure levels of performance; The goal is improved performance."

I grew excited thinking about my potential as a leader at Creekside.

~

I was well on my way to being an outstanding teacher, but I knew it wouldn't be easy, even under the best conditions. And the conditions around me were changing.

Half-way through the year, the Veteran accepted a new central administrative position so she could, "Do some real good." Whatever "good" the Veteran did, our school didn't feel it. She began working in her new position almost immediately, and left a vacuum of leadership for a notoriously negative staff (my mentor speculated my positive attitude was a big reason she hired me), and students who struggled with bullying (particularly in lower grades). The district hired an interim principal who helped with paperwork for a few months, but did nothing for the eroding morale of teachers and staff.

Also, my 5th grade teammate decided to leave for personal reasons. And although the Veteran assured me the new teacher and I would be fine, it was rumored he wasn't very good.

While signing the contract for a third year, the Veteran expressed concerns about my grading and feedback. Confused, because nothing was written under "Areas of Concerns" on either of my evaluations, I asked if she saw improvement. When she paraphrased what's in my evaluation—improved feedback in all subjects, especially Language Arts—I knew my grading and feedback would continue to guide and improve my instruction in every subject. Still, I worried because I was a year from earning tenure.

Tenure for teachers is controversial. Teachers argue that teaching has so many variables it's difficult to evaluate performance and most could get fired for arbitrary reasons. So tenure ensures that teachers receive detailed expectations and evaluations. But some argue that since administrators don't have the time or resources to do the paperwork, planning, and feedback, firing teachers is too difficult. And when teachers can't be fired, they become lazy.

I vowed to stay on my new teammates' and new principal's good side.

I'm not going to let anything stand in my way. After two years I knew I'd built a strong foundation, and understood this to be the beginning of a career that has the kind of impact I always dreamed of.

Climate

I hoped to make the most of my strengths with diversity in my second year as well.

I signed up for the District's "Equity Cohort" with a few other Creekside teachers. The cohort raises awareness about differences: race, religion, class, culture, sexual orientation, politics—all differences that can serve as excuses to divide us. We met once a month for a year (including an overnight retreat in Estes Park). 2007 was the ninth annual, and since reactions to the first eight were overwhelmingly positive, they doubled the number of participants from 50 to 100.

The Cohort creates a safe environment. Support groups, personal experience panels, and dyads allow people to candidly share thoughts and ideas about sensitive topics. Success depends on participants adhering to rules: Everyone gets equal time; When listening, don't interpret, paraphrase, analyze, give advice, or break in with a personal story; When speaking, don't criticize or complain about the listener or mutual acquaintances; Maintain confidentiality. I'd worked and studied with this kind of curriculum for decades, including graduate courses at CU, an MA short course; and an MFA degree completion. After everyone in my small group introduced themselves, I looked forward to the year.

Still, I had two concerns, so I spoke with the Cohort's directors. One concern was our group leader. She raved about the cohort, "It'll blow your mind. Ground breaking work that no one in the nation is doing!"

I thought it was great she loved it, but was uncomfortable being led by someone who didn't know this kind of work had been happening for decades. I didn't want her kicked out, but when the directors spoke to our group about how they could use her elsewhere, our group decided we'd do fine without a leader.

My second concern was with one of the Cohort's guidelines, "No one is born prejudiced."

"I'm a mixed-race American man, who is identified black, raised in a white community by a white mother and grandmother from Germany," I told them. "About six years ago, after three decades of reflection and study, I was finally able to forgive my own and everyone else's bigotry," I said, "because I realized that you—me—everyone—we're all born prejudiced."

After a brief discussion and getting permission from the Veteran, the cohort directors invited me to the Administrator's Cohort retreat in Estes Park, a two-day session run by the cohort creator Julian Weissglass. I would be the only teacher, but they needed more minority representation, and I could have dinner with Julian to discuss why he included this guideline.

~

Julian struggled with academics in elementary school but graduated second in his class in high school and became a National Merit Finalist. He knew something was wrong with our schools and society (having grown up during the civil rights and anti-Vietnam war movements), but never saw himself as a leader for educational or social change. In the 1970's he taught at University of California, Santa Barbara. He was assigned to teach mathematics for elementary teachers and became deeply concerned while teaching students of color because even though they were smart, he found they did poorly and seemed doomed to fail in a system that wasn't addressing their needs. For the next 30 years he focused on educational change, and has traveled the world to work with people hoping to change inequities faced in classrooms and schools.

"I love the work you're doing," I said to Julian, "if people are going to overcome our violent and oppressive history, we need a safe place to openly and honestly speak, listen, and honor our differences."

"I'm glad you feel that way," Julian replied.

"I also like many of the guidelines,' I continued, "like how we must talk about race, class, and gender bias, not to lay blame, but to figure out better ways of educating children. And that assumptions, values, and practices of people and institutions from the dominant culture disadvantage the minority. Or how we must improve alliances between educators from different races, genders, and classes. And that nothing will change until we listen attentively and release emotions that arise when we try to make sense of our own and other's experiences."

"But, I take exception to the first guideline: No one is born prejudiced," I emphasized, "I agree with part two: All forms of bias—from extreme bigotry to unaware cultural biases—are acquired, actually imposed on the young person. Still, I believe we're all born prejudiced."

"Well, they're guidelines not rules," Julian responded, "they're meant to promote thought and discussion on emotional topics."

"I get the idea," I said, "it's important to recognize people's good nature and assume the best," I continued, "I've seen people struggle with racist family and friends, as you wrote, 'It is painful for a young child to see prejudice among loved ones or find out about injustice and then be forced or manipulated into deferring to it in order to be accepted in a family or a community. This pain is one of the causes for people's passivity when confronting prejudice and discrimination.'"

"Yes," Julian said showing all the signs of a great listener.

"Still, it's important to recognize that everyone is born prejudiced," I continued, "Merriam-Webster defines prejudice: *to injure or damage by some judgment or action of another in disregard of one's rights; esp. detriment to one's legal rights or claims.* I worked with two, three and four-year olds and they made judgments and actions in disregard of each other's rights all the time. Not because we taught them to, but because they wanted to. And, if newborns could do more than eat and poop, I'm sure they would too."

"I think prejudice is more about preconceived and adverse judgements and opinions," Julian emphasized.

"Yes, Merriam-Webster states that too," I continued, "but judgments begin in the womb. Probably before 24 weeks of age, but certainly after we develop ear drums and start to hear voices and language. That means we are all born with preconceived opinions."

"I don't understand," Julian replied.

"My family confronted fascists in Germany," I continued, "I faced prejudice personally in Kansas, Colorado, and Florida, and have read much about it. Books like Shelby Steele's <u>The Content of Our Character</u>, and Robert James', <u>And don't call me a racist!</u> led me to conclude that racism is everywhere."

"I don't understand," Julian said.

"I'm not demonizing people, everyone has a great deal of good-will. Maybe think of being prejudiced like breathing," I said in a last ditch effort, "we aren't born breathing but if we don't start, what's the point? Ergo—we're born prejudiced too."

"I don't understand," he said and I grew uncomfortable in the silence that followed.

I appreciated that Julian didn't tell me I was wrong. He made it clear it was ok for me to think we're all born prejudiced if it helps me forgive myself and others. And since I don't remember much else about our conversation, I imagine it turned to small talk and awkward silences. I ended our time together by thanking Julian for all his great work.

~

I was surprised how much it hurt that Julian didn't recognize that we're born prejudiced.

On the drive to Estes I thought about how saying we're born prejudiced is like saying we're born running. It takes years to actually learn prejudices toward race, gender, culture, religion, whatever. But we begin determining what we like and dislike—what's good and bad—in the womb. And while it may be a stretch, the poet in me thinks it makes sense to say we're born "prejudiced" because we're born "that way."

Most importantly though, that implies that everyone needs to learn how to apologize and forgive; and that everyone would benefit from workshops like Julian's. So I told myself to give it a shot, but not to get my hopes up too high.

I walked the shores of Lake Estes, took deep breaths, and watched night wash the snowy peaks of the Never Summer Range in indigo, scarlet, and slate.

Julian has led successful workshops with people all over the world for 30 years. Many of the participants agreed to his guideline that no one is born prejudiced. But they also understood that we start learning our place in this often violent and oppressive world as babies. In other words, there's agreement that we're constantly developing the second part of the dictionary definition of prejudice: Adverse opinions or leanings formed without just grounds or before sufficient knowledge. *Participants honestly shared and honored other people's experiences with diversity. While recognizing that good intentions alone aren't enough to overcome centuries of institutionalized bigotry.*

Be patient, I thought taking solace in other times I believed I had the answer but found I couldn't change my girlfriend's racist parents in college; or write a book on overcoming prejudice in either my twenties on the AVP or in my thirties in graduate school. Then I remembered the Veteran, an avid fisher.

She's right, next time I'll remember to bring my pole. Because even though I prefer the skills it takes to fish a river, it'd still be nice to simply stroll the shore, find a hatch, present a fly, watch one rise, reel her in, give her thanks, and let her go.

I hadn't discovered the magic potion. Still, my melancholy faded. In the morning I'd be speaking on the minority panel. Telling district administrators about experiences that might cast me as weak, paranoid, or not that smart. But I'd do it, because sharing is the first step.

~

"I'm a black man, raised by whites and a largely absent black father," I began, before sharing the time when my dad told me he was trying to keep me from his and his family's "toxic" anger and hate. And that I think his actions helped me endure decades of racist verbal assaults with a nearly unblemished record of actively nonviolent responses.

I made a connection with a Latino assistant principal who spoke on the minority panel too. He talked about the prejudice his friends, family and he had faced growing up in Texas, and how his anger made him a great football player. He listened closely to his coaches, refused to accept failure, ignored pain, and tried to destroy whatever he hit. I told him about how anger over prejudice motivated me to be a national champion and pro beach volleyball player.

Being at the administrator's retreat reminded me of six years earlier, when I thought about speaking to the assistant superintendent about being male in work place dominated by women as well as black in white Boulder. But, after cussing over her refusal to make contracts transparent, I was afraid that if she parroted BVSD's usual mantra of "being concerned about struggling minorities and doing what we can," I might have let a few more unproductive words fly.

So I thanked the Cohort directors numerous times for the opportunity to share. And when a few principals and I were hanging out Friday night, one said he'd heard about my outburst six years earlier. He assured me he would've handled the meeting differently and not put me in that position, which eased my embarrassment and worry.

~

The Superintendent spent a couple of the workshop sessions in the back: legs and arms crossed, looking everywhere except at who was speaking. He seemed bored or annoyed or both. His body language struck me because it was such a contrast to when he introduced himself to me last year. He said he'd been an assistant principal at Boulder High and complimented me on how well my volleyball teams always conducted themselves on and off the court. But his posture at the retreat told a different story, and had he been one of my students, he would've gotten a look that would've had him sit up and at least look like he cared.

Concerned, I asked the Veteran what she thought of the Superintendent and she assured me he was aware and committed to ending inequity and prejudice.

Still, I'd see similar displays from the Superintendent three more times. Once was after he'd fired every teacher and the principal at one elementary school while hundreds of irate teachers, staff, parents, and students demanded an explanation. Another came when I met with him and the Director of Human Resources to appeal my being fired. The final time was in a school board meeting, after a board member complained about the district's poor diversity awareness towards Jews.

~

Fall of my second year is also when I watched the first in a series of PBS News Hour reports on the Washington DC school district and its new superintendent, Michelle Rhee—the young and determined administrator out to show America how to shape up our failing schools. And the more I watched, the more I worried that my ideas about doing what's best for all people, in all communities, would negatively impact my career.

In the 1960's, 70's and 80's, a lot of liberals chose a career in public education because the work required patience, compassion, and a willingness to be underpaid. Decades later the pay is still not great, and teachers, their unions, and public education are attacked for having taken political correctness too far and creating overly sensitive, uneducated, lazy citizens. But that narrative is overplayed, and diminishes the priceless contributions made by teachers who are caring, intelligent, and hard-working.

Michelle Rhee had three years teaching experience and none in administration. Still, Rhee burst onto the scene like a superhero. She claimed to know what DC needed and promised to get it done. Rhee also bragged about being able to judge people within five minutes of meeting them. And how she had the bravado to publically embarrass those who didn't meet her standards.

"I'd say that I have a tremendous will," Rhee boasted, "Some people would call that being very willful, or stubborn. But when I know what needs to get done, very, very little, if anything, can stand in my way."

Rhee was DC's eighth superintendent in ten years. The decade-long revolving door began with retired three-star General Julius Becton. Becton and Rhee had the same motto, "Children First." "Our goal is to build an environment that fosters success," Becton said, "Remember, children first. Failure is not an option." Becton had survived three wars, but resigned after 16 months saying he'd never come across a more difficult job than reforming DC's schools. When Rhee was asked about the social and personal problems hindering academic progress in DC she responded, "You can address the needs of the souls of these kids in the classroom through the power that we have as educators. You can't teach in a vacuum. You've got to meet them where they are. You've got to take that into account. But you can never, ever, ever let that be an excuse for the kids not achieving at the highest levels."

Hunger; Friends shot and killed; Lack of sleep because you can't afford heat in the winter—those aren't excuses. Those are reasons! Sure, some kids excel in academics under those circumstances (some people can run a mile in four minutes). But most students who are malnourished, sleep deprived and/or depressed will struggle with academics.

"I believe that the public is behind me in an unbelievable way," Rhee continued, "I mean, to the level that, you know, on the weekends I'm in the grocery store. I am like in my flip-flops, and people come up to me, and they say, 'Thank goodness you're doing this. You can't do it quick enough. Don't give up.'"

Rhee's clueless, I thought, remembering fifth graders in Kansas who clowned me for selling out to "The Man." And a camp in high school, when black kids from Denver questioned my keeping my shoes untied like slippers. "What if you have to run to keep from getting beat down or shot?" one asked. "Boulder brat," another joked in the stereotypical nasal tone of whites.

Not everyone in DC is going to trust a woman walking around their rough neighborhoods in slippers. Besides, desperate people are easily seduced by promises of success.

Like when the Taliban fought the Russian military to a decade-long stalemate in Afghanistan and our military insisted we'd be out in a few years. Ego and arrogance will be the root of Rhee's failure too.

It'd been ten years since I first noticed conservative media intensify their attack to delegitimize "politically correct" language, (despite PC language being the product of a time when Americans were more integrated than ever).

It'd been five years since I read Bernard Goldberg's <u>Bias</u>, a liberal bashing liberals without making it clear that he still believes in liberal values. Now we get Rhee, another Democrat who says and does things older white male conservatives have traditionally said and done.

A new age of political correctness has arrived, I realized. Then vowed to speak against it.

~

I took a lot of deep breaths during the teacher's cohort. In one session, we discussed closing the achievement gap between whites and minorities. The conversation focused on how to work smarter and harder. I grew frustrated thinking about the decades of teachers giving heroic efforts, while the achievement gap remains.

"Teachers can make a difference," I said near the end of our discussion, "but many students face inequities so great that to succeed they need systemic change. We also have to spend time convincing those with power and resources to invest more."

"That's just a waste of time," one white female teacher insisted as I argued otherwise, "The powerful never listen. We need to focus on ourselves and the students."

"We need to do both," I said with my heart rate urging an expletive. Afterwards I asked a cohort leader if there was a program more suited to my experience and skills, like a Diversity Cohort II. She told me there wasn't.

I took more deep breaths during the teacher's retreat in Estes. Like when I was talking at my table about things that haven't changed. A young white male teacher at another table overheard and jumped in, "What are we doing in this cohort if things haven't changed?" he questioned and cited examples of a few high profile wealthy blacks. Then turned back around.

I continued the conversation at my table by bringing up minority home ownership and other statistics of upward mobility being the same as 50 years ago, before the Civil Rights Act. Those still listening nodded. Especially as I talked about a slave owner's convention in the 1850's, and the slave owner who shared his secret to success, "I used to have problems with rebelling slaves," he said, "Until I gave light skin blacks a few privileges and brought them into the house. Then dark and light skinned blacks started fighting with each other." Yet another dimension of 'divide and conquer.'

I wanted to berate the teacher for jumping in and out of our conversation (focusing only on the old self-congratulations for how far we've come, which keeps us from looking at how far we have to go). Not to mention I'd been doing these kinds of workshops for decades, and between the good old fashion prejudices, and the growing number of "reverse discrimination" claims, there's no shortage of examples showing that people continue to discriminate—and worse.

Later, the teacher who jumped in and out of our conversation spoke in front of the entire cohort. He said he'd learned a lot, and has a better understanding of how institutionalized bias and prejudice affects him and his students. He also wanted everyone to understand that white men aren't the only ones who speak and act with bias and prejudice. "I used to get women's phone numbers and dates all the time when I had a lucrative job," he explained, "But now, when I tell women I'm a teacher, they just walk away."

Part of me still wanted to tell him off. But I was glad he liked the cohort and I wanted our connection to remain positive. So when I spoke with him, I didn't mention the women who walked away from me for being black, and told him I'd gone through similar experiences after leaving pro beach volleyball. We shrugged and smiled.

~

The best part of the cohort was how close the Creekside teachers grew. We were excited to teach our curriculum to the whole Creekside community. Still, one teacher said the Veteran didn't want us getting carried away with it, because many in central administration didn't want too much time and effort going into diversity work.

I was surprised to hear that. The district motto is, "Excellence and Equity." The Veteran did the cohort and said she deeply valued it. She also knew about my extensive background with this kind of work and praised my skills with students, coworkers, parents and more. Like how I handled conflict between a Jewish and an Islamic student in my class. We did the work: researched facts, gave presentations, invited a parent to come in to speak with the class about how their faith promotes peace. And we found common ground.

When I asked, the Veteran denied that anyone wanted to limit diversity work, then paraphrased what she wrote in my evaluation, "Curtis, faculty appears to respond to your leadership and direction when you offer your opinions and express your thoughts. Your thoughtfulness is evident when you do share in a larger group ... You have taken a leadership role in our school in the area of equity ... Your insights and willingness to share your personal experiences adds a tremendous value to our faculty and our growth as educational professionals."

Sunset

I was one of a dozen on the interview team for our new principal. We rated candidates in several standards and criteria. I was shocked by who was eventually hired. She was by far the least articulate. And though she'd taught elementary and was an assistant principal at Boulder High, seemed most like a rookie. I spoke with others on the interview team and no thought her most qualified. Still, I empathize with those who struggle in interviews. Especially after having had to learn English as a second language, she might have a lot to offer. So I kept an open mind.

Originally, our staff's main concern was that we'd get a principal who wanted to dictate our every move. But after a few weeks teachers began to express concerns about how the Rookie gave almost no expectations or guidance. Poor communication aside, what disturbed many teachers and staff was the Rookie's constant tardiness (something she was renowned for at Boulder High). I wasn't too bothered until the secretary said the Rookie often arrived to school after first bell. The Veteran arrived early, helped with everything from shoveling the sidewalk to classroom preparation, actually showing all of us how much can be done to help staff and students be their best when the opening bell rings.

~

After accepting a new administrative position in the district half way through my second year, the Veteran's leadership all but disappeared. Then came a summer of relentless news coverage of America's failing teachers and schools. After eight months without leadership, Creekside's teachers and staff began the year anxious.

Then central administrators called Creekside's teachers into a meeting. They informed us we were on "probation" because last year, for the first time in many years, our students performed poorly on the annual standardized test, the CSAP. They explained that consequences accrue over the course of three years. First year, additional paper work and planning. Second, they'd bring in outside consultants, students would be allowed to open enroll and leave our school, and they'd give us additional funds and resources (we joked about evaluating students without standardized tests, so they'd learn but fail because of the foreign test format, then we'd cash in). Finally, if scores don't improve by the third year, everyone could be fired.

Our staff's main concern was our high percentage of second language learners and special education students, whose standardized test scores didn't accurately reflect our teaching. The central administrators empathized and told us to focus on teaching to the test and completing the paper work to be sure students are given appropriate accommodations. It's nerve-racking to be under the gun when there's no way to predict how many and what kinds of students might walk through your doors. Still, we were confident our student's scores would improve once we spent a little more time studying CSAP rules and regulations, and became more familiar with exemptions, accommodations, and the tests themselves.

~

Losing my 5th grade teammate's planning and organization was significant. Still, with two fat notebooks filled with two years' worth of daily plans and lessons, I felt comfortable leading someone who wasn't familiar with the curriculum. And though I'd heard that some in my teammate's old school were happy to be rid of him, I remembered 1999-2000, and the quality work I did with another male teacher others didn't like. Plus, since 10 out of 12 of the classroom teachers in kindergarten through 4th grade were women, I thought students would benefit from an all-male teaching team in 5th grade.

It didn't take long to see why some teachers and administrators might not like my teammate's teaching. Keeping updated posters and examples of student work on the walls for more instruction and feedback had been a weakness in my first year with noted improvement in my second. But my teammate's classroom walls were virtually empty—just a few pieces of student art. His students also spent a significant amount of time in self-run assignments and assessments. I don't think my contract would've been renewed if I refused to use wall space and gave so little direct instruction. But my new teammate was tenured.

My teammate's sterile, self-directed classroom probably wouldn't top the list of most principals' favorite. Even I didn't mind the extra effort of hanging posters and student work for inspiration and instruction. Besides, I thought it was important to remind students about expectations and connections more regularly. But my teammate showed me how using wall space can be over-stimulating. And that students can excel when they're allowed make their own expectations and connections. He also gave thought-provoking and artistic lessons in music, art, writing, and math, had an excellent, dry sense of humor, and could quickly and accurately evaluate a student's needs. I admired how he taught his self-reliance and authentic creativity.

I also appreciated how my teammate prioritized his personal life. Few jobs can consume you as completely as teaching. Students, parents, teachers, administration, staff—there's *always* something more that can be done. And the competition to be the kind of teacher who goes the extra mile is fierce. Not having time for one's self, spouses, and friends is a big part of why half of all teachers leave the profession by their fifth year (just when they start to get good).

I went into school to work on most Sundays for two years. Half-way through my third year I improved my lessons, rubrics, time management and got the work done during the week. And while I could've continued to come in on weekends, I nurtured other important relationships.

~

My five teammates: one 5th grade, two 4th grade, and two specialists, combined for nearly a century of teaching experience. At our weekly meetings we spoke of concerns for our principal's lack of feedback and direction. My new 5th grade teammate was particularly concerned, "I've seen administrators get rid of teachers for no good reason." They also warned that administrators often act like vindictive members of an exclusive club—so never get on their bad side.

I wasn't too concerned. I took the lead in mapping and planning (curriculum, Outdoor Education overnight retreat, Fundraisers, field trips, and more). My grading and feedback were better than ever. And with more students telling me they had a new love for Language Arts than in previous years, my poetry and social studies units were steadily improving, too.

Twice, I came back from a break to find central administrators had dropped in unannounced to watch me teach. As usual, lessons and classroom were prepped. Objectives clearly written and stated. Introduction and follow- up engaged students. Students worked in small groups and individually. They demonstrated their understanding of the scientific process by recording experiments in colorful, detailed journals. In math they expanded vocabulary and number concepts by discussing and solving the same problems in different ways.

I considered inviting the administrators back because their presence put my students on their best behavior. Then, thought it was too bad the administrators didn't have a chance to see one of my best skills— refocusing students when things go awry. They never saw how effectively my own language and version of my supervising teacher Millie's "Dead Eye Dan" recaptures a student's attention.

"Do I need to remind you how lucky you are to be getting an education?" I'd ask making eye contact with everyone. And by the end of the year, they'd jump back to work before I could finish the sentence— anything not to hear me ramble on about that again.

Or I'd bring out the good stuff. Remind them hard work earns rewards: read aloud, drawing, board games, computer time, or extra recess.

~

The Rookie wanted one of our literacy specialists and me to spend the months leading up to the CSAP test team-teaching. We were surprised but played along. I watched her teach two lessons using a new projector that made it easy for students to share and edit together. Then she watched me teach a couple similar lessons.

"I don't know why [the Rookie] wants us teaching together," my teammate said after calling me into her office, "watching each other teach is a waste of time. Most students understand and like our lessons. So if it's ok with you, let's go back to me taking a few who need help with some basics back to my office, and the other 20 or so stay with you."

"That's fine," I replied, "but thanks for showing me those lessons and that projector from the library. I've thought up a game and rewards I think they'll like."

"My pleasure," she said, "we just bought the projector. You can check it out from the library. I found the lessons on line. Teachers in Texas created them after finding out how standardized tests were scored."

"Cool," I responded, "well, you're always welcome in my class, but let's do what's best for our students ... and us."

"Good," she agreed.

Aside from a respected literacy teacher with two decades of experience telling me I was doing great, my confidence soared because my students told me her lessons were boring. And though my games and connections made the formal essay lessons a bit more fun, what really kept my students working hard was my promise that once we aced the CSAP, we'd start the end of the year "literary celebration." A chance for students to write their dreams in their favorite genre: poetry, report, short story, journal, magazine, comic, or skit. Then we'd celebrate each other.

~

Michelle Rhee made a lot of changes in DC. On the positive side, she quadrupled spending for teacher development (though given how little was being invested to begin with, it wasn't as significant of an investment as "quadrupled" might imply). Rhee also changed evaluations for improved feedback and greater accountability.

On the negative side, Rhee judged with extreme bias and boasted about publically shaming people for failings that, by and large, were the result of circumstances beyond their control.

I thought two images in Time Magazine's article about Rhee accurately portrayed her impact. Within the article pages was a small picture of Rhee working with a bunch of students, everyone smiling. But the glossy 8" x 11" cover pictured Rhee standing in front of an empty teacher's desk, holding a broom, chin and chest raised, stern face—a dictator.

In an April 2008 PBS report, Rhee said she gave annual standardized tests scores more weight when measuring teacher, principal, and school performance. Even though standardized tests give limited feedback on students' needs, they do make great headlines. And Rhee seemed to relish negative ones. She fired half the district's principals and closed 23 schools.

DC teachers tried to take refuge in a plan negotiated in 1999, to keep principals from the too common practice of firing teachers for the wrong reasons. In that plan, struggling teachers had to undergo a 90-day evaluation with clear goals and expectations to determine if they can hack it. Rhee and her supporters claimed that plan made it near impossible for administrators to do their jobs. Principal L. Nelson Burton spoke with PBS. Burton wanted massive lay-offs and had only three teachers on the 90-day plan.

"Where the real difficulty comes is when half of your staff falls into that range," Burton complained, "how do you fire half of your staff?"

Rhee's and Burton's problem is the same as their teachers: not enough time and resources. The whole community, students, teachers, principals, assistants, parents, staff, everyone deserves the best organization, evaluation, and feedback. There's the fatal flaw in the "Children First" motto touted by Rhee and the three-star general a decade ago—making laws without allocating resources to enforce them.

~

Mid December 2008, Boulder's Superintendent shocked the district when he announced that since students at Columbine Elementary had done poorly on the annual CSAP test three years in a row, he was firing every teacher and the principal there. It was particularly surprising because just two years earlier, the Superintendent kicked off his tenure with a $50,000 pep rally in which he gave a speech saying that standardized tests won't be given much weight when evaluating a school's performance.

Columbine's population was 83 percent Hispanic (most English second language learners) and 14 percent white. Teachers and parents picketed and chanted, "Save our school," "We love our teachers," "We are here and we are happy." A petition to reverse the decision circulated online and hundreds of teachers, other employees, and parents throughout the district signed. The community demanded the Superintendent hold a meeting and explain. I attended hoping to gain insight into how our school might avoid a similar fate.

Angry community members talked about their love for the principal, teachers, and school. They explained, in a variety of ways, how most second language learners are overwhelmed by language in primary grades. So naturally their test scores lag behind, especially on assessments like the CSAP, based heavily in language and cultural references. But in secondary and higher education, as students master fundamentals in both languages, scores improve exponentially.

Our Superintendent thanked the Columbine community for their concerns and assured everyone he also wanted what was best. But his tone and body language told a different story. I was reminded of him sitting in the back of the administrator diversity cohort in Estes last year, looking like he couldn't believe he had to be bothered. Like many attending the meeting, I left feeling cheated.

The Superintendent sparked further outrage when he hired a new principal without community input. A complaint was filed with the US Department of Education's office of Civil Rights.

The Superintendent completely ignored Columbine's community input. Maybe that's how the least articulate candidate, his former colleague at Boulder High school, became our principal at Creekside.

~

We talked about Columbine in our 4th, 5th, and specialists team meeting. One specialist, a friend of the principal, said she knew personally the

Columbine staff were great educators, had been there for years, and had built a program tailored to their population.

I talked about how I presented a week-long Poetry to Celebrate Life workshop at Columbine. The teachers were first-rate. They loved my curriculum. We had a great week. And after being fired later that year, I figured it wasn't a coincidence that both Columbine's and my curriculums were considered expendable.

Worried Creekside might meet a similar fate, our teaching team doubled down on our commitment to the CSAP content and format. We were optimistic. In part because we had fewer second language learners than Columbine. Still, it remained nerve-racking. We did have many second language learners and special education students, plus, no way of knowing how many more might walk through our doors in the next couple of years.

In 4th and 5th grade classroom teacher's team meetings, I was surprised by the amount of time we spent discussing how best to deal with BVSD leadership's contradictions when it comes to diversity. Being a 41-year old minority who grew up in Boulder and whose strength is diversity, I volunteered to write a letter to the Superintendent. I'd explain that we want to be held accountable, but measuring our effectiveness requires looking at many kinds of evaluations. My three teammates, half a century of teaching experience between them, thanked me for taking the lead.

Over winter break I wrote the letter and changed some lessons to be CSAP-centric. One teammate read my letter and cheered as I walked down the hall to set up a meeting with the Rookie.

"I wrote the letter on behalf of the 4th and 5th grade team," I told the Rookie to kick off the meeting, "and we'd like your input."

The letter opened with how tests like the CSAP are heavily biased in language and cultural references, which means socio-economic status determines success more than anything else. I included that our students' long-term needs often aren't served by short-term success on the CSAP. And concluded with how our Superintendent seems to be caught up in a national trend of unjustly and unnecessarily demoralizing individuals and communities.

The Rookie agreed with the short-comings of teaching to, and measuring our success with, one biased standardized test a year. But she gave me a look of concern after reading the part about our Superintendent's actions mirroring the unfortunate national trend.

"There are bad teachers out there," she said, "Why shouldn't I just bring in a young, talented replacement."

"Well," I replied, "teaching takes years to master, even talented rookies (like quarterbacks coming into the NFL), struggle with the amount of information and the speed with which teachers communicate and make decisions. So replacing experienced teachers results in a loss for students for a few years. Plus," I continued, "half of all teachers quit by their fifth year, just when they start to get good. Factor in the large numbers of teachers about to retire across the nation, there's going to be teacher shortages in no time."

The Rookie nodded, but looked unconvinced.

Knowing that I wasn't tenured yet, teaching positions in Boulder get hundreds of applicants each, and she might not care about the big picture, I began to feel uncomfortable.

"I'm doing a satisfactory job, right?" I asked, "Because this is a dream job. And, I'm willing to put in the extra hours—after school, weekends, and summer—learn Spanish. I'll do what it takes."

"You're doing fine," she replied, "your goals are appropriate and you're getting better."

~

The next day the Rookie dropped in for an unscheduled observation. BVSD mandates all new teachers schedule at least four observations and conferences with their principals during each of their first three years. In my case, the Rookie was late to *every* scheduled observation. She actually witnessed only half of the two—Science and Social Studies—scheduled for 40 minutes each. So the impromptu observation plus the conference accounted for our longest professional interaction at any one time.

Originally, I planned a two week unit using the Investigations curriculum right after winter break. But after what happened at

Columbine, I planned a unit using the Scots/Foresman curriculum. Investigations is heavily language based, focused on exploring and discussing associations between different math concepts and a variety of ways to problem solve. Scots/Foresman focuses more on algorithms and rote memorization.

"Why aren't you using the Investigations curriculum adopted by the district?" she asked.

I was confused because I wrote "Improved CSAP scores," as one of the goals for the lesson on the board. And during the lesson, I repeatedly stressed to the students how this rote, algorithm work may be boring, but sometimes you just have to drill numbers and procedures.

"Well, like our conversation yesterday," I explained, "after Columbine, we're concerned about doing well on the algorithm-loving CSAP."

"Yes, but in the long run," she fired back, "these students (we divided the fifth grade into two groups, my teammate taught advanced while I taught the basic with more English as a second language learners) do better with Investigations."

"Sure," I responded, "but if we don't improve our test scores, our Superintendent and School Board aren't going to care that we built a foundation for their success later. We're all going to get fired."

"Well," she said with a look of concern, "I guess you have to decide if you're going to do what's best for our students."

"I always keep my students best interests in mind," I replied thinking most students don't get a confidence boost from failing a test that gets their teachers and principal fired.

"Good," she said, then asked for a copy of their homework and left.

I thought of my teammate's advice about staying on administrators' good side. And how the Superintendent had already heard most of what I had written in the letter (like at the Columbine meeting). I decided not to send the letter to the Superintendent.

I also moved an Investigations unit to the beginning of February. I would have done more Investigations, but after evaluating my students' performance in the two-week Scots/Foresman unit after break, they needed the work. So, not to let my students, colleagues, and school down,

I planned another <u>Scots/Foreman</u> unit. The Rookie dropped by for an unscheduled observation during one of those follow-up lessons on January 27. She came late and left after ten minutes.

~

The most memorable looks our principal gave me came in February.

One came in a team meeting. We talked about the movie our principal had us watch, "Stand and Deliver." Edward James Olmos plays a high school math teacher who changed the expectations in a poor Latino neighborhood by having his students take AP Calculus as seniors.

We were all inspired. But I also brought up how Olmos' character worked so hard he had a heart attack (though notable Hollywood embellishments were that their teacher had an inflamed gall bladder instead, and students who took AP Calculus as seniors *could* do basic multiplication as freshmen). Then I remarked on the scene where the teacher's son yells and pleads for him to give his family a fraction of the attention he gives his students.

"I hope we all give our best effort," I concluded, "but I don't think any of us should sacrifice our personal or our family's well-being for this job."

While teammates nodded thankfully, she looked at me, stone-faced.

The other came after President's day, when I went golfing with three male teachers on a gorgeous, sunny, 50-degree winter day. One in our group was a retired teacher from Creekside, and a go-to sub for many teachers. I called him because my students liked him, they got their work done, and he encouraged me to leave him papers to grade. On the course he told me the Veteran had been hiring him to organize the State's standardized testing material. But the Rookie didn't want to pay him and would have secretaries and other staff do it instead. My sub told the Rookie it's a lot of additional work but she wouldn't listen.

"She's going to regret it," my go-to sub said walking up the tenth fairway.

The next day I saw the Rookie and told her I a great day golfing with the guys. She straightened her shoulders and rocked back like I'd inched into her personal space though I hadn't. I told the Rookie how the Veteran had hired the retired teacher to prep the testing material for years. I mentioned he'd taught for a decade at Creekside, was a reliable sub and always did a great job, "If he says prepping the materials requires help it probably does."

She smirked and assured me she had it covered.

~

Though the Rookie's looks and body language regularly concerned me, there were also reasons to turn off my alarms.

There was a mad rush to begin CSAP testing. Everyone scrambled on breaks and after school to prep materials, further stressing teachers and staff already dealing with a large percentage of second language and special education students.

"Next year," the Rookie said to me, "I'm going to heed the advice the retired teacher and you gave me."

In the fall teachers debated whether or not to celebrate Halloween with parties and a parade throughout the school. Some teachers thought Halloween had little academic or cultural value, needlessly pumped our students full of sugar, and exacerbated economic divides (the coolest costumes were usually expensive). But some teachers thought dressing up and having some treats was a positive experience. We voted to skip Halloween festivities that year.

With some obviously disappointed, we talked about revisiting the issue next year.

"Cultures throughout the world celebrate ghosts, spirits and other transformations. Like The Day of the Dead," I said. "We could base costumes on social studies or literature units."

Many teachers nodded. But our principal's brow grew stern, like she was confused or concerned. I didn't want her to think I was likening The Day of the Dead to Halloween, so I spoke to her later. "It could be a good excuse to do some research. Learn about differences and find some common ground. Like including Catholic All Souls Day. And if we tie it to curriculum, maybe students can make costumes in school."

"That's not a bad idea," she said.

~

In the beginning of March I met with the Rookie to go over my evaluation. I had serious concerns.

First, she wrote, "...is beginning to utilize some instructional strategies to enhance learning. I have seen Curtis use graphic organizers in writing, support students one on one, provide multiplication charts in Math, and use questioning techniques in Reading." And, "...is beginning to use some summative and formative assessment such as writing rubrics."

"I've been using and improving rubrics in all subjects since my first year," I said, "along with questioning techniques and aids: from vocabulary to critical thinking. And after being warned by 3rd and 4th grade teachers about this class having particularly diverse emotional and educational needs, feel like I've done a good job."

"Well," she responded, "I can only comment on what I observed."

I remembered the Rookie apologizing for being 20 minutes late to *two* 40-minute observations. Saying she wished she saw the parts of the lesson that got my students so excited about the Civil War and water conservation.

I was also concerned because under 'Areas for continued professional growth', the Rookie wrote I needed to work on "implementation of RtI [Response to Intervention] and PBS [Positive Behavior Support]."

"You also noted I was one of a few Creekside teachers to attend the RtI and PBS workshops," I said, "and led staff meetings on how to implement this new curriculum in our hallways, playgrounds, and classrooms. So are you saying," I asked, "I'm a respected leader, striving to be better, and will continue to be an important role model for our community?

"Yes," she said.

My last concern was based in having received lower marks in six of eighteen categories on my evaluation. Yet the Veteran and Rookie regularly told me I was improving.

"A third of my evaluation is marked lower this year," I emphasized, "So I was wondering if you consider the evaluation pass/fail?"

"The evaluation is not pass or fail," she replied.

"So, I'm doing a satisfactory job?" I asked.

"Yes," she said.

"Is there anything you need to see me do to keep my dream job?" I pressed.

"No," she ended our conversation as she had our meeting about the letter I wrote to the Superintendent, "You're doing fine. Your goals are appropriate and you're getting better."

~

My new teammate said he connected more with me than any teacher in his 18 years. He also thanked me for my leadership, and said he'd contribute more next year now that he knew what to expect. I liked how we brought a "male" tone—appreciation for sarcasm, more authoritarian discipline and consequences with fewer frilly rewards—to our classrooms. I was certain some students felt more validated with us than in their previous five years at Creekside. I saw a valuable place for growth and connection with how my teammate taught students to breathe (good for everyone, especially those with a lot of testosterone). The best part was how we talked about getting together that summer to get to know each other better. And talk about ways to make next year far better.

That spring I had more than my quota of flying dreams, and woke up energized, ready to take my career, and Creekside, to new levels.

On Thursday, April 30th, at 9:26 pm, with only one month left in the year, our principal e-mailed me saying we needed to meet and discuss my contract on Monday. On Friday, we planned to meet first thing, after I drop my students off at music.

The national and local climate were unsettled. Greedy, criminal bankers had plunged millions across the world into poverty. America was in the worst economic turmoil in 80 years. The news regularly blamed teachers for failing schools. BVSD's Superintendent devastated many in the Columbine community, firing a principal and all the teachers. Teachers and principals throughout BVSD were being fired and communities were responding in protest. Students walked out at Boulder High.

Still, lawsuits and petitions helped rational minds prevail and the Superintendent rescinded his order to fire *all* Columbine teachers. I'd made it clear to the Rookie that this was my dream job. My commitment to growth and professional development were undeniable. In their final CSAP practice tests, my student's growth in Reading and Math were equal to their growth under the celebrated 4th grade teachers, and they grew more in Writing. My students demonstrated better understanding between my Social Studies units and bully prevention. My students cheered when I said it was time to begin our end of the year Writing unit. My colleagues said I was an excellent teacher. The Veteran and Rookie said I continually improved all aspects of teaching and my worst were "satisfactory." Plus, the Rookie scheduled the meeting with a month left in school, first thing Monday. I was confident my contract would be renewed.

Unlike when I left Kansas in 1991, LA in 1997, teaching in 2000, coaching in 2003, and poetry workshops in 2005, I was ready to begin a long career to significantly impact my community. I was home.

Darkness

"This isn't going to be an easy conversation" the Rookie began and then said I was fired for not being, "the right fit." And concluded, "I'm not obligated to explain any further."

You got to be fucking kidding! My heart pounded, mind flooding with expletives recounting endless examples of what a shitty principal she'd been.

I made a list when most of my colleagues said they'd back me and I was thinking about suing: the Rookie was tardy to the start of most school days, planning meetings, *all* my observations, and more; she gave few expectations to me, other staff, students, and parents; office staff often had to deal with discipline and other problems because they didn't know where she was; the Rookie made two highly inappropriate jokes, one when staff expressed concerns about her schedule causing confusion which resulted in students being left unattended on the playground, another after the Rookie was bitter because in a meeting, the male administrator talked a lot more than the female administrator. We also never practiced an important safety drill.

When I got back to my empty room, I screamed, cussed, and whipped a few markers at the wall. Then went across the hall to talk to my teammate.

"That's messed up," he said, "I had no idea. Did you ask her why?"

"She said I wasn't the right fit," I said, "and that's all she had to say."

"I don't know what to say Curtis," he concluded, "I'm shocked."

My students came back from music and we began our morning routine. I struggled to manage my sense of shock and grief. I apologized to my students if I felt distant to them and told them I had been fired. They were shocked and saddened too.

The morning was a blur, I just kept taking deep breaths and saying to myself "keep my students on task."

At lunch I drove to the top of NCAR. I looked over my old elementary school, Jr. and High school. My church, the sand volleyball courts. Home.

"Goddamn, stupid, ignorant, mother fuckers," I screamed, punched the steering wheel, and cried. After some deep breaths I looked back to the familiar Flatirons. The trails and canyons, meadows and streams, cool damp ravines where broad leafed ferns thrive in our desert climate. Then, once again, the mountains told me everything would be ok if I charged back downhill like a warrior. So I vowed to finish the year strong and find a teaching job in BVSD next fall.

~

The next day, I found out the Rookie had fired another of the three male classroom teachers that the Veteran hired two years earlier. He felt blindsided too. He couldn't believe she had the right to say he was "not the right fit," let alone that someone would actually be so "unprofessional." He contacted our Union rep who said the deadline to file an appeal *and* hold a hearing was in three days. They had set up a meeting and were putting together his defense.

My 5th grade teammate asked the remaining male teacher if he knew why the Rookie kept him. The Remaining Male thought of a meeting he and the Rookie attended together.

That meeting was led by a male and a female. Afterwards the Rookie made a remark about the man doing most of the talking. The Remaining Male took offense at the remark. He said he talked to the Rookie and they came to an understanding. But he also thought the incident probably influenced her decision to keep him.

"The more I think about it the angrier I get," Remaining Male said after I'd been fired, "if you want to fight this, you can count on me." (In fall of his fifth year he decided to quit and leave Boulder saying, "I'm just sick of all the BVSD bullshit.").

I thought of earlier in the year, when the Rookie said she might have to make cuts to school staff. How other teachers mentioned that the Veteran said the same thing every year, and she always found a way to keep everyone. Some teachers even responded by saying they'd work less to give FTE time so other teachers might keep their job and remain a part of our community during the worst economic crisis in 80 years. The Rookie nodded, but didn't look convinced.

The Rookie e-mailed me late Thursday to schedule a meeting on Monday! Three days before the deadline to appeal amid a crush of deadlines for the teachers—projects, report cards, graduation. A majority of the Creekside community supported me and the district had had enough bad press.

So this was an old school hit job! The institutional equivalent of being snatched out of bed in the middle of the night and disappeared in the swamp. Shameful shock and silence is the only response.

For the next three weeks the Rookie perpetuated the silence by rarely being in the building and skipping staff meetings. This way she didn't have to face a room full of confused and angry teachers. And justify her behavior, which most thought was unprofessional and unproductive.

I set up an appeal on the last day possible. And with only two nights to prepare, along with the end of the year work load, I wrote a quick outline and planned to speak from the heart.

~

Thursday May 7, I gave a lesson, dropped my students off for music and PE, and drove to the Education Center.

The Superintendent, the Director of Human Resources and I walked into a small room.

"I want to make one thing clear," the Superintendent said as we sat, "there is no appeal process. Your principal's decision was final. Still, we're willing to hear you out."

"*What a load of shit!*" I thought and took a deep breath thinking now they can end my career claiming they gave me fair shake. Or worse, that the overly sensitive minority man who wasn't a very good teacher needed a therapy session, and they helped me understand the "real" world out of the goodness of their hearts.

"[The Rookie] was a weak leader" I started, "She's tardy more often than not, communicates poorly, and struggles with student discipline. She marked one third of my evaluation lower than [the Veteran]. Most notably, categories I've excelled in my entire life: Commitment to educate students; Commitment to ongoing professional growth; and Continues to increase knowledge of equity and diversity issues and recognizing their effect on student achievement." I ended the first part of my defense with, "[The Rookie] also made highly inappropriate jokes on two occasions."

The Superintendent's posture and face remained still, but his eyes rolled. The Director of Human Resources looked concerned.

"But I'm not here to focus on her," I said and the Superintendent and Human Resources Director said they thought that would be best.

"[The Veteran] said my strengths were outstanding," I continued, "And both [the Veteran and Rookie] regularly said my weaknesses improved. I've improved at evaluating students and giving feedback in every subject. And though it's not an official score, my students performed well on their practice CSAP. My books show I did my part to keep us off probation. You're welcome to look at them if you like [they didn't]."

The Superintendent crossed his legs, leaned back and nodded like, "And?"

So I began my grand finalé, relying on what BVSD administrators made clear in 1999—my contract is with the district, not Creekside.

"I'm a tremendous asset to BVSD," I continued, "born and raised in Boulder, I've always dreamt of teaching. Half white, half black, but identified as black, a graduate level education, with unique and powerful insight on diversity and BVSD's motto: Excellence and Equity."

I brought out the Equity Cohort book and placed it on the table. When I saw the look the Superintendent and Director of Human Resources gave each other I knew I'd lost them.

I might as well walk out right now, I thought, but vowed to see the fight to its end.

"'Dealing with people very different than myself caused a shattering in me of preconceptions I scarcely knew I had.'" I read the James Baldwin quote at the beginning of section 24, Leadership and Equity.

"Forty years as a bi-racial person has taught me we all have preconceptions we scarcely know we have," I continued, "and I have a good understanding of the four stages of development Julian describes. First comes *Resistance* – thinking education has no business addressing teacher's beliefs or emotions, or institutionalized racism or sexism. Second is *Awareness* – reading to reflect on and discuss beliefs, and listen and talk about experiences with inequity. Third is *Commitment* – realize progress will require considerable personal and social transformation."

"After decades of studying diversity and teaching at Creekside, Fairview, CrestView, Lafayette, Columbine, and many more BVSD schools, people have often praised my leadership as stage four, *Strategic Action* – able to take greater risks, to speak out more forcefully on equity issues to help people use the structures and develop strategies for change."

"Section 12 in the district's diversity workbook," I continued turning the page, "is titled, Teachers Deserve Respect and Support, and states 'Any educational change effort must, at its core, provide intellectual and emotional support for teachers.'"

"You shocked teachers across the district when you fired everyone at Columbine," I said frankly to the Superintendent, "It was predictable that in the highly educated town of Boulder, many would protest and demand you retract such an unproductive decision."

The Superintendent shifted in his expensive chair and looked confused, like he couldn't understand what Columbine had to do with anything. Then he leaned back further, raised his arms, linked his fingers behind his head and asked "You were a coach, right?"

"Yes," I answered.

"Well Curtis," he continued like a two bit businessman, "I just see it like a judgement call."

Right, I thought, *a really fucking bad one*. I then turned to the Director of Human Resources, who was looking at him with a Mona Lisa smile before turning to me and nodding.

"Boulder is my home," I tried to stay on track, "I've worked in the district for two decades. My current position is ideal for a litany of reasons. But if I'm not reinstated, I want to pursue other positions in the classroom, or in Art or PE, utilizing my skills as an artist, former pro athlete, trainer, and coach. Unfortunately, I do not yet have an official endorsement. I'll pass the tests no problem," I assured them, "but they're not offered until the middle of summer. So I'd appreciate any advice you might have about the best way for me to stay in the district."

"It's difficult for a third year non-renewed teacher to get another job, especially in the same discipline," the Director of Human Resources said and the Superintendent agreed (those who used the term "blackballed" included my mentor, the Veteran, my principal in 1999, and the president of our teacher's union). And because BVSD schools get so many applications, as soon as principals see you're not endorsed, they'll throw the application out. So I wouldn't waste my time."

Still, the Human Resources Director said she'd be happy to help me prep my file and look for another job.

The Superintendent wished me luck.

I thanked them for their time and told the Human Resources Director I'd be in touch.

~

"We feel more angry every day," my teammates said at our next planning meeting. Teachers, staff, students, and parents throughout the school were talking about ten months of the Rookie's questionable and unprofessional judgement.

"I'm a lost cause," I said to my teammates, "between the crashed economy and the nation-wide teacher bashing, any argument I'd make to the School Board would fall on deaf ears. I'm not going to fight this. And I'd be careful about getting on the bad side of this Superintendent and School Board."

"I'm just staying positive and moving forward," I continued, "I'll contact teachers and principals I've worked with in the past and introduce myself to new ones—do what it takes to be working on the first day next year. And I would appreciate it if you all would write me a letter of recommendation."

"I'll get right on it," each one said.

When I got back to my room I looked at my evaluation.

The Rookie did note the right dates and amount of time for her observations. But she did not note if her observations were scheduled or not. She also left out times she was scheduled to arrive, and that she missed half of two planned 40 minute observations. Plus, seven out of ten observations were for 10, 15 or 20 minutes, which means she only saw three complete lessons. Not to mention her unclear, passive-aggressive feedback.

If there's ever been a time to write my story it's now. Still, as an educator, and a man who can provide for himself and his family, I'm first going to try to salvage a career.

~

PBS News Hour ran an update on Washington DC's schools that highlighted the effects of Superintendent Michelle Rhee's words and actions.

"It created a culture of low morale," said teacher union president George Parker, "one that was the lowest that I've seen since I've been in D.C. public schools, and I've been here for 25 years."

English middle school teacher Ronald H. Brown talked about effects in the classroom, "There will be students who will start your day off saying, 'Oh, yeah, I've read the article. You all are getting fired anyway.' And they absolutely believe it. You can't really be accountable when you're undermined."

~

The Creekside community was confused and angry too.

The Rookie sent out in an email on Tuesday May 19th. "Dear teachers, Parents have asked me to do a presentation about the school's vision and goals next Thursday, May 21st from 6:30 pm to 7:30 pm. Please let me know if you will be able to attend. Attendance is not mandatory."

The flyer said, "We would like to have an opportunity to share with you the school's vision, core values and goals [*actually, parents had demanded the meeting*]. Please come to learn more about our continued efforts to create a school where students and families can embrace a culture of high expectations, a culturally responsive environment, collaboration [*my personal specialties*], effective instructional practices and relevant professional development [*I was one of four to attend the professional development workshops and presented our vision at staff meetings*]. We will explain how our practices, policies and procedures are changing to reflect what we believe in, how you can support us and how we are working together to achieve our goals."

~

Immediately following the meeting, parents from two families wrote a four page letter on behalf of those in attendance. They sent copies to the Superintendent and the Superintendent of School Leadership.

"Three rapidly developing issues at Creekside Elementary involving our principal have us alarmed and deeply worried," the parents began, "Any one of these would prompt a letter to you; to have all three unfolding simultaneously has us requesting your full attention and prompt response."

"The bottom line is parents felt their son was being bullied," is the first concern mentioned, "[the Rookie's] response left them so upset they have decided to pull their second-grader and incoming kindergartner from BVSD. The parents were heavily involved in the school and PTO. Dad had an extraordinary touch as a soccer coach and was spearheading Creekside's effort to improve school lunch; Mom helped with the read-a-thon and was one of the primary supporters of the effort to fill Creekside's 'late start' hour with health-based curriculum. Their son was in Creekside's tiny 'Talented and Gifted' student program."

"No school can afford to lose active parents or gifted children," the parents continued, "Creekside especially so ... We have since learned – third- or fourth-hand, of a second bullying incident where the parents also ultimately opted to withdraw from Creekside."

"Bullying is a huge issue for Creekside. During last year's search for a principal, Creekside parents identified as a high priority the need to swiftly and properly address, diffuse and curtail bullying incidents. At last night's visioning meeting, where parents gathered in a breakout session to discuss how Creekside can create a more culturally responsive environment it surfaced again as a top concern."

"The second issue concerns the layoff of two provisional teachers … We found [the other teacher] to be an engaging teacher and a well-liked part of the Creekside community. We're less familiar with Mr. Griffin. But his background as a poet brings a crucial dimension to the school; as read-a-thon coordinators, we planned to work with him to make poetry the central theme of next year's event."

I was going to introduce my poetry workshops schoolwide. I'd reinforce bully prevention curriculum and lay a foundation for when students reach 5th grade and I teach them about the good and bad in our Founding Fathers. We'd prove MLK Jr. was right—the potentially violent 10% have little impact when 90% speak out against hate. And the surest way to create a nonviolent environment is to learn to like others. But my main goal was to get as many students as possible to fall in love with language and its power to make dreams come true.

"Both men are assets for our elementary school," the parents continued, "[our] community hired these two teachers because they were seen as an excellent fit for our vision of the school … [the Rookie] has let them go without offering a clear vision why … [in the meeting] she failed to enunciate why teachers acceptable to the community a year ago are no longer a good fit … [the Rookie] hopes to lead Creekside through transformational change … But to seize this opportunity she needs a committed community that supports and understands her efforts. She has instead fostered dissent, bitterness and rumor among parents and teachers."

"The final issue concerns the late start," the parents continued, "the district is squandering an opportunity to get students and families excited and involved in what could be an enriching part of the school day. We had hoped that this hour could become a part the schools regular curriculum—an hour of intramural sports or gardening or music or chess or any of a number of educational but non-traditional activities."

Like my goal setting, anti-bullying, language skills developing and community building poetry workshops, overseen by me and taught by talented and enthusiastic 5th graders.

"Instead, it appears the YMCA will handle the bulk of the children deposited at school by parents unable to keep children at home," the letter details, "And that the divide between bused and neighborhood kids – already acknowledged as a problem at Creekside – will only grow ... this rushed effort is creating division: those with options and means to keep their children home will do so; those who must work or rely on the school bus will send their children off to an environment that is, essentially, daycare ... It strikes us as a terrible way to create a culturally responsive environment, one that undermines many of the gains to be realized by collaboration."

"We want to emphasize that we support [the Rookie's] efforts and appreciate the challenges confronting her," they conclude, "We don't expect to be privy to every detail ... But we want assurances that fundamental needs are being met. We want to feel our kids are safe, that they're learning and developing social skills in a productive way within a diverse community, and that the teachers and principal are working together as a team."

Since I (and the other male teacher) had been providing exactly the kind of learning environment the parents were asking for, I thought again about taking a stand against the clear injustice of our being fired. I could go to the media and courts of law. I'd let my teammates help (they offered individually and in groups). A friend taught in another BVSD school and said he'd get people to picket at Creekside. Still, I worried because winning in these situations requires making the other look worse.

Instead, I went to the Rookie on the day she promised to have my letter of recommendation ready. She placed her hand on my forearm, shrugged, giggled, and apologized for not having it done. I smiled and said no worries. But the instant I was alone, threw a backhand that would've landed on the Rookie's jaw and shouted, "Don't fucking touch me you incompetent dumbass!" I'd never been more ready for a war. And part of me took pleasure knowing I could use words to devastate the Rookie, Superintendent, and Director of Human Resources.

Thankfully, I had help with staying positive. Many co-workers told me they were certain I'd get rehired (even if it took until August when schools get their final student counts and FTE worked out). Plus, everyone I asked to write a letter of recommendation said they would. And they were pouring in.

Dawn

"I have watched Curtis get involved in some very important conversations," wrote BVSD Executive Director for Institutional Equity, "He was always respectful and even though he may have had a different point of view he made the other point of view feel honored. This active listening made it possible for him to gain trust and often impact the person's thinking through well timed questions which prompted the people to reassess their thinking."

"Curtis is also a student-centered professional," the Director of Equity continued, "willing to be involved in professional development opportunities. His impact in the sessions was powerful ... I never heard him be negative or disengaged. Curtis was a leader by example ... I think every group needs someone who can lead by example."

~

"I have been very impressed with Mr. Griffin's dedication to his class," one parent wrote, "preparation for parent teacher meetings, and especially his ability to provide attention and assistance to the broad spectrum of student abilities I know are in his class ... I attribute much of the development of a voice in [his daughters] writing to Mr. Griffin's encouragement and teaching ... [his daughter] also explained Mr. Griffin has the ability to talk about subjects so that they actually make sense ... and has skill at dealing with children who misbehave as well as the ability to turn school work into games that are fun."

~

"One of my duties is to supervise Curtis' 5th graders during lunch recess and their lunch," wrote a coworker whose son was in the other class but came to me for math and poetry, "When I inform Curtis of disciplinary problems ... he deals with the issues immediately and finds fair solutions ... I often hear him praise the good behavior ... [her son] would come home excited about the poetry, saying that Mr. Griffin explained everything ... made poetry fun [he'd never enjoyed writing before] ... he also loved the math ... Mr. Griffin always took the time to explain things until he understood ... now in middle school [her son] is in advanced math and advanced language arts. I believe that Curtis had a great deal to do with how well he progressed ... I regret that my other son will not have the benefit of Curtis' knowledge and skill as a teacher."

~

"Curtis is an excellent teacher," wrote a first grade teacher at Creekside, parent of one of my students, "who continually demonstrates amazing patience, creativity, skill, love of learning and empathy for his students and colleagues alike ... Curtis exhibits effectiveness in teaching to the standards and possesses strong classroom management skills, exemplified by the vast amount my son learned in the safe, calm, yet exciting learning environment created by Curtis ... With Curtis's guidance, my son became a student who to this day enjoys reading and writing for pleasure, and for that I will always be grateful."

~

"Curtis is a dependable and responsible teacher," wrote my 4th grade teammate, "He comes in on weekends to plan and prepare ... He is thoughtful about the activities that he presents to his students, using his strength in writing with his students ... As we participated in our Equity Cohort, I saw firsthand that Curtis is thoughtful and handles complex issues in a sensitive and appropriate manner. I have seen him use these skills as issues arise with the students ... He takes the time that is needed to debrief incidents with students in a way that makes them feel heard."

~

"Curtis approaches every situation with a level of maturity, integrity and attention to detail that is uncommon in this profession," my 18 year veteran teammate wrote, "His students feel safe to express themselves and are willing to take chances ... Curtis is able to dig beneath the surface and look for the deeper meaning when it comes to student and parent needs ...

I would have been honored to have my own children (and now, my grandchild) in his class."

~

I received other letters too. A 4th grader's parent wrote that he was "appalled" to hear about my firing and that he thought I was a "VERY good fit" for Creekside, and if I needed *anything* to contact him.

"Thank you for all your hard work this year," another parent wrote, "[Her son] really took in your lessons about the real things in life ... being a compassionate, engaged citizen. You've got a lot of skills, a kindness, and ease that some other school will be lucky to get."

"Thank you very much for teaching me great stuff and preparing me for middle school," one student wrote, "I really appreciated it. Thank you also for teaching me about things in life, and how life is, and the valuable lessons of doing the right things. One other thing that I had a fun time learning was social studies, mostly about slavery. I hope you have a great summer and hope you find a good job."

~

When I told my 4th grade teammate I was going to discuss my file with the Director of Human Resources she rolled her eyes like I was wasting my time. Still, I was optimistic. At least until about 30 seconds into our conversation.

"I have five letters of recommendation," I said, "a principal, teachers, parents, and more are on their way. I've also been in touch with principals and teachers I've worked with in the past, and have applied for some Art and PE positions," then quipped, "even though you and the Superintendent told me not to."

"Now Curtis," she snapped like I was an unruly child and concluded condescendingly, "I didn't tell you 'not' to apply. I said principals probably wouldn't look at your application if you weren't endorsed."

My heart beat against my rib cage like a mallet on a bass drum – demanding an outlet – You're scolding me? Are you fucking kidding? I am a man and know what you said you dumbass! That's why I'm busting my butt to customize applications and making contacts anyway! And more importantly, when BVSD's Superintendent and Human Resources Director say applying would be a "waste of time," it's not a fucking stretch to assume their telling you not to.

"Right," I said but the discomfort between us would remain palpable for years.

I continued by emphasizing teaching in Boulder is my dream job. Also, as a minority who has lived and worked in this community for decades, and who receives praise when he speaks out about difficult issues, both the district and I would benefit from my receiving the job security that comes with being tenured.

Then I spoke about the Rookie's poor job performance. A parent's letter summarizing, "[The Rookie] has fostered dissent, bitterness and rumor among parents and teachers." Another male teacher called her "unprofessional." A different male teacher saying, "She said something sexist." And the 20-year veteran and I determining that *not* following The Rookie's professional directive would better serve the students.

"You could write a letter that disputes the Rookie's evaluation and include it in your file," The Human Resources Director said, "I'd be happy to review it if you'd like."

Then, in a very thoughtful voice, The Human Resources Director named a few near-by districts that I could apply to.

So fucking helpful! Using Google is so fucking hard! I came way too close to barking out loud and then realized, *my teammate was right about how useless this conversation would be.*

I decided not to deal with the Human Resources Director again. Though I broke that vow less than two years later, after the Boulder Daily Camera Newspaper ran an article, "Boulder Valley Makes Small Gains in Minority Teachers." I just had to sit with her, face to face, and hear her explain the things she said to the reporter.

I also chose not to write a letter contradicting the Rookie's evaluation because I thought nine highly positive letters of recommendations (including the Veteran and Rookie) would speak for themselves. Instead, I researched schools, customized cover letters, practiced interviewing, reconnected with teachers and principals I'd worked with in the past and made phone calls to introduce myself to new ones (my teammate rolled her eyes at most of those ideas too).

~

"I mentored another African American," my mentor said trying to wrap his head around my being fired and how to find a path forward, "she was so tired of insensitive comments that she said she just had to leave Boulder. So, if you feel like you have to leave Curtis, then I understand."

I appreciated all my mentor had done, but even he didn't seem to get that I had nowhere to go. This is my home. The place where I best understand people and they best understand me. In other words, where I'd be the most effective teacher.

"I'm sorry this happened," my mentor continued with something like what he'd say for the next five years, "I don't understand … your principal and I took the first Equity Cohort together and she was a respected teacher … if I had only known."

"I feel blindsided and confused too," I said, "the only comparable feeling is when people acted with blatant prejudice towards me."

"We'll get together again and prep for interviews," my mentor assured, "If you need anything else just give me a call."

"I will," I said, "thanks."

~

I got an interview for a fourth grade classroom position at Kohl Elementary. I almost didn't go because of the role Kohl's principal played in the disaster at Columbine Elementary.

After the Superintendent fired all the teachers and principal, he assigned Kohl's principal to be Columbine's Superhero. In the Boulder Daily Camera article, "New Columbine Principal Passionate about

School," the Superintendent boasted that his Superhero has "so many skills I don't know where to start."

"It's about student achievement," the Superhero said in the same article, "and there are multiple measures of achievement. CSAP is just one of them. And it doesn't give a real picture. It's just a snapshot."

Why would the Superintendent fire everyone in a school for failing the CSAP, I wondered, only to then place a principal who thinks the CSAP doesn't give a "real" picture of student progress?

In December, the Superhero left a school she'd led for seven years "with a heavy heart," but excited because Columbine offered "a wonderful opportunity." In January she started with an assistant and 25-member "visioning" group claiming she was "cognizant of the feelings and emotions involved when a principal is placed." A few months later the Boulder Daily Camera ran an article about schools that were breaking CSAP rules. An internal investigation found the Superhero broke that year's newly implemented rules but that the infractions probably didn't influence student performance. Not long after the article, the Superhero left Columbine and was back at Kohl.

There are warnings not to totally trust the Superhero. But maybe the lawsuit filed with the Education Department of Civil Rights had forced her out. Besides, I need a job and if nothing else, the interview would be good practice.

The interview went well until the Superhero asked why I left Creekside. "Well," I said, "students, teachers, staff, principals, and parents said I was a great teacher, as you can see in my nine letters of recommendation. And many thought [the Rookie] struggled with communication and discipline. Some parents, a long-time music teacher and secretary left Creekside too. So I'm happy to be out from under an inexperienced principal."

"Yes," the Superhero sounded empathetic, then referred to the few months she spent at Columbine, "I know what it's like to work at a *bad* school."

Wow, it struck me, *what a horrible thing to say*.

~

On May 12, the Veteran wrote me a letter of recommendation, "Because of our extremely diverse demographic student population, our instructional programs require highly competent instructors. Curtis was able to bring his previous college work, his master's degree work and practicum experiences to his classroom and he worked to improve the many qualities he already possessed during the first two years of his tenure ... During observations Curtis was able to demonstrate his knowledge of sheltered instruction and content standards; he provided supports for vocabulary building, models and demonstrations for the children (especially second language learners) to better understand the activities."

On June 9, the Superintendent wrote a letter explaining why I'd been fired, "As you know, Creekside Elementary is a unique school with a diverse population. In particular, Creekside has many struggling learners and needs teachers that are exceptionally strong in the implementation of curriculum and instruction. Unfortunately, the District was neither satisfied with your implementation of the basic components of effective instruction in all areas nor with your ability to shelter and differentiate instruction for all students in the classroom."

Over the summer I applied to every position I qualified for in BVSD and half a dozen neighboring districts. I received hundreds of rejection e-mails. No offers.

~

The first day of school, along with the opportunity to earn tenure and a reasonable shot at a job for the year, came and went.

PBS ran an update on the D.C. school district. "I am not a career superintendent," Rhee said after three years with at least as many set-backs as successes, "This is going to be my one and only superintendency. So in that way, I'm lucky, because I don't have to worry about, you know, well, what's going to happen to my reputation or something like that."

Well that's fucking poetic. That egomaniac with three years teaching and no administrative experience gets hired by some fool democrat and gets national news coverage because she spouts hard-line crap that inspires fair-weather liberals, conservatives, and racists to demonize public education and minorities without ever addressing the real underlying problems. And now that she's failing, she's happy to be able to walk away unscathed.

Then I thought about staff meetings when I led the Equity Cohort curriculum. After one, the male PE teacher and the Remaining Male (who was offended by the Rookie's inappropriate joke but was not fired), walked down the hall and joked about how the cultural and racial sensitivity stuff is mostly nonsense.

Nice guys really do finish last.

Light

Angry and determined not to finish last, I wrote almost every day that fall and winter. I let the pen fly, stories from childhood to adulthood. People who called me nigger. Women in education acting as sexist as men in corporate America. Co-worker's ignorant questions and comments. Conservatives and fair-weather liberals acting like cold hearted assholes.

~

That spring I called the Veteran and asked if we could get some coffee and talk. I was hoping to gain perspective on what "good" the district had done since she left Creekside.

Again, the Veteran assured me the Superintendent was a good man, aware of the inequities, and doing his best. He might have been a "good man," but I had no evidence of the other two qualities she cited as being true.

"I'm going to have to write about this," I said towards the end of our conversation.

"Good," she said, eyes lighting up (she knew I'd always wanted to write a memoir).

"But," I responded surprised at her enthusiasm, "this is the kind of thing that makes people go out and get a gun."

"You wouldn't get a gun, would you?" she asked.

I immediately regretted the comment. I was hoping she'd see my dilemma, and in my head the gun reference sounded better than, "But how do I write about it without calling you all ignorant prejudiced mother fuckers." Still, when the Veteran worried enough to ask if I would get a gun, it was clear I'd misjudged how well she knew me.

Six months later, in November and December, I worried about my gun reference again. I saw a news story in Florida. A woman had been fired from a school district she taught in for twenty years. Her ex-husband went to a board meeting, pulled a gun, and started shooting at board members.

So when I saw the Superintendent shift uncomfortably in his expensive chair after seeing me walk into BVSD board meetings, I wondered if the Veteran had told him what I said, and he'd heard about the shooting in Florida.

"My commitment to nonviolence is as strong as always," I said in the coffee shop to assure the Veteran, "from being a kid who couldn't hurt anything larger than an ant, to a man that became a conscientious objector and peace activist."

The Veteran nodded but her eyes seemed worried. So to emphasize my taking positive steps, told her that I had an interview with a private school that showed promise.

"I think you're a good teacher," the Veteran said doing her best to reinforce my being positive. "We should get together again soon." She said before saying good-bye.

I never heard from the Veteran again. I tried to get in touch with her about a year later, after reading a Boulder Daily Camera article, "Boulder Valley Makes Small Gains in Minority Teachers." Seeing the same empty words that I'd heard for decades, it took me an hour to calm down. Then I called the Veteran. When no one answered I left a message asking, "How clueless can BVSD leadership be?" and then insisted that we talk. When she didn't return my call I wondered if my tone and the gun comment were part of the reasons why.

~

I was certain the essays I wrote that fall expressed the truth. But by spring, I was equally certain that my use of context and offensive words wouldn't do much good.

Family, close friends, a former lawyer who said I had a compelling case, and a few hard-core liberals would read these essays and empathize. But a third of the readers would say I was being overly dramatic, "playing the race card." Another third would think my being male and black probably didn't help, but since the economy crashed and whites were getting fired for no good reason too, I'd better just put on my big boy pants.

With teacher hiring season on the horizon, and at a loss for how to express myself and still deliver a positive message, I decided to get back to my strength and work with kids. So I put more energy into researching schools, customizing applications, and making phone calls. I also did a few things that are taboo. I put the picture the Boulder Daily Camera used for my "Coach of the Year" article on the back of my cover letters. I also applied for positions I wasn't qualified for (they may think I'm incompetent but after twelve months and around a thousand rejection e-mails, it's worth taking a few shots at getting a foot in the door).

Breaking the rules produced mixed results. The first call-back I received was for a special education position. Given her exasperated tone, I'm pretty sure she thought I was incompetent. Then I received a call from a private school in Broomfield, 20 minutes east of Boulder.

They needed a long term substitute in the fall. I could also teach and coach in summer and afterschool programs, substitute teach, and tutor. I had an interview. Then I prepped and taught a math lesson to the students I'd teach in the fall. The principal and 1st grade teacher observed. Afterwards we discussed the student's and my lesson's strengths and weaknesses. A few days later I was offered and signed the contract.

~

I was worried because sometimes I talked over the heads of my 5th graders, and I only had a few months to get it right with these second graders. So I decided to focus most of my time and energy on the students: curriculum, lessons, and other daily activities.

My students took to my more authoritative style and grew academically and socially (especially several boys). I also enjoyed having just 13 students, which gave me time to do detailed weekly newsletters. And since the school's motto was "Individualized Instruction," allowed me to give my students first rate evaluations and feedback.

Tuition at the private school was thousands of dollars more per student, per year, than what's allocated for each student in public education. I knew parents would feel entitled and using my time to focus on student needs could risk alienation. So I told myself not worry too much about critical parents. Plus the principal, teachers, and staff were nice. Which is why I was surprised by how much the community influenced my decision to let go of a life-long dream and stop trying to teach within institutions and rules governed by biases and prejudices.

BVSD had built the coffin. But a few moms regularly drove nails into the lid. Before school, when every grade and their parents hung out on the black top, waiting for their teacher to arrive and walk them back to the classroom. The moms looked at me like they'd taken a gulp of sour milk.

A self-proclaimed "helicopter" mom drove more nails into the lid. She, her husband, and I had a meeting a month into the year. They were primarily upset that their second grader received only 30 minutes of homework a night. They wanted him to have 90 minutes of homework.

I would've imploded if I had 90 minutes of homework in 6th grade, I thought and agreed to include extension worksheets in his take-home folder. Helicopter mom and I ended on a good note, but I don't think she regretted my decision to leave either.

Another mom hammered a couple nails by attaching a note to her son's homework. She wrote about how I must be "incompetent" for sending students home with work based on a math concept that the student has never seen or heard of before.

I had explained and demonstrated the activity! I put them in groups, watched, and questioned each student as they discussed and practiced for 20 minutes. Everyone did it. PLUS, the lesson was on the math concept I introduced as part of my interview last spring!

I'm glad the CEO dropped in on a math lesson and said I did an excellent job. But I want nothing to do with a woman who slanders my professional integrity over the word of an eight year old who regularly forgets most everything: jacket, backpack, lunch, and spelling of basic words. Including the answers to his own questions moments after I had him read them aloud, "oh, I see ... oh, no wait ..."

Especially when I have impeccable references and still can't get a full time position, I didn't need this mom inspiring others to begin their own witch hunt and further undermine my career.

Yet more nails were driven by a teacher. We talked about education in America. She admitted she didn't know the first thing about public education because she attended and taught at private schools. Nevertheless, she loved Michelle Rhee in DC and the movie "Waiting for Superman." I appreciated the movie's goal of bringing awareness to failures in public education. But it did more damage than good because it demonized teachers and distracted from societal failures that even great teachers can't overcome. Shortly after talking about the movie, I heard administrators ask my co-worker if they could place a special-needs student in her class—a sibling of someone already enrolled.

"Oh, I *can't* take her," she responded, "I just don't see what I have to offer."

> *You only have EIGHT students—figure it out! Public Education has outstanding infrastructure, makes good use of resources and teachers—as evidenced by their being required to take three or four times as many students, work with thousands of dollars less per student annually, and have no choice about which students they get. Work harder. Students deserve real superheroes!*

But the final nails pounded into the coffin did not come from the Broomfield community. There was the person or persons who painted racial slurs on a bathroom wall in Boulder High School. I imagine many in Boulder didn't think much of it, shrugging it off as just another of the countless mean things kids do. But for me, it was the last straw.

~

I told everyone at the private school I wouldn't be back after my sub contract because I was going to drive a bus and write a book.

The CEO said I shouldn't worry about the parents, all teachers get put through the ringer initially. And with how much the staff and administration liked me, he was certain they'd come around. Then he said he'd find me hours to work this year and with their plans to expand, I could get my own class next year.

The principal said she understood. She had worked with a twelve-year veteran who left because he was sick of defending himself against wrong minded parents.

The teacher who said she often listened in on my class (we shared a small two room building), tried to talk me into staying. She also spoke to the principal to insist that more be done to keep me. In the end, she offered to write me a letter of recommendation.

Another teacher who was also being hounded by helicopter parents said she admired me, and hoped one day she too would have the courage to walk away.

At 41 and with a baby on the way, it might be selfish foolishness.

But each morning I was waking up energized. My dreams weren't as detailed as in the weeks before being fired at Creekside. Never-the-less, like at Creekside, I often felt like I'd just woke from a flying dream.

Mission

I don't know much about the Boulder Valley School Board. But they must have played a role in how I've been run, and kept, out of BVSD.

I went to board meetings for months. I did not go with an open mind. But since I knew there would be a battle to contain the hateful words flying around in my head, I made it my top priority to remain silent.

My bias began five years earlier, 2006, with my first year at Creekside. When the Board signed off on our Superintendent throwing a $50,000 dollar pep rally on the first day of work. All BVSD teachers commuted to the Broomfield event center (seats 10,000 and is located in the very south/eastern corner of our geographically huge district). We were given a t-shirt and a cheap bag of swag. Some played silly games. A few won prizes. We danced with pep bands and cheer leaders. And heard mediocre speeches (including the Superintendent saying CSAP scores won't be given much weight when evaluating teacher and school performance).

Afterwards, I sat on the hood of my car for twenty minutes. I was waiting for the poorly designed parking lot to clear, and cursing over how I didn't get to spend the morning getting to know my teammates, students' academic history, and what to do with our share of the $50,000. Because instead of a pep rally and cheap bags of swag, the Superintendent and School Board had prioritized resources and collaboration that directly impacts our student's academic achievement.

So as I pulled into the Boulder Valley Education Center's parking lot to attend the Board meetings, my heart was pounding. My anxiety was also fueled by decades of walking through those doors as a coach and teacher, bridging racial divides by being myself and hoping to make noticeable progress. But the student achievement gap and percentage of poor and dark skinned people who think Boulder sucks were the same as forty years ago. Then I grabbed my pen and notebook, reminded myself I was at war, and walked in.

The battles were nasty from the start. In the first meeting of the year, each member began by congratulating each other for having gotten rid of "bad" teachers, and taken real steps towards fulfilling BVSD's motto: "Excellence and Equity."

Spoken like racists who learned from the Civil Rights movement— you can't just say you want to get rid of minorities anymore. But if you call them "bad" and boast about fulfilling goals of Excellence and Equity, you can still fire them. Even if the minorities and their communities respond in protest!

~

The Board had one clear Alpha (at least in public). She had an advanced degree, was hard-working, and I imagined she considered herself a progressive democrat. She reminded me of DC's superintendent Michelle Rhee, a democrat who's big into politics and demoralizing people. They seemed to relish the kinds of words and actions I usually associate with older, white, conservative males. Alpha was President during the Columbine debacle and my being fired.

When I listened to Alpha, I kept in mind the Native American medicine man who said that there's a good wolf and a bad wolf in each of us, always fighting for control. Since most of Alpha's words were like throwing large chunks of raw meat in front of my bad wolf, his wisdom reminded me to take deep breaths and feed my good wolf. And helped keep me from jumping up and screaming in the middle of numerous meetings.

On the December 14th, 2010, Alpha boasted that she and others were introducing a Bill for the State Legislature to assure the best principals and teachers for our students. She was concerned that teachers and their union (which she called incompetent), and BVSD hadn't taken the opportunity to learn together, adding "the best way to feel like legislation isn't being done to you is to join the process." Then Alpha asked the Board be given a presentation on how we currently determine the effectiveness of educators and school leadership.

Are you fucking kidding!? BVSD keeps that shit ass principal at Creekside, fires two strong male teachers (one black), and other minorities throughout the district. And now, two fucking years later, you're preaching about the need to look at evaluations and come together? You people are acting like fucking dumbasses!

But earlier meetings prepared me for staying outwardly calm while my heart and mind race over their dismissive arrogance. So I took deep breaths and wrote.

~

In September, Alpha complained to the Superintendent about poor communication on Jewish holidays. She said she'd objected for years and had gotten the calendar committee, CHSAA (Colorado's high schools governing board), and the Anti-defamation League involved. And still, teachers needed to do a better job with appropriate accommodations.

"We value equity," Alpha said, "we talk about tolerance and culture ... we certainly are very good at looking at it relative to issues of ethnicity. But, I think it's broader than ethnicity, and it's about religious, just like it's about gender and sexuality as well."

"Ethnicity" refers to racial, national, cultural and religious background. So if BVSD was "very good," you wouldn't be complaining! And actually, when adding up the complaints of Jews, Latinos, blacks, and men, this Superintendent and Board have a verifiably poor record.

Why doesn't Alpha think her religion is ethnic? I wondered the next day. Then I looked up "ethnic" in Merriam-Webster's Collegiate Tenth Edition Dictionary and found a possible answer. The first definition is "HEATHEN."

Alpha and the Superintendent seemed close, often nodding in agreement and laughing at each-other's jokes. Still, not long after Alpha began her call for greater diversity awareness towards Jews, the Superintendent jumped in.

"There's a lot more being done than putting dates on a calendar," he said before assuring her he'd get her that information. He then added, "But trying to communicate with 2000 teachers is a daunting task."

"I would really appreciate [the information]," Alpha responded, "and then maybe we could talk about ideas ... maybe appeal to leadership in the Jewish Community."

The Superintendent rocked back in the over-priced chair while nodding sheepishly.

I've seen that body language several times before. At the Administrator's Equity retreat in 2007, the public meeting after the Columbine firings in 2008, my appeal in 2009. And now. Again.

With Alpha, the Superintendent looked like he thought he'd been reprimanded by the leader of the pack. All the other times, the way he leaned back and raised his eyebrows made him look more like he couldn't care less about what the speaker was saying.

~

Three moments in my life stand out as being my most energized and calm at the same time.

The first came on the pro beach volleyball tour, while placing 7th at the 1995 US Championships in Hermosa Beach (my home away from home).

Another came on a warm winter day in 1997, shortly after deciding that if I wasn't ranked in the top 20 at the end of the next AVP season, I'd find another career. I planned to work out on the steep half-mile of road and trail to the water tower behind NCAR: sprint and rest in 10-second intervals, up and down three times. As I came to the end of my first sprint interval I felt so light and powerful I decided not to stop. I felt just as good 10 seconds later, so I kept sprinting. I didn't stop until reaching the water tower. Then I jogged down and sprinted back up to the water tower non-stop, three more times.

My third most energized and calm moment came November 9th, 2010. It was the first BVSD board meeting since someone had written racial slurs in a bathroom at Boulder High School.

Alpha began by praising students who had given a presentation to the board, "Our teachers must be doing an excellent job teaching students more than just how to pass the CSAP, but also to participate in our democratic government. That it's important for all of us to consider the perspective of all the stake holders that could be affected."

Teachers, staff, students and parents at Creekside said that that's exactly what I did for them.

Then Alpha admonished people who, after the district made sudden cuts in the equity department, organized like good democratic citizens and shared their voices in a meeting the board created specifically for, "Broad-based listening."

"I would be very concerned," Alpha said, "if we gave up our goal to meet the needs of a group that is perhaps trying to hijack our process because they were upset with decisions that were made around the equity department," Alpha continued spinning, "Because that is what happened at that meeting [or so she heard, Alpha wasn't actually there]." Alpha then cited e-mails as proof these citizens were hijacking the Board's process and summarized, "We cannot be all things to all people. We have to stick to the goals we invested in."

Is she talking about people speaking up for four Latina women who were fired from the Equity Department, I wondered? Then my thoughts rolled, the Superintendent acted like a supreme dumbass when he wrote that I was fired because the district wasn't satisfied with my ability to, "shelter and differentiate instruction." Not only was that directly contradicted by the Veteran (who supervised my weakest years), but I got better at sheltering and differentiating instruction because one of those Latina women they fired had taught me and my class. We received lessons in language, hard work, and commitment to education while growing up in a migrant farming family. The Veteran and Rookie complimented me for bringing her into my classroom!

My mentor told me an assistant Superintendent had told the Latina women they were fired. The Latina women demanded to speak to the Superintendent, to tell him they were leaders in the community and he was sending a bad message. The Superintendent barged in and admonished the Latina women for thinking they were leaders. My mentor was so horrified he met with the Superintendent to tell him such behavior was unacceptable.

Alpha continued to comment on the racial slurs incident at Boulder High, "[Another central administrator] said to me 'It's too bad I'm not a parent at Boulder High anymore.'"

"I'm thinking really?" Alpha's voice grows sarcastic, "Empty nester vs. boys in high school … um … I'm thinking empty nester," Alpha chuckled, then peeked at the Superintendent who laughed boisterously.

"But it's unfortunate," Alpha continued sounding serious again, "that I am not an active member of that school community anymore."

Maybe being a resident and having boys that are alumni isn't enough for you to get involved. But you are a fucking member of the School Board! You've had experience trying to improve diversity awareness through the calendar committee, state governing board and the Anti-defamation League! And all you can come up with are jokes and empty threats?

Then Alpha praised Boulder High and district leadership for how they denounced racism.

Which was fine. But most people do that, I thought, before taking a deep breath, puzzled by the same old problem. *We can't blame this incident entirely on our Superintendent and School Board. Hateful things happen in Boulder. Still, BVSD leadership should have set a stronger example and instead wasted resources and fired educators that could help people value others.*

"What are we doing?" Alpha began to preach, "What kind of messages are we as parents giving our children that allow them to believe that acts of hate and discrimination are ok? We all have ownership in this. The parents, the administration, the students."

Bullshit! I wanted to scream examples of times when BVSD leaders had not taken ownership. But I took deep breaths and as Alpha stepped on her soapbox, let my pen fly.

"I think it's time for our community to really look at what kinds of things we're looking the other way on," Alpha lectured, "And what kind of behaviors we actually want to promote in our children [*You mean like the Superintendent firing and scolding Latina women?*]. I frankly don't think we should be the kind of community that tolerates any kind of racial, sexual, ethnic, religious [*Not that again!*] slur among our students and our schools ... And I'd like to see us start talking about that at the School Board because I don't think it's ok anymore to look the other way [*Are you saying you used to think it was OK to look the other way?*] ... It's just upsetting to me that in a community that is as well-educated and as progressive as Boulder that we have things happen like what happened at Boulder High. We have a diversity curriculum. We teach this stuff. It's time for adults to start modeling this behavior."

> *Does she really not realize?* I asked, heart beating like a Union soldier arriving at Gettysburg. *If I had spoken to this Board two years ago—with a community behind me—citing what happened to Columbine teachers and me as proof of institutionalized prejudice, Alpha probably would've defended her words and actions. And in doing so, labeled me a "hijacker." Maybe added something about my being a nice guy who works hard but just doesn't have what it takes. And conclude with how well-spoken I am, though I'm selling snake oil because when it came to issues of "ethnicity," BVSD was, "very good!"*

~

Board meetings weren't the only things that made my transition from teacher to bus driver/author both difficult and easy at the same time.

I also researched and compared CSAP test results from my last year at Creekside, with those of the following year. I was interested in the Annual Yearly Progress (AYP), because it's the most accurate measure of teacher effectiveness. My students excelled (scoring similarly to their final practice tests). Next year's students performed notably worse.

In my third year, 5th graders went from a 4th grade teaching team with 20-yr and 12-yr veterans who had worked together for years, to a new team that consisted of a two-yr. veteran leading the 18-yr veteran because he had never taught the 5th grade curriculum. Despite our team's relative inexperience, our student's Reading and Writing scores improved substantially.

"Unsatisfactory" scores in Reading were cut in half -21% to 11%. "Unsatisfactory" scores in Writing were eliminated -14% to 0%.

Our specialist teachers played a significant role in those scores. For example, when one suggested we ignore the Rookie's direction while she continued to develop lessons for the worst performing students and teach them in her office. Still, all students participated in many of my language arts lessons, including my poetry workshops. Plus, I reinforced language arts skills in math, social studies, science, and more.

The year after I was fired, "Unsatisfactory" scores in Reading and Writing made minimal to virtually no gains: 19% to 15%, and 19% to 18% respectively.

In math, I taught students who had scored "Unsatisfactory," "Partially Proficient," and "Proficient." All three categories remained within three percentage points (plus and minus) of their previous year's scores. Given that math is my weakest subject, I was happy my students kept pace with the progress they achieved under the 4th grade teachers everyone loved.

The year after I was fired, "Unsatisfactory" scores in Math nearly tripled, from 8% to 21%.

That doesn't mean the students didn't learn. Maybe the Rookie made the new teacher do the language-based "Investigations" curriculum (as she had passive-aggressively told me to do), and the new teacher's students were just lost in the CSAP format.

Seeing the Writing scores of students I taught directly (because the specialist and I ignored the Rookie) was one of the most memorable moments of my life. Although advanced students dropped from 13% to 11%, that drop might have happened because administrators told us to focus more on struggling students until we get off probation. Plus, the needs of my advanced students led me to cover voice and rhythm, skills the CSAP doesn't measure well. But what *really* made the moment was that 8% of my students had gone from "Partially Proficient" to "Proficient."

The countless D's and F's I received in writing while growing up, my boring lessons while student-teaching in Kansas, and the Rookie and others who couldn't see the benefits of my poetry workshops ... I'd overcome them all!

The best revenge is a life well lived, I remembered. Then danced. But my joy quickly turned to rage as my thoughts shifted to what a great 5th grade teacher I would've been. And if one of BVSD's powerful few had been transported into my office, I would've beaten them senseless.

The year after I was fired, "Advanced" and "Unsatisfactory" scores in Writing remained the same while 5% of the scores went from "Proficient" to "Partially Proficient."

What's really sad is that teaching to the CSAP is not even my strength! I was successful because I promised my students that if they worked hard and pre-tested well, I'd get back to the "real" lessons they enjoyed so much.

~

Though I left the private school to write a memoir, comparing test scores got me thinking about teaching. Again. I was done talking to the Superintendent and Director of Human Resources. But I hadn't talked with the Superintendent of School Leadership (who supervised principals, including the Rookie). The Creekside parents sent her a copy of the four page letter detailing the Rookie's poor performance. And though she remained silent then, perhaps now, if I sent her a letter showing my data vs. the next year's data, along with details behind my celebrated leadership and life-long record of professionalism and improvement, she might know a principal and school who'd like to benefit from my skills as an educator.

I sent Superintendent of School Leadership a letter detailing my excellent resume. Then called or dropped by her office a few times a week for a few weeks. She was never available and didn't return my calls.

Still a Pillar of Silence.

~

Wealthy corridors of power drove the narrative that led to hard-working teachers across America being fired. Hoping to better understand the academic, political, and economic forces that were devastating teachers and communities across our nation, I turned to reading.

The Schools Our Children Deserve: Moving Beyond Traditional Classrooms and Tougher Standards by Alfie Kohn. I have loved Alfie since the Peaceable Schools conference, when he said discipline is on a continuum from Negative reinforcement: hitting, timeout, exclusion, to Positive reinforcement: rewards, compensation, bathing with praise. Negative suppresses creativity, questioning, and risk taking. Positive gives students the impression they won't succeed on their own and authority doesn't trust them. Most students learn from both Negative and Positive reinforcement. Great teachers artfully complicate their student's lives using both.

I agreed with the praise Jonathan Kozol received for The Schools Our Children Deserve, "A powerful, crisply written assault upon the mad excesses of the educational 'standards' movement. Kohn cuts against the grain and takes on adversaries without fear, and yet with a mature and rational sophistication. He draws upon a rich tradition, citing the work of Dewey, Bruner, Piaget, and Holt, among others, but he now takes his proper place within their ranks."

I read most of <u>The Deliberate Dumbing Down of America</u>, (heavy on statistics and long) by former Senior Policy Advisor in the Department of Education during the Reagan Administration, Charlotte Thomson Iserbyt. And I agreed with teacher Jerome Brown, "I applaud Iserbyt for her shocking, completely documented expose ... evidence shows school reform, supported by all political stripes, to be a totalitarian plan using Skinnerian behavior modification and other equally manipulative psychological techniques to subjugate future generations in a state of ignorant bliss."

Two books that stood out were: <u>The Death and Life of the Great American School System: How Testing and Choice Are Undermining Education</u>, by Diane Ravitch; and <u>What Ever it Takes: Geoffrey Canada's Quest to Change Harlem and America</u>, by Paul Tough.

Diane Ravitch was a Research Professor of Education at New York University, senior fellow at the Brookings Institution, former Assistant Secretary of Education and Counselor to Secretary of Education in George W. H. Bush's administration. She supported No Child Left Behind's high stakes testing and punitive accountability in 2000. And I was moved by her account of how not only had student performance not improved after a decade of No Child Left Behind, but teacher morale plummeted with cheating, segregation, and the rich getting richer all on the rise.

Still, I was most struck by what happened to the first class that was supposed to graduate from schools in Geoffrey Canada's "Promise Academy." Like Michelle Rhee, Canada is featured in the movie "Waiting for Superman." He's also passionate, intelligent, and did what few would dare to do. Canada started K-12 schools in Harlem called Promise Academy. He even re-branded a few blocks of Harlem—The Harlem Children's Zone—which was open to all children, not just the lottery winners who got to attend his schools. Canada guaranteed students in his schools would graduate from College, with his academy helping every step of the way. Canada created hope and prosperity. But doing "what-ever it takes" also meant having to break his promise.

~

Promise Academy started with Kindergarten through 5th grade in elementary school, and the first year of Jr. High.

Elementary students showed the most improvement. Wanting still greater gains, and after seeing how much kids learn before turning five, Canada expanded Promise Academy and changed the lottery system so every student started in his preschool at two or three years old. They also knew strong parenting and good health play important roles in a child's education, so they added programs to educate parents and provided access to quality medical care.

Problems with "bad apples" in Jr. high were harder to solve. The longer kids are exposed to things like malnutrition, sleep deprivation, murdered friends, and family members in jail, the more difficult it becomes to change their behavior. Canada was idealistic and thrifty in the first year. He didn't hire an assistant principal for discipline. He also told the principal she could not suspend or expel students (too many consider the time-off a vacation). As a result, the year produced many discipline problems, poor test scores, and Canada and his investors fired the principal and many teachers.

Canada's thrifty idealism disappeared the second year as he hired an assistant principal for discipline and allowed suspensions and expulsions. The new hard-knocks approach began with an assembly for the previous year's 30 worst offenders. That year they expelled at least one student and test scores, morale and overall behavior improved.

The previous year's principal and teachers might have been just as successful if they could've disciplined in the same manner.

Canada kept the same administration and rules the following year and discipline and morale continued to improve. Unfortunately, they did poorly on their practice tests. In March, majority investors convinced Canada that their brand image couldn't take the bad headlines of such poor scores. So the group that started in 6th grade, would graduate from 8th and then be disbanded.

Canada told the students and parents that he and his staff were to blame. But in order to keep his promise of helping all his students graduate from college, he had to break that promise with some of them. The decision to disband the grade came late in the year, meaning his students had missed application deadlines to many of the best schools. Still, Canada helped students find new schools. And everyone noted it was great that none of their students had to enroll in *the* worst school in the area.

"As it turned out, the eighth grade had done better than the preliminary estimates had indicated," Tough wrote about the official test scores, "Their reading scores hadn't stayed where they were the previous year, after all: they jumped from 24 percent on grade level to 33 percent on grade level. Those weren't stellar scores, but … the students had gone from being twenty points behind the city average to nine points behind."

"Back in 6th grade, just 9 percent scored on grade level in math. In seventh grade 34 percent did," Tough wrote about student performance that could've made headlines: <u>Promise Academy Students Begin High School Bearing Fruit</u>, 'Now, in eighth grade the number had jumped all the way to 70 percent. The eighth-grade scores weren't just impressive when compared with the abysmal place the class had started from; they were impressive by any measure. [They] beat the state average on the math test by twelve points, and city average by twenty-four points."

> *I feel you kids—screwed while excelling. And I feel you too Canada, you didn't really want to get rid of those kids, you just needed people's money.*

~

Canada never shared his politics so he could court the rich, liberals and conservatives. He won praise from Obama, the Clintons, and Mitt Romney. His fundraising was essential to Promise Academy's success. It helped pay for medical support, classes for parents, pre-school, and after school programs open to every kid in Harlem, not just his lottery winners.

Canada spent most his fifteen minutes of fame humbly accepting praise for Promise Academy's success, but would emphasize that from his neighbors in Harlem to many in LA, millions of minorities across America are not so lucky. Then he'd plead for people to find ways to invest in the well-being of children and their families.

Americans who deserve help. And neither liberal nor conservative media spent much time covering that part of Canada's message.

~

"And I think adults have an ownership here." Alpha said responding again to the racial slurs incident at Boulder High's, "And I think it's time for us to be a community that really fosters responsible behavior. And I'd like to see us start talking about that at the School Board."

Although Alpha reeked of insincerity, her words were right, so I started putting together a presentation about my experience. I also decided to attend more meetings, to get more comfortable with the environment and process. The meetings on January 25th and February 8th were diamond bullets—right through my forehead.

~

Anyone presenting to the Board is allotted two minutes. A person who is at the meeting can give their two minutes to another speaker. No one gets more than four minutes.

Six people from Columbine went on January 25th. Two parents and a teacher gave a 12-minute presentation on the Columbine "turn-around" plan. It was largely an account of the Superintendent, Alpha and the Board unfairly scapegoating Columbine.

The first parent began speaking about a staff who worked just as hard as when the Board and the Superintendent tried to fire everyone two years ago. Four teachers were National Board Certified. One won an award from the Governor. Another was the *only* teacher in Colorado nominated for, and would later win, a National teaching award.

Next, the parent quoted Alpha (something all three presenters would do), "Why aren't we looking to make sure that Literacy Squared [reading curriculum] is still being implemented with, you know, true implementation, when we're not seeing results in these programs?"

"Literacy Squared is a reputable curriculum," the parent explained, "proven by independent research and Columbine making AYP in Reading on the CSAP." Then she invited the entire Board to their school and see their environment, curriculum, and data.

You guys are screwed if this Board is anything like the Superintendent and Director of Human Resources, who completely ignored an invitation to see my data.

The second parent stepped to the mic and quoted Alpha, "I am concerned that the students in your school are not getting the education they deserve or the education I believe they would get at a different Boulder Valley School."

The parent then presented data that points to the Superintendent and School Board having been on a witch hunt. In the last 7 years, six schools performed *worse* than Columbine: one school failed 7 out of last the last 7 years; four schools failed 6 out of 7; and another failed 5 out of 7. Columbine was also just one of six schools to have failed 4 out of the last 7 years. Still, only Columbine was subjected to public ridicule and the attempted firing of their entire staff.

The white, female, National Award winning teacher who looked like an aged hippy stepped to the mic for the final four minutes.

"Hello," she waved, "you know me well, third seat on the left," she pointed to where she'd been sitting since the Board started their witch hunt a couple years earlier, "When we looked into math growth scores we noticed the District showed a significant decline, but Columbine did not: our Hispanic score of 51 was higher than the district's 44; ELL of 47.5 was higher than District's 45. Latino ELL of 51 higher than District's 43; meal assistance of 49 higher than District's 45; in reading growth scores, our Hispanic was 52, higher than the District's 44."

And if the Board ignores your data like Superintendent of School Leadership (Pillar of Silence) recently ignored mine, you're still screwed.

The national award winning teacher continued by quoting Alpha, who said, "I noticed that elementary schools are using the <u>Advantage Math</u> curriculum. I know there are two math curricula in the District, is that necessarily the best curriculum for your students? It might be worth looking at other curriculum. It might serve the students better."

"So," the national award winning teacher sighed, "The two math curriculums for the district are <u>Scots/Foresmen</u> and <u>Investigations</u>. <u>Advantage Math</u> is *not* a curriculum, it is an assessment framework. Which means that in addition to providing diagnostic assessments, it also gives a research-based progression on how mathematical concepts around numbers develop … [<u>Advantage Math</u>] is a big reason why we made AYP in Math."

"Both suggestions about doing something different than <u>Advantage Math</u> and <u>Literacy Squared</u>," the national award winner concluded, "at a time when we are showing improvement, would be counter-productive to the gains we have made."

All levels of BVSD leadership are acting like dumbasses, I thought, *though not sure whose worse: Alpha, for not knowing the difference between the district's assessment and its curriculum; or the Rookie, for passive aggressively telling me to use curriculum that doesn't prepare students for the CSAP.*

~

The Board President thanked Columbine's teacher and parents, adding that they always like to hear from the community. Then he called for Board Communications and asked who would like to start, though everyone knew he should've just given the floor to Alpha.

Alpha chided the two parents and national award winning teacher for calling her, "The Board Member," saying they could call her by name because she was proud of asking ignorant questions that wasted people's time.

"I come from the place of these questions for caring about each and every student in BVSD," Alpha explained, "I am concerned and continue to be concerned, not just about Columbine but about the performance of the district as a whole and our ability to close the achievement gap … I am passionate about public education."

Where was this passion during the racial slurs incident? I questioned. *Instead, we got jokes and assurances that district leaders who no longer had children at Boulder High and are enjoying the freedoms of an empty nest, aren't going to confront racist behavior like they otherwise could and would.*

"I also believe it is the Board's role to ask these questions," Alpha doubled down, "I'm glad to see that our asking these questions have brought members of the community forward telling us how they're using their data."

Never mind that your questions were grossly misleading and riddled with ignorance.

"And supporting the new leadership," Alpha spouted like the staff at Columbine had been trouble makers.

Never mind that the last principal was placed and the current principal is more qualified!

"And paying attention," Alpha's spin machine was now in full effect, "so that I'm glad to hear that you as parents have the same focus and are creating a culture in your school of focusing on performance that this Board has been trying to provide leadership on for a number of years."

Trust me, your questions are not what motivated those teachers!

"And I thank you for letting us know that you've gotten that message," Alpha concluded one of the greatest hijackings I've witnessed, "and those who are listening to this tonight in other schools, I hope you recognize the importance of using data."

When you tried to fire everyone at Columbine two years ago, they used data of progress (just not CSAP-centric). My male co-worker at Creekside presented his progress with data and was still fired. I had data of progress too, and mine was CSAP-centric!

~

"What is the outcome?" Alpha asked on February 8th, "Can we find a way for every single child to find passion and inspiration in their lives through learning? And we know an effective teacher finds that and cultivates it in every student … And I think sometimes we get caught up in the deliverables, the process, and we forget about the outcome we're looking for."

The revolving doors keeps spinning, Data and rhetoric mean nothing in the wake of bias and prejudice.

Then I inhaled. And exhaled. And walked out.

Back to Breath

Shortly after the February 8th Board meeting, the husband of a Creekside teacher gave me a Boulder Daily Camera article, <u>Boulder Valley Makes Small Gains in Minority Teachers</u>. It had comments from the Director of Human Resources, a minority PE teacher who'd been in the district for two years, and a community activist. I also read the online comments. Then sat for an hour, dismayed over how little has changed in forty years.

"It's an ongoing challenge," the Human Resources Director said of trying to find minority teachers who want to work and live in Boulder, "A diverse teaching staff adds value to the educational experience."

The Human Resources Director boasted to the reporter that she'd applied for a grant: $25,000 to train 16 principals; $5,000 for a graduate student to lead discussions with minority teachers. Five years after receiving the grant BVSD saw a 1% increase in minority teachers, and a 9% *decrease* in minority administrators.

The Human Resources Director also told the reporter how minorities had confided in her. Saying some of the major road blocks for minority teachers coming to Boulder is not being able to afford to live in Boulder and having few other minorities around.

The same fucking things minorities said in 1980 and 1990. The same fucking things discussed each year in the BVSD's Diversity Cohort since it began a decade ago. And if you add, "Having to speak on behalf of all minorities," still the same fucking conclusions your grant is going to find.

"Schools are making an effort not to overwhelm minority teachers by asking them to serve on a plethora of committees because they can provide minority representation," the Director of Human Resources said to cover all her bases, "Providing a good support system is key."

Actually, I was constantly asked to take a leadership role. I was the only teacher at the administrator's Equity Cohort retreat and during the teacher's Equity cohort. Throughout my three years in the halls and classrooms at Creekside, I accepted responsibility for three reasons: I'm highly trained; the majority learns more quickly when they hear directly from the minority; and I had a support system. The Cohort directors, my teammates, staff, administrators, students, parents all thanked and praised me for speaking out.

Human Resource Director also told the reporter that BVSD tries to recruit minorities by talking to student-teachers in Boulder (*since CU has so many minorities coming and staying*), and educator licensing programs for minorities looking at teaching as a second career, "The district's focus is mainly on recruiting local candidates."

I am a fucking successful, celebrated and experienced local candidate! I yelled, jumped up, and paced around my apartment.

Then I read about BVSD's "small" gains. "Small" being generous since seven elementary schools didn't have a single teacher of color. There were no teachers of color at a school where 37% of the students were minorities. And at a school with 68% of the students being minorities, less than half of the teachers were of color.

~

The same rationale that drove me to finish Bernard Goldberg's book Bias, got me in the habit of reading people's reactions to articles on line. So I went to the comment section for the Boulder Valley Makes Small Gains in Minority Teachers. There were 20.

With BVSD hiring minorities at a two percent increase every decade, the teacher population will match the student's in the year 2111. Still many comments implied that minority teachers were flooding the district.

"This must be so comforting to read for those people who are not of color and studying to become teachers."

"For as silly as it is to base someone's opinion on another person using their race, our government sees fit to do so all the time. So do the so-called colorblind liberals."

"This article is not about teachers, it is about a racist school district policy of hiring teachers based on their skin color and not their ability to teach. I am not saying that teachers of color do not have the ability to teach. The most important part of hiring a teacher is their teaching ability, not their skin color."

Most of these people would see me, a black man demanding that BVSD improve diversity awareness, I thought, *and yet totally miss my point: **everyone** needs to be heard. They'd only hear that half the cards in my hand are black, and make me fold an ace/king full house.*

Of course Boulder's liberals chimed in on the article. First of all comments was, "Watch out below for all the posts from uncultured morons using any chance they can get to bash teachers."

"Shhhhhhh" another chided, "the truth is Boulder is Racist … a subtle racism Boulder is almost a totally White liberal fortress. Where are the Black areas of town? Where are the Hispanic areas of town? Where are the Asian areas of town? White, white, white … oh they shout about equality and open borders but when it actually comes down to it … Minorities are for 'other' cities."

"The city of Boulder is the perfect example of unearned white privilege," a third detailed, "It's admirable that they want to undo the damage of institutional racism, but I can't help but think it is too little too late. It's kind of like a billionaire trying to emulate the life of Christ. The only way for him to do that is to quit being a billionaire, but there is no way he will willingly make that sacrifice. Likewise Boulder wants to be a diverse and affordable community, but they will never give up their rich white privilege for it. So they just make token out of touch gestures like complaining about kids painting themselves black for football games and trying to give a few people of color teaching jobs."

Yes, but my story goes deeper. Then I saw a comment to explain.

"We want the teachers to reflect the students?" one asked and clarified, "Then let's fire a bunch of female teachers and hire more male teachers. The male/female ratio is greater than the minority ratio."

~

"I don't get it. Now BVSD is catering not only to minority children, but minority teachers?" one comment began "My 'white' children have been turned down for classes because of their color. There are clubs at school they can't participate in because of their color, the schools bend over backwards to have minority children succeed but when white parents ask for the same thing they are either ignored or turned down. What's next?"

There's the rub; conservatives think BVSD is going out of its way to hire minorities, liberals think BVSD is trying to give a few people of color teaching jobs. And BVSD gets to fire and blackball me, a racial minority who calls Boulder home, has proven data, dozens of recommendations, and a life-long record of learning. No wonder the statistics aren't improving.

"I went to a high school that was 80% Hispanic," someone wrote about how mandating diversity can benefit many, "I was offered opportunities because I was white. They needed to meet their racial quota and didn't have enough whites. Not saying that is good or bad, just pointing out that it goes both ways."

A few comments focused on how BVSD should simply hire the top candidate, best summarized by, "Agreed, usually the person most qualified for the job should get the job. I didn't see in the article where it said lesser qualified minorities would be hired though."

After reading the comments, I thought of comedians Tim Allen and Roseanne Barr. How they get laughs for mocking Boulder's liberals as soft hearted hypocrites ruining America. But of those who commented on the article, 14 chose a side, and the liberal to conservative ratio turned out as it often does. Six supported BVSD hiring minorities, while eight called the policy racist. With Boulder's majority silent, that makes a 57% to 43% conservative win. Plus, only fifty percent of the "liberals" mentioned that a two percent increase every decade was slow. The other half seemed satisfied with reaching equity in the year 2111—right around my 150th birthday.

Then I imagined what people would say if BVSD announced that progress was too slow, so in the summer of 2011, they would hire 20% more teachers—all minorities.

~

I did agree with the article's conclusion, which emphasized that it takes a variety of talent to serve a variety of needs.

A community activist who ran a Latino group for middle school boys said there are many reasons why it's important they have Latino teachers.

"It's easier to communicate with Latino teachers because they better understand them ... from how they address each other to how they make eye contact ... they often have personal experience with historical events like Cesar Chavez Day, such as having farm workers in their families who struggled to earn a fair wage."

"The students say," the activist continued, "'It's important for us to see people like us who are successful, who have good jobs.' These are all people who are inspiring to them." The activist summarized his point saying the best educator at their school isn't a teacher, but the Latino head custodian, who happens to have a master's degree. "He knows how to listen to them and relate to them. He reminds them of their family members."

~

I thought about my white mom and Oma. And the mostly white, female Creekside staff who, more so than any time in the last 40 years, made me feel like I could honestly share the impact that prejudice has had on me. Then I thought about the grizzled 15-year veteran who had parents from Germany, was part of our Diversity Cohort team and said, "I'd sue the

District." And the 25-year veteran who held my hand, looked me in the eye and said, "At least *you've* acted like a professional."

I called my mentor. He was glad to hear from me (like always). I told him I was done with BVSD's education department and was driving buses and writing a memoir. Then asked if he'd read and comment on a few essays I'd written.

Over the next three years I got feedback from co-workers, friends, and family. One is a former high school English teacher, who my mentor said is one of the best writing teachers he's known. He and I met a couple of times a month reading and discussing books and essays by Ralph Ellison, James Baldwin, John McPhee, James McBride, Michelle Alexander, Michael Fleming, the list goes on. He was instrumental in shaping the chapter Nigger, which in turn shaped my entire memoir. Six months after Nigger he read a chapter from my pro volleyball years.

"This is great Curtis, your writing is strong," he said, "Still, I hate to be the bearer of bad news, but I think you may just be getting started."

~

When it was time for my daughter's bottle and nap I also read. One of my favorite books was, You Are What You Speak: Grammar Grouches, Language laws, and the Politics of Identity, by Robert Lane Green. It's smart and funny (I highlighted on a third of its pages).

"A Georgia student visiting Harvard asks a passing student," Green shares one of his father's favorite jokes, "'Excuse me, can you tell me where the library's at?' The Harvard man says, 'Here at Harvard, we do not end a sentence with a preposition.' The Georgia boy thinks for a second and tries again, 'Sorry, can you tell me where the library's at, *asshole*?'"

"English rules were taught to me as self-evident and logical," Green further illustrates problems with associating "proper" language with intelligence, "yet people broke them all the time speaking the 'correct' version of their own languages. Were French and Danish illogical, or were the rules I had been taught in English based on something else besides logic?"

"Language is a powerful marker of our identity: our social group, our class, and our nation," is a point Green illustrated in numerous ways. My favorite is, "Too many people are too angry about language too much of the time. That time could be better spent listening, learning, and enjoying the vast variety of human language around them."

While I enjoyed Green's insight, reading his book wasn't always fun. I often got the same message I got when I read Bill Bryson's, <u>the mother tongue: english and how it got that way</u> – Don't use language to exclude or hurt others.

Still, my melancholy faded—overrun by the joy I felt when looking at my daughter lying perfectly in the donut pillow on my lap, our chests steadily falling and rising.

Closing

After three decades of study and practice, I'm still amazed how difficult it is to follow Gandhi's advice, "Be the change you wish to see in the world."

I apologize to everyone who feels my thoughts and feelings plunge the knife too deep.

When BVSD fired me, I started an "in house" relationship with another teacher (now my wife), which some principals don't like. The Rookie often said she was uncomfortable communicating in English, and still showed potential as a leader. Plus, being a principal is hard, few decisions make everyone happy and like first-year teaching, rookie mistakes happen. I also got the feeling that the Rookie would have fired other teachers if they hadn't been tenured.

I don't think the Superintendent really wanted to get rid of me either. Perhaps the economy and No Child Left Behind forced his hand. So maybe he targeted one of the worst performing schools (Columbine) while keeping other communities together whose CSAP scores also didn't reflect the strong foundations their teachers had given their students.

When Columbine refused to be the scapegoat and I was the seven hundred and something person to sign the petition demanding the Superintendent retract his order to fire everyone, I thought about the crashing economy, criminal bankers, and rising unemployment. How millions of many races, religions, and nationalities were plunged into poverty.

'Divide and conquer' 101 I lamented: *create anger and hatred by screwing people who don't deserve it.*

Signing this petition, I reasoned, *draws targets on minorities across the district. Still, they won't come after me, a successful minority (race and gender), who has called Boulder home for the last 40 years.*

The vast majority at Creekside (and many at other schools) thought I was an ideal fit for BVSD. A powerful few didn't. Those powerful few may not have been prejudiced in their personal lives, but they spoke and acted on behalf of those who were sick of "failed" liberal policies favoring minorities. And many more who remained silent while I was blackballed.

I don't know what played the greatest role, being black, male, or an outspoken leader willing to challenge authority. Like most prejudices, it was probably a cocktail of all three. Still, the flavor is irrelevant. The poison they fed me was institutionalized discrimination.

And whether it's war, volleyball or social justice, I play to win: a "kill shot" is warranted.

~

I have a natural disposition to feed my good wolf and have worked hard throughout my life. Still, while writing this book, I was often surprised by how much my language was influenced by the news, politics, and work. Like after bus driver in-services in 2015 and 2016.

In 2015, the speaker was a former driver who worked hard, rose through the ranks, and now traveled across the nation giving inspirational speeches. Making the big bucks, "If she can do it—anyone can!" I again marveled at how people can focus on the fact that *anyone* can climb the narrow ladder to wealth and power, while ignoring the fact that if 300 million Americans do, that ladder is guaranteed to collapse (I mean, how many presidents can the US have?). The speaker also made ignorant comments about identity, but then quoted the Dalai Lama and Henry Ellis in her conclusion. I was so dismayed I wrote a letter to the district (like a few other drivers). Remembering the speaker had just come from an engagement in Oklahoma helped keep my letter civilized and on point. It also motivated me to get back to my memoir.

In 2016, the speaker was a high school principal who studied how the brain develops. He said children use less evolved parts of the brain: stem, cerebellum, and temporal lobe, which mostly sound alarms like fight or flight. As children develop, they start using the top parts of the brain: frontal and parietal lobes, which influence concentration, memory, planning, and problem solving. The speaker also said ideas travel along synapses, and like muscles, synapses grow stronger the more they are used, and weaker the less they're used. Which reminded me of 15 years earlier. A panelist at the Peaceable Schools conference had studied the brain too. He added that when we stop using negative stereotypes, they'll shrivel and die.

The speakers made me feel like I'd been spinning my wheels for decades. When I wrote in the weeks following each, I took extra deep breaths because I noticed my language was more derogatory and I was striking the keys like I was trying to drive nails.

I got better at softening my touch, from gently tapping the keys to minimizing and eliminating many people's worst words and actions. Including what actually came to my own mind when listening to BVSD administrators and school board. A colorful array of offensive words were toned down to "dumbass." And instead of calling the *person* a "dumbass," I used it to describe their *behavior*.

~

My roots as a peace-maker go deep. White mother, Oma and Opa from Germany, black father, grandmother and great-grandmother from America's slave trade. Many have called me the whitest black man they'd met. I've coached and taught for decades. In the spring and summer of 2000 I quit a teaching position in BVSD and went to a Peaceable Schools conference. I read my poetry at an open mic. Two women praised my writing, then offered advice.

"Remember," the black one said, "White people want *you* to think *you* are crazy."

"Keep writing!" the white one said, "Just go somewhere and write, write, write."

Also at the conference, Dr. Ulric Johnson planted the seed to my greatest personal revelation—*Everyone is born prejudiced*.

"Stereotypes are like records," Dr. Johnson said, "Deeply grooved tracks guiding the needle to play the same old song." Then he had the audience do exercises to help us explore and discuss our personal biases and prejudices.

> *Language is an imprecise tool—like using a bowling ball to cut cake. Still, it's the only tool we have.*

Dr. Johnson then spoke about the lead article in the core readings, <u>The Ten Cs: A Model of Diversity Awareness and Social Change</u>. How to navigate our world, ripe with centuries of violence and hatred based on race, nationality, class, religion, culture, gender, and more. They've guided me for two decades.

The first five C's are what to be aware of: *Color, Culture, Class, Context,* and *Character.* The next five C's are about creating positive change:

Conflict – refers to the reflection, struggle and creative tension that promotes growth and justice. Conflict is a positive and necessary part of the process of change.

Courage – the ability to take action in spite of fear. Taking risks is essential when communities, politics and other institutions present social, economic and other consequences for confronting norms and laws.

Confidence – faith in yourself and your abilities, and the belief that you, alone and with others, can make a difference. Positively defining personal and group identity and abilities builds confidence and unleashes creativity that can enrich and enhance life for all people.

Commitment – focus, strategy, determination, and consistency driven by passion for justice and love for humanity, grounded in accurate education about history and culture from multiple perspectives, especially stories that have been silenced.

Community – people working collectively and collaboratively, finding ways to value and affirm human diversity for each individual and the whole. Community helps us connect with allies, which encourages and sustains us through difficult times.

~

My life is filled with irony. My success as a black man is rooted in white privilege. In some ways I've received more than some whites. Still, I'm angered when whites don't acknowledge their privilege. I also know things are better than ever, yet get aggravated when people cite change in a few successful individuals of color, while ignoring the masses in ghettos and mass incarcerations across our nation.

Perhaps someday people won't have to think about how myths, illusions, and lies impact us. But for now, in order to heal from the histories we've been taught—filled with poverty, violence, and different heroes—we need to have honest conversations about how race, class, religion, nationality, and gender influence our personal and institutional lives. And if we're going to go to war, everyone needs to work as hard as those on the front line. Because we may need armed forces, but few win when hatred burns. And when we learn to like others, we extinguish prejudice.

I wish BVSD's past and present powerful few and I had had a chance to think about illusions and lies. If we could have had honest conversations about race—if we could have worked hard together to extinguish prejudice—I believe it's a good bet we always had, and still have the same goal: We want everyone to succeed.

I've found immense joy in the love and support of my wife, daughter, and family. I'm a near scratch golfer and fish the most spectacular mountains anywhere. I'm no musician, but know a few strums, a lot of chords, and feel heaven when playing the Blues.

I do have a couple of regrets. First, that my memoir isn't based on a decade of teaching with BVSD students, teachers, staff, administrators, and parents. Second, that I gave all my drawing and painting time to writing. I estimated I'd finish the memoir in three years, and the artist in me will never forgive myself for it taking eight.

Still, I've addressed the difficulty of being human, and finished a book with a message I've tried to convey for 25 years: Talk about the *good* and the *bad*! Because charting a peaceful path requires knowing *both*.

Way to finally man up.

~

Human capital is the most powerful capital on earth. And while I harbor no illusions about the intractability of some conflicts, I'm equally convinced that millions value the ability to hold opposing views in our minds at the same time. And can start a revolution to spend more time celebrating: *We are the ones we've been waiting for!*

Be honest. But minimize negative language because while the truth may be painful, you can communicate it with calm and care.

Speak. Listen. Read. Write. Apologize. Forgive. Invest in yourself and others. Be happy.

I strike the floor with a stick, BAM!—Now!

Appendix

Page -

9 - Dr. Ulric Johnson and Patti DeRosa, <u>The Ten Cs: A Model of Diversity Awareness and Social Change</u>, Core Reading, Peaceable Schools Institute, Lesley College, 2000.

17 - Bill Bryson, <u>the mother tongue: english and how it got that way</u>, Perennial, 1990.

25 - Merril D Beal, <u>I Will Fight No More Forever: Chief Joseph and the Nez Perce War</u>, University of Washington Press, 1963.

27 - Robert C Tucker, <u>The Marx-Engels Reader</u>, W. W. Norton & Company, 1979.

48 - Jas Obrecht, <u>Early Blues: The Music Before Robert Johnson</u>, 1992.

48 - Stefan Grossman, <u>Early Masters of American Blues Guitar: Mississippi John Hurt</u>, Alfred Publishing Company.

67 - David J Eicher, <u>The Longest Night: A Military History of the Civil War</u>, Simon Schuster, 2002.

93 - Francis Coppola (Director), <u>Apocalypse Now</u> (movie), United Artists, 1979.

113 - Hugh Hudson (Director), <u>Chariots of Fire</u> (movie), Warner Bros., 1981.

128- Alan Gottlieb, <u>Klan to Rally Again at Capitol on King Day</u>, Denver Post, 1992.

128- Documentary Series, <u>30 for 30: The Gospel According to Mac</u>, ESPN Films, 2015.

134- Dr. Charles A Garfield, <u>Peak Performance: Mental Training Techniques of the World's Greatest Athletes</u>, Tarcher Inc./Houghton Mifflin Co., 1984.

143- Arnold Rampersad, David Roessel <u>The Collected Poems of Langston Hughes</u>, Vintage Classics/Random House, 1995.

143- Stephen Mitchell, <u>The Enlightened Heart: An Anthology of Sacred Poetry</u>, HarperPerennial, 1989.

Page -

143- Mary Oliver, West Wind: Poems and Prose Poems, Houghton Mifflin Company, 1997.

151- James McBride, The Color of Water: A Black Man's Tribute to His White Mother, Riverhead Books, 1996.

151- Andrew L Shapiro, We're Number One: Where America Stands—And Falls—In the New World Order, Vintage Books/Random House, 1992.

152- Jonathan Kozol, Amazing Grace: The Lives of Children and the Conscience of a Nation, HarperPerennial, 1995.

152- Shelby Steele, The Content of Our Character: A New Vision on Race in America, St. Martin's Press, 1990.

154- Thich Nhat Hahn, Be Still and Know: Reflections from Living Buddha and Living Christ, Riverhead Books, 1996.

158- Cameron Crowe (Director), Jerry Maguire (movie), TriStar Pictures, 1996.

159- Thich Nhat Hahn, Being Peace, Parallax Press, 1987.

159- Jon Krakaur, Into the Wild, Anchor Books, 1996.

165- Thich Nhat Hahn, Being Peace.

169- Chief Niwot: The Story of "Left Hand" and the Boulder Valley Curse, visitlongmont.org

170- Cheyenne Arapaho Hall, https://ipfs.io

171- Tony Horwitz, The Horrific Sand Creek Massacre Will Be Forgotten No More, www.smithsonianmag.com

177- Terrence Malick, (Director), Thin Red Line (movie), 20th Century Fox, 1998.

202- Curtis M Griffin, The Goals of Peacemakers are Clear, Colorado Daily, 2003.

203- Sam Hamill, Poets Against the War, Thunder's Mouth Press/Nation Books, 2003.

209- Howard, Famous Indian Chiefs, St. Nicholas Magazine, 1908.

209- Helen Addison Howard, Saga of Chief Joseph, Bison Books, 1965.

209- Arthur H R Fairchild, The Making of Poetry: A critical Study of Its Nature and Value, Knickerbocker Press, 1912.

Page -

210- John E Hill, <u>Revolutionary Values for a New Millennium: John Adams, Adam Smith and Social Virtue</u>, Lexington Books, 2000.

210- Frederick Douglas, <u>What to the Slave is the Fourth of July?</u> freemaninstitute.com

210- Langston Hughes, Arna Bontemps, <u>The Poetry of the Negro 1746 - 1949: An Anthology</u>, Double and Company Inc., 1949.

211- June Jordan, <u>Affirmative Acts: Political Essays</u>, Anchor Books/Doubleday, 1998.

211- Simon J Ortiz, <u>Fight back: For the Sake of the People, For the Sake of the Land</u>, Institute for Native American Development, 1980.

211- Tupac Shakur, <u>Only God can Judge Me</u>, Death Row Records/Interscope, 1996.

212- Richard Greene, <u>Words that Shook the World: 100 Years of Unforgettable Speeches and Events.</u> Prentice Hall Press, 2002

213- Stephen Mitchell, <u>The Enlightened Heart</u>.

214- Warner Home Videos, <u>500 Nations: Attack on Culture</u> (movie), 1999.

220- Jon Krakauer, <u>Where Men Win Glory: The Odyssey of Pat Tillman</u>, Doubleday/Random House, 2009.

231- Bernard Goldberg, <u>Bias: CBS Insider Exposes How the Media Distorts the News</u>, Perennial/HarperCollins, 2003.

263- Julian Weissglass, <u>Ripples of Hope: Building Relationships for Educational Change</u>, Center for Educational Change in Mathematics and Science U of C, Santa Barbara, 1998.

269- John Merrow, <u>Learning Matters Michelle Rhee Series</u>, PBS News Hour, August, 2007.

278- John Merrow, <u>Learning Matters Michelle Rhee Series</u>, PBS News Hour, April, 2008.

293- Julian Weissglass, <u>Ripples of Hope</u>.

295- John Merrow, <u>Learning Matters Michelle Rhee Series</u>, PBS News Hour, May, 2009.

304- Vanessa Miller, <u>New Columbine Principal Passionate about School</u>, Boulder Daily Camera, February, 2009.

Page -

306- John Merrow, <u>Learning Matters Michelle Rhee Series</u>, PBS News Hour, August, 2009.

315- <u>Boulder Valley School District School Board Meetings</u>, (52:03), December 14, 2010.

316- <u>Boulder Valley School District School Board Meeting</u>, (44:09, Superintendent 47:05), September 14, 2010.

317- <u>Boulder Valley School District School Board Meeting</u>, (46:14), November 9, 2010.

321- The Colorado Department of Education, <u>CSAP Results</u>, http://www.schoolview.org/SchoolPerformance

324- Diane Ravitch, <u>The Death and Life of the Great American School System: How Testing and Choice Are Undermining Education</u>, Basics Books/Perseus Books Group, 2010.

324- Paul Tough, <u>What Ever it Takes: Geoffrey Canada's Quest to Change Harlem and America</u>, Mariner Books/Houghton Mifflin Harcourt, 2008.

327- <u>Boulder Valley School District School Board Meeting</u>, (28:37), January 25, 2011.

332- Amy Bounds, <u>Boulder Valley Makes Small Gains in Minority Teachers</u>, Boulder Daily Camera, February, 2011.

337- Robert Lane Green, <u>You Are What You Speak: Grammar Grouches, Language laws, and The Politics of Identity</u>, Delacorte Press, 2011.

342- Dr. Ulric Johnson and Patti DeRosa, <u>The Ten Cs: A Model of Diversity Awareness and Social Change</u>.

ABOUT THE AUTHOR

Currently, Curtis can be found working on his breathing. With family: playing games, singing, reading, camping, dreaming, and more; transporting children to and from school safely; in a river searching for the perfect cast with his bamboo rod; on the links, looking for a swing that feels like butter, and gets the ball to explode off the face of the club.

And of course, as he continues to write, he's hoping to pen a magic spell—a potion that enables people to talk about hard truths, and still find ways to like each other.

Curtis invites you to engage in the conversation by visiting his blog https://wordpress.com/home/sixdegreestotruth.wordpress.com.

Made in the USA
Columbia, SC
09 June 2020